"One Day We Are Going Home"

The Long Exile of Elizabeth Mafeking

Holly Y. McGee

Catalyst Press, El Paso, Texas

Published by Catalyst Press.
(www.catalystpress.org)

Copyright © 2020 by Holly Y. McGee

All rights reserved. No part of this book may be used or reproduced in any manner whatsoever without written consent from the publisher, except for brief quotations for reviews. For further information, write to info@catalystpress.org.

In North America, this book is distributed by Consortium Book Sales & Distribution, a division of Ingram.
Phone: 612/746-2600
cbsdinfo@ingramcontent.com
www.cbsd.com

In South Africa, Namibia, and Botswana, this book is distributed by Protea Distribution. For information, email orders@proteadistribution.co.za.

First edition, first printing

10 9 8 7 6 5 4 3 2 1

ISBN 9781960803399

Library of Congress Control Number 2025936327

Dedicated to

Mrs. Elizabeth Rokie Mafeking, who finally came home.

Lala kahle, qhawe la maqhawe.

Table of Contents

List of Figures vi

Map ix

Acknowledgments x

"Where is Mrs. Mafeking?" 1

1 Unbridled Insinuation and Unproven Charges 42

2 Unlikely Alliances 119

3 "God Made Liz Abrahams" 187

4 A Dangerous Embarrassment 258

5 "One day we are going home" 332

Conclusion 409

Epilogue 417

Appendix: The children of Elizabeth Mafeking 438

Index 448

List of Figures

1.1 The Mafeking family pictured outside their home in Paarl, October 1959

1.2 The Mafeking home at 34 Barbarossa Street in Paarl, South Africa

1.3 This image of the poorly maintained entrance to the isolated farm of Mafeking's proposed banishment was one of many critics labored to publicize.

1.4 These three isolated shacks were originally constructed to house political exiles, and Elizabeth Mafeking was assigned here to serve out her indefinite banning orders.

1.5 Mafeking pictured at a FCWU meeting in the late 1940s giving the "Afrika" salute

1.6 Mafeking discussing the party newspaper and selling it to workers

2.1 Mafeking with Nimrod Sijake (far right), Patrick Molea (with hat) and two other comrades

2.2 This 1955 headline started a firestorm and contributed to Mafeking being labeled "the most dangerous threat to native administration" in the Western Cape.

3.1 A *New Age* political cartoon satirizes Mafeking's proposed banning to Vryburg in Southey.

List of Figures

3.2 The morning Mafeking's banning went into effect, hundreds of supporters filled her front yard in a show of solidarity for the married mother of eleven.

3.3 Supporters were delighted to learn Mafeking and baby Uhuru had evaded Security Forces and escaped to Basutoland.

3.4 Newspapers featured Mafeking and baby Uhuru in special interest stories during their first few months of exile.

3.5 Mafeking's dramatic escape to Lesotho made her and baby Uhuru famous.

3.6 Mafeking and her infant, Uhuru, were instant celebrities upon arrival in Lesotho, and they frequently found themselves in the pages of local newspapers.

3.7 Lilian Ngoyi holds baby Uhuru aloft during a speech in Basutoland.

3.8 Mafeking speaking to a crowd at a BCP rally about the evils of Apartheid in South Africa.

3.9 Mafeking and baby Uhuru at their first BCP rally in Lesotho where they earlier shared the stage with party leader Ntsu Mokhehle and Lilian Ngoyi

3.10 Mafeking eluded authorities to the delight of her supporters, and political cartoonists mocked frustrated Apartheid leadership like M.C. De Wet Nel and H.F. Verwoerd, who wanted to make an example of the activist.

List of Figures

4.1 Mafeking's first application for a residency permit in Lesotho made headlines with this image and Mafeking confidently declaring, "I see no reason why I should not get it!"

4.2 The early years of her banning had little effect on Mafeking's activist spirit, and she routinely participated in local politics.

4.3 Mafeking and Mrs. N. S. Maphathe conferring prior to Maphathe's departure to Copenhagen, Denmark to participate in the Women's International Democratic Federation's (WIDF) annual conference.

5.1 Nomathemba "Themsi" Nkewu and Koko Ndinisa at the Mafeking home in Mbekweni (Summer 2017).

5.2 Elizabeth Mafeking makes her grand entrance into the banquet hall where friends and family prepare to celebrate her 90th birthday, which was hosted and fully sponsored by FAWU.

5.3 Elizabeth Mafeking dancing with her eighth child, daughter Catherine Nomsa.

5.4 Mafeking's enduring admiration for the ANC was reflective in many elements of her 90th birthday celebration, most especially the cake.

A.1 This treasured family photo hangs in the Mafeking home in Mbekweni. In the center is Elizabeth Mafeking, surrounded by images of nine of her eleven children.

Map

FM.1 Map of South Africa, Lesotho, and Paarl in the Western Cape

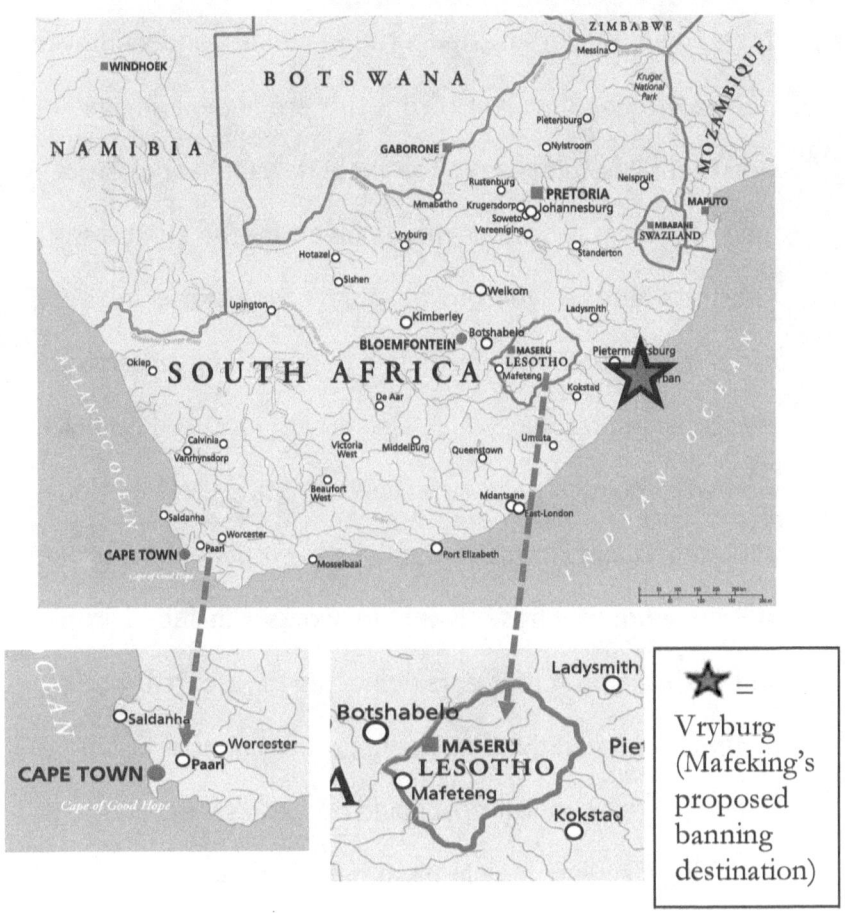

Acknowledgments

I have been enamored with the untold life story of Elizabeth Mafeking since 2004, shortly after first seeing her photograph in an archived newspaper at the University of Cape Town. Her bright smile, round cheeks, and kind eyes were a striking departure from the predictable images of woe that filled the pages of national newspapers of African men and women who seemed cowed by the strictures of Apartheid and resigned to their devolving status in South Africa in the 1950s. I'd only begun to undertake research for my dissertation topic, which was broadly focused on black women's political activism beyond state and national boundaries, and Elizabeth Mafeking eventually became one of four women whose lives and works I included in my study. Throughout the years dedicated to research, writing, my first hire, and into the revision process for dissertation-to-manuscript publication, I could not stop seeing Elizabeth Mafeking's smiling face in my mind's eye, nor could I stop wondering about the unknown personal life of an activist whose public persona cost her everything. After much

Acknowledgments

deliberation I settled upon a radical idea: to turn ten pages from my dissertation into a full manuscript project. A former committee member pointedly warned me "not to jettison three quarters of [my] dissertation" in lieu of going back to the drawing board to write a manuscript about Elizabeth Mafeking, reminding me of the time and work it might take to re-create the wheel. While it has, indeed, been difficult to re-create the wheel for the past seven years, *"One day we are going home"* has been more than worth the effort.

    I have been honored to work with dozens of scholars, archivists, language instructors, and laymen who have enriched my life both personally and professionally in the course of this project, and I would like to offer my humble thanks for their amazing aid, guidance, and direction at various points in my journey. First and foremost, my most sincere thanks to the Mafeking family. Words cannot express how much I appreciate you welcoming me into your family and allowing me to present your mother's complicated life story. I will always be grateful for your candor in our conversations, and sincerely

Acknowledgments

hope I have done justice to the memory of your mother with this manuscript. Many scholars have played a part in this work, and it is with a heavy heart that I can only thank a small number of them here. Thank you to Christina Greene (UW-Madison), Richard Pierce (University of Notre Dame), James Campbell (Stanford), Gemma Beckley (Rust College), Chris Dunton (National University of Lesotho), David Ambrose (University of Cape Town, *Emeritus*), and Shireen Hassim (University of the Witwatersrand), for all of the constructive feedback that substantively shaped *"One day we are going home."* My utmost thanks to the many archives/archivists whose work made it possible for me to dig into the life and times of Elizabeth Mafeking: University of Cape Town (Archives and Special Collections; Jagger Reading Room), University of the Witwatersrand (Historical Papers Research Archive), University of Fort Hare (Liberation Movement Archives of the National Heritage and Cultural Studies Centre), the Alan Paton Centre & Struggle Archives, Stanford University Library and Archives (particularly the ladies in the vault!), and Mercia Sais at the Paarl Library in the Western Cape. I am truly indebted to a

Acknowledgments

handful of amazing language instructors whose patience and dedication to their craft afforded me the opportunity to learn and utilize three of the most beautiful language the Continent has to offer. *Enkosi kakhulu, Titshalakazi Nolutho Diko, ndiyabulela ngesiseka esihle kwiXhosa. Abafundisi bami baseZulu bahlanganisa noMary Gordon, Baba Nelson Ntshangase, Sandra Senah, noFrancis Fanyana Lukhele. Nina nonke ngabafundisi abahle kakhulu! Qetellong, matichere a Sesotho, Malira Thetso le L. Phafouli, kea leboha ka ho nthuta "Basotho ke batho ba hlomphanang hape ba ratanang. Ba boetse ba a tsotellana."* Any omissions in my thanks are truly inadvertent, and any linguistic inaccuracies are entirely my own.

Finally, these acknowledgments would be incomplete without expressing my gratitude to two entities at the University of Cincinnati. Generous summer funding from the Charles Phelps Taft Research Center provided crucial language training and archival research in Lesotho in the final stages of writing. Finally, sincere thanks to my colleagues in the Department of History. It has been a joy to work such wonderful people, and I thank you for

Acknowledgments

consistently providing guidance, support, and sage wisdom at every opportunity.

"Where is Mrs. Mafeking?"

> I was shocked at the change in Elizabeth. The woman I had known had been handsome and lively. Now she was careworn and anxious; her new life was a hard one [and she] had been reduced to real privation . . . She had become embittered by the unending poverty and anxiety, feeling that she was forgotten now by the workers whose battles she had fought for so many years.[1]
>
> – Helen Joseph

In 1962, Helen Joseph traveled from South Africa to Basutoland (modern day Lesotho) to visit her dear friend, Elizabeth Mafeking, who had escaped banishment orders in South Africa three years earlier to live in self-imposed exile. Joseph – an anti-apartheid activist who was a founding member of the Congress of Democrats (COD), National

"Where is Mrs. Mafeking?"

Secretary of the Federation of South African Women (FEDSAW), and one of the main leaders of the 1956 Women's March – could not believe the toll exile had taken on Mafeking, who pleaded with her comrade to tell supporters back in South Africa how much she suffered in isolation. Only three years earlier, Elizabeth Mafeking had been one of the most well-known and respected trade union organizers in the Western Cape. Now, however, the once-proud activist with the "expressive, strong, humorous, [and] beautiful face" was desperate, noticeably breaking under the pressure of exile and facing a sad, slow demise.[2]

For more than a decade, Mafeking – a married mother of eleven children who was employed in the canning industry – had slowly worked her way up in union circles, eventually becoming President of the African Food and Canning Workers' Union (AFCWU), the National Vice President of the African National Congress-Women's League (ANCWL), and a trusted comrade of movement stalwarts like Ray Alexander Simons, Rebecca "Becky" Lan, Oscar Mpetha, and Liz Abrahams. In October of 1959, however, the Apartheid government labeled Elizabeth

"Where is Mrs. Mafeking?"

Mafeking "the most dangerous threat to native administration in the Cape," and served her with banishment orders that decreed the activist move from her home in Paarl to a desolate farm in Vryburg – more than 600 miles away.[3] Banning and banishment – forms of punishment utilized by the South African government against those who challenged their power – was one of the most effective ways of silencing dissent because offenders could and were shipped hundreds of miles away from their homes/lives/families for an undetermined length of time. Rather than submit to her banning orders the day they went into effect, however, Mafeking escaped Paarl before the South African Police (SAP) could take her into custody and fled to neighboring Basutoland. The home of Elizabeth Mafeking's heart in South Africa, though politically contested terrain, was lost. Even more tragically, historically speaking, this is where the story of Elizabeth Mafeking has traditionally ended. It is, however, where my book begins.

"One day we are going home" is the biographical oral history of Elizabeth Rokie Mafeking – a recognized

"Where is Mrs. Mafeking?"

South African women's leader and trade union president identified by white civic and political leaders in 1959 as head of "the most militant trade union in the country."[4] Mafeking is vital to histories of South African women, resistance politics, banishment studies, and exile, but in spite of her influence and significance to the making of protest politics at the dawn of Apartheid in South Africa, her story has never been fully explored. Scholars of South African history routinely acknowledge (or at the very least footnote) Mafeking's centrality to the trade union movement, and her name is always at the forefront of conversations regarding the phenomenon of banning. Her lived experiences, her time in exile, her fate, and her activist legacy, however, have effectively been reduced to marginalia.[5] Indeed, Elizabeth Rokie Mafeking is as absent from the formal, activist history of South Africa as she was from Paarl the morning her banning orders went into effect. Unlike her absenteeism in 1959, however, Mafeking's historical invisibility in the annals of South African history makes little sense. She was a senior leader of crucial trade unions and within the ANCWL, and her name and her story are frequently mentioned in histories of pass protests in the Cape – but the discussions lack the depth and detail necessary to truly understand her centrality to anti-apartheid politics in the mid-twentieth century, and the price she paid in service to the struggle.[6] This biography positions Elizabeth Mafeking where she historically belongs – amidst a host of recent efforts to broaden and deepen our understanding of the long road to liberation in South Africa beyond the narratives and experiences of "great men" who – in their own time – looked to Mafeking as an example of effective organizing. Moreover, it finally brings to the fore the important struggle of a heroine whose experiences as a worker, a woman, an activist, and a mother in exile reveal the intersectionality of race, class, and gender in the anti-apartheid movement.

Positioning "*Me'* Rokie"[7]

South African scholarship regarding the activist work of women has grown tremendously in its scope since the international beginning of the study of women's history as

"Where is Mrs. Mafeking?"

a discipline in the 1950s and 1960s. The survival of the Apartheid regime and repression of ideas in South Africa meant this radical form of historical writing did not begin influencing scholarship in the country until more than a decade later in the 1970s, with social history, recuperative history, and feminist theory dominating the early wave of this scholarship. Issues that reflected the concerns of radial social history – pass laws, women's involvement in protest organizations, and women's roles in emergent township issues – provided a historical perspective that was in explicit opposition to the development of Apartheid from above. In keeping with global trends and conversations, the growth of the field in the 1970s meant feminist theory influenced the making of history in the era, introducing and problematizing "motherhood" as a useful category of analysis. It was not until the early 1980s that gender history as a discipline allowed for the study of the social construction of male/female social roles and social identities. South African social histories in particular filled a distinct void regarding the lack of writing on women in previous decades.[8] Class analysis supplanted racism as a focus, and scholars began to pay less attention to the formal political organizations that characterized anti-apartheid struggles and more to popular protest.[9] Black resistance history in South Africa was not formed with women in mind, but with the veritable explosion of women's history in the 1990s, scholars made a concerted effort to re-imagine just that.[10] This was a truly radical moment in South African women's history when feminist scholarship – long marginalized – finally realized validation. Scholars posed questions regarding the ways in which race and/or class structured the Apartheid state, criticized the lack of theoretical developments in the field, considered the status/position of non-traditional communities, and articulated new potential areas of analysis.[11]

South African historian Shireen Hassim and American sociologist Gay Seidman look at the emergence of women's movements in South Africa during the last two decades of the twentieth century and posit that time as *the* period of black women's political internationalizing and cognizance of gender-specific needs and rights.[12] As the life and work of Elizabeth Mafeking demonstrate, however, there are both chronological and ideological challenges to these presumptions, and this study provides an additional interpretation of South African women's history that understands the post-WWII era as one of radical political mobilization and acculturation for women. The activist work of African women humanized freedom struggles in the very important eyes of the international community and demonstrated a surprising level of savvy regarding gender-specific claims (even, admittedly, if not while using explicitly feminist terminology).

In recent years, both activists and academics have begun to push South African women's history beyond traditional conversations regarding domestic pass protests to include themes like labor and union organizing, armed struggles, and challenges facing women since the country's transition to democracy.[13] New methodological approaches – particularly oral histories – characterized scholarship of the early 2000s, encouraging people to voice their experiences under Apartheid as a means of confronting the merciless policies and practices that dictated their lives. Forced removals, self-representation, trade unionism, exile, and "the question of women," all benefitted from this new methodological approach, providing unique insight into women's political and economic struggles.[14] In this regard, the introduction of Elizabeth Mafeking into the historical narrative is particularly timely in its advancement of exile studies in that it builds upon new scholarship of political repression and women in exile by including the experiences of a woman trapped in the first wave of political banishments that swept through South Africa in the mid-twentieth century.[15]

Oral history and memory

"One day we are going home" views oral histories as a unique and underused source base that is vital to uncovering the story of Elizabeth Mafeking.[16] As such, it employs author-conducted interviews of family members, activist comrades, work colleagues, and community members of Mafeking to help uncover her place within the larger social movement of the era. From 2012 to 2017, I conducted interviews with all four of Elizabeth Mafeking's

surviving children and a handful of their extended family members, political comrades, and friends. I conducted interviews in South Africa and Lesotho. Depending on the subject's preferred language, interviews were conducted in English, isiXhosa, isiZulu, or SeSotho.[17]

The settings for the interviews varied and there were no set questions for any of the exchanges. My initial intent was simply to ask what – if anything – Mafeking's children recalled about growing up in Lesotho and what they understood about their mother's place in South Africa's anti-apartheid history. Our initial exchanges all began the same way: I would produce an enlarged copy of a newspaper article, photograph, or government document I had come across in my archival research and ask one question, "What do you remember about this?" My documents – from a picture of their mother's smiling face in a 1955 newspaper to a family photograph taken to commemorate Mafeking's release from prison in 1959 – always stimulated an emotional response from Mafeking's children, ranging from laughter to tears. I retreated as much as possible in these moments, allowing whatever emotion

"Where is Mrs. Mafeking?"

that filled the space to do just that, and resisted the urge to press for more information during silences. Doing so gave those interviewed the freedom to process their emotions without pressure and provide a more thoughtful response to my queries.

Oral histories tend to evoke an automatic suspicion of the reliability of memory, the identity of supposedly authentic sources, and pointed (mis)representations. Many of these trends held true for this book: most interview subjects recalled events accurately and vividly, and things forgotten were due to either age or a purposeful decision. Uhuru Zikalala Mafeking was only 2 ½ months old when her mother spirited her away to Basutoland, so many of the details of Uhuru's early life in the territory are lost in childhood.[18] Sophia Mafeking, however, the eldest daughter left behind in Paarl when her siblings were smuggled across the border to their mother in 1960, outright refused to speak about certain subjects. Memories were incredibly painful and when Sophia could not objectively discuss something she determined to lessen the psychological influence of those negative episodes by dismissively saying she did "not want to talk about the bad times."[19] Memories of the past can also be incredibly unreliable and details about the same event or moment in time can vary greatly depending on perspective. Ultimately, in spite of the disadvantages, the inclusion of the personal narratives of Mafeking's family and friends contribute to a larger, more vivid, picture of the life of a nearly forgotten activist.

Sources

My method of analysis is interdisciplinary in that it combines aspects of oral history, historical, political, and cultural inquiry, and engages varying sources such as organizational records, print media, government publications, and personal correspondence. Source documentation for the manuscript spans three continents, four countries, and almost one dozen archives. I first met Elizabeth Mafeking in the pages of newspapers archived in the African Studies Collection at the Chancellor Oppenheimer Library at the University of Cape Town (UCT).

"Where is Mrs. Mafeking?"

The periodicals and newspapers housed here and in the Manuscripts and Archives Department, and the supporting documents in the Jagger Reading Room, whetted my appetite for more information on a woman whose name I had frequently read, but whose face I had just seen for the first time. The Department of Historical & Literary Papers in the William Cullen Library at The University of the Witwatersrand in Johannesburg has one of the most extensive collections of individual and organizational papers in the country. Records of FEDSAW, the FCWU, the AFCWU, and the personal papers of Helen Joseph and Ray Alexander yielded information instrumental in reconstructing Mafeking's life events and work.

The Alan Paton Centre & Struggle Archives at the University of KwaZulu-Natal in Pietermaritzburg is a rich and invaluable resource. It houses a broad collection of the papers of almost two dozen political parties like the Liberal Party and Communist Party of South Africa and non-political organizations like the South African Institute of Race Relations. The African National Congress-Women's League records at the University of Fort Hare in the Eastern

"Where is Mrs. Mafeking?"

Cape provided helpful insight into the structure of the organization. The National Archives of South Africa has retained the original banning orders for Mafeking and other anti-apartheid activists, and these documents have been vital in reconstructing events. Both the Paarl Public Library (Drakenstein Municipality) and the South African Institute of Race Relations in Johannesburg provided much of the statistical information found within the manuscript.

In the United States, the Cecil H. Green Library at Stanford University holds a bound, nearly complete collection of original *Drum* publications, which afforded a direct, unhindered glimpse into the past, and the Hoover Institution Library & Archives houses a surprising number of primary source documents specific to "The Mafeking Affair." The National University of Lesotho in Roma, Lesotho, has an unparalleled collection of both SeSotho and English-language newspapers from the period under study, which were vital in piecing together the first few years of Mafeking's life in exile. The Morija Museum and Archives has an impressive collection of monographs from the early to mid-twentieth century that were helpful in providing context for Lesotho politics in the 1960s and 1970s. Finally, the British National Archives in London has a surprising amount of information on Mafeking's exile, offering a first-hand glimpse into the level of surveillance and scrutiny Mafeking was under during her first few years in exile. Recently declassified government records demonstrate the shifting levels of regard British authorities actually had for Mafeking's plight, and show just how close the activist came to being delivered back into the hands of South African authorities.

Limitations

I have undertaken to write as comprehensive a life history of Elizabeth Mafeking as possible, but there are specific historical and methodological limitations. The overwhelming majority of sources utilized for this manuscript are primary rather than secondary, which, some might argue, subsequently lends the project to meager and superficial assessments of critical themes. I suggest, however, that in understanding the work of Elizabeth

"Where is Mrs. Mafeking?"

Mafeking it is more important to understand *that* she advocated for higher wages, rather than *the amount* of said wages. Moreover, the vast majority of secondary sources that specifically deal with Mafeking do not offer any new information that would (or did) substantively alter the current project. They merely repeat the brief but dominant narrative of the Mafeking Affair with more variation in the spelling of her surname than in the story itself. There is little to no parity in those versions of Mafeking's exit from the activist spotlight: the reporting of her banning outweighs any critical assessment of the work that preceded it, or an examination of her life following it.

While this manuscript makes great strides in uncovering those epochs in her life, not all aspects of it are treated evenly. For example, while her faith and work in the AME Church was a crucial element in the personal makeup of Mafeking, there are simply no records, correspondence, diaries, or so on relevant to her that might provide a more concrete view of the religious underpinnings of her actions. It is truly unfortunate that there is little more that can be said of Mafeking's specific institutional connection to the

AME Church because knowing the more intimate details of this facet of her life might provide an even more well-rounded portrait of a woman whose life seems to suggest that the political overrode all else. Even Mafeking's familial relationships in the early years of this manuscript are simply lost in time. She gave birth to a child every other year for two decades while simultaneously rising in the trade unionism ranks, but outside of an errant comment made by one of her surviving children in a 2016 interview, there is no way of knowing what kind of impact these factors had on Mafeking's relationship with her husband, Moffat Henry Mditjane. His feelings about her work, their conversations and compromises, and how she navigated gender and cultural expectations within her marriage, can only – given the lack of evidence – be left to speculation.

Finally, and perhaps most importantly, while this is the critical history of a woman who was central to the political activities of trade unions in the Western Cape, it does not seek to provide a comprehensive history of specific trade unions or the trade union movement. Those accounts have been done elsewhere.[20] Ultimately,

Elizabeth Mafeking's story illuminates not only the condition of working women and the challenge of trade unionism, but compels a consideration of the more intimate details of self-imposed exile for a married woman with eleven children, which is the central focus of this manuscript.

Narrative Arch

This biography consists of five chapters, each of which explores a distinctive epoch in the life of Elizabeth Mafeking and retraces her path from the infamy of banishment into exile and back. Chapter One looks at the phenomenon of banning in Apartheid South Africa and details the shocking moment when authorities served Mafeking – the married mother of eleven children, the youngest just 2 ½ months old – with banishment orders. The chapter discusses her origins, political development, importance, and influence in trade union circles of the 1940s and the growing anti-apartheid movement. Mafeking's prominence in the ANCWL, FWCU, and most particularly the AFCWU, was derived – in large part – through her ability to connect women's local activism in the fruit canneries of the Cape with larger currents of international anti-apartheid activism. Mafeking managed to negotiate complex relationships between African and Coloured workers in the Cape during a period in which the government was discriminating against both but also seeking to privilege so-called Coloureds over Africans. "Unbridled insinuation and unproven charges" explains the ways in which race and gender were central elements of the organizations to which Mafeking belonged and how she used these to promote a radically different vision of South African society during the early years of Apartheid. It also introduces Ray Alexander as a vital component to Mafeking's changed understanding of the economic, social, and political aspects of the lives of working African women and demonstrates Mafeking's ascension to local and national notoriety.

Chapter Two demonstrates the 1950s was *the* decade of political activism and agitation in South Africa, most especially for African women, but government regulations and restrictions governing African participation in trade unions effectively silenced the organized dissent of one of the most radical segments of South African society. After more than one decade of tireless efforts leading a trade union considered the "backbone of organizing among food and canning workers," Elizabeth Mafeking fell victim to just such machinations in 1959.[21] "Unlikely alliances" also introduces motherhood as a theme central to the personal, cultural, and societal identity of Elizabeth Mafeking and demonstrates how the activist purposefully utilized motherhood as a political tool aimed at reconstructing a positive social and political identity of African women. The government's 1959 attack against Elizabeth Mafeking was a crucial moment to publically – and definitely – consolidate a dominant construction of African motherhood as largely irrelevant, and Mafeking's dramatic escape from South Africa in defiance of her banning orders speaks to the evolution of the socio-political identity of African women as mothers.

"God Made Liz Abrahams" utilizes interviews of Mafeking's children to begin the first full reconstruction their mother's elaborate escape and the days and weeks immediately following her flight from Paarl. Chapter Three also examines the response of Mafeking's community to what it perceived as an attack on one of their own: first petitions and demonstrations, then eventually a two-day riot. No amount of violence could reconstitute the Mafeking household, however, and this chapter details the ways in which an entire multi-racial community worked together to support Mafeking's broken family and bewildered children in her absence. Her departure was devastating for her family, an embarrassment for the South African government, a cause for diplomatic concern for British officials in Basutoland, and more than a mild irritant for local officials in Maseru. Mafeking was a refugee *first* and a mother second, thus, this chapter also introduces the complication of the changing legislative relationship of Basutoland with South Africa in the 1960s that compelled the High Commission Territory to broker some semblance of understanding and peace with the sea of Apartheid that surrounded it.

With a husband and eleven children, Elizabeth Mafeking's flight into exile increased the pressures of motherhood exponentially.[22] Mafeking was one of only eleven political exiles – and the only woman – who fled South Africa for freedom in Basutoland in the mid-twentieth century. Unlike the vast majority of her male compatriots, however, Elizabeth Mafeking refused to allow Apartheid to sever her parental rights, and elected to smuggle eight of her youngest children into exile alongside her. Mafeking's banishment shined a harsh light on the true cost of Apartheid politics, most especially on her children whose only crime was being born to a parent in protest. Chapter Four analyzes the realities of life in Basutoland for Mafeking and her children, exposes the unique vulnerabilities of women in exile/banishment, and discusses the complexities of changed family forms and intimate relationships.[23]

Political refugees threatened the tenuous links between Basutoland, South Africa, and Great Britain, and Mafeking's particular plight (and technical status as an exile) was a catalyst for immigration policy that helped to preserve the diplomatic ties of those closely dependent nations.[24] Elizabeth Mafeking's presence in the territory also provides an opportunity to explore the origins of the underground networks of support created by the ANC and allies like Ray Alexander. Alexander was the key organizer of the FCWU and the South African Communist Party (CPSA), and was a central conduit for information-sharing between women in exile and those still inside South Africa. Alexander ensured cadres remained active through these connections, but more importantly, these links were part of the care that the ANC and SACP began to develop in the 1960s as more of its members went into exile. As "A dangerous embarrassment" demonstrates, however, Elizabeth Mafeking's ill-timed exile meant that she suffered through the early years in Basutoland as Alexander and others scrambled to initiate an organizational welfare system to maintain solidarities with the dispossessed and their global allies.

Exile in Basutoland held its own special challenges for Elizabeth Mafeking and the children she raised. The final chapter, "One day we are going home," continues the discussion of family imbedded throughout the manuscript, paying particular attention to the experiences of the

"Where is Mrs. Mafeking?"

Mafeking children in exile and the resultant crisis of cultural identity upon returning to South Africa in the early 1990s. Mafeking's children – most of whom were very young when they arrived in Basutoland in 1960 – struggled to understand their mother's longing for a country and a people that seemed to care nothing for her. Exile had brought out the best (and the worst) in their mother, and returning "home" meant confronting old, personal demons, negotiating new cultural expectations, and disrupting the only family many of the children had ever known. This discussion of family with regards to Mafeking's banning-turned-exile begs an examination of the lives of her children in exile.[25]

Elizabeth Mafeking spent thirty-two years believing in and repeating to her children the singular promise that one day they would all return to the Cape. When the family did return to South Africa during the transition to democracy after more than three decades in exile, it was less than glorious. Some family, friends, and former comrades of Elizabeth Mafeking were appalled to see how little the new, ANC-led government seemed cared for the returned icon. It was widely felt that the organization failed Mafeking in the final years of her life, and in detailing these slights, Chapter Five considers the memory of Mafeking within activist circles, questions the value of her sacrifices, and reflects upon her enduring legacy within the South African freedom struggle.

***

The story of Elizabeth Mafeking is one of radical, working-class consciousness and brings into focus a struggle figure who has been neglected in the existing scholarship on trade unions and women's organizations in South Africa. This vital work follows the political and personal life of Elizabeth Mafeking to elucidate dimensions of the agency of women activists, the types of local and international networks that they accessed to pursue the goal of publicizing Apartheid's ills, and – for the first time – details the life and exile of a forgotten activist, a victim of "the cruelest and most effective weapon that the South African government [had] yet devised to punish its foes."[26]

Notes

1 Badat, Saleem, *The Forgotten People: Political Banishment under Apartheid* (Leiden: Brill, 2013), 189.

2 Blumberg, "The Mafeking Affair" in *Africa South* vol. 4, no. 3 (April–June, 1960), 40.

3 Digital Innovation South Africa (DISA), "The Lonely Exile of Elizabeth Mafeking," November 14, 1959, 2, www.disa.ukzn.ac.za/index.php?option=com_displaydc&recordID=Ctv2n2359 (accessed March 2007).

4 Ibid.

5 Lodge, Tom, *Black Politics in South Africa since 1945* (New York: Longman, 1983); Walker, Cherryl, *Women and Resistance in South Africa* (New York: Monthly Review Press, 1982); Simons, Ray Alexander and Raymond Suttner (eds.), *All My Life*

and All My Strength (Johannesburg: STE Publishers, 2004); Patel, Yosuf and Philip Hirschsohn (eds.), *Married to the Struggle: 'Nanna' Liz Abrahams Tells Her Life Story* (University of the Western Cape, 2005); Scanlon, Helen, *Representation and Reality: Portraits of Women's Lives in the Western Cape, 1948–1976* (South Africa: Human Sciences Research Council, 2007); Badat, *The Forgotten People*; Theron, Jan, *Solidarity Road: The Story of a Trade Union in the Ending of Apartheid* (Johannesburg, South Africa: Jacana Media, 2016). Helen Scanlon and Saleem Badat are exceptions to my contention that Elizabeth Mafeking's story has yet to receive the attention it so richly deserves. Scanlon provide a two-page summary of Mafeking's plight, relying upon the same, sparse documentation frequently cited and re-cited by other scholars. Badat, however, offers a five-page treatment of Mafeking that utilizes newly uncovered sources offering rich detail surrounding the impetus for her banning.

6 Scanlon, *Representation and Reality*; Sibeko, Archie, *Roll of Honour: Western Cape ANC Comrades 1953–1963* (Cape Town: University of the Western Cape, 2008); Yosuf and Hirschsohn (eds.), *Married to the Struggle*; Malherbe, V.C. (ed.), *Paarl the Hidden Story* (South Africa: Black Sash, 1987).

7 "*Me*" (pronounced "may") is a SeSotho word used to communicate *mother*, *Mrs.*, or *ma'am*, and is the culturally appropriate way to refer to or speak to a female elder. The courtesy title also serves as an indication to the speaker that s/he is connected to the person being addressed – if not by blood most

certainly by cultural expectations of respect and propriety.

8 Bozzoli, Belinda (ed.), *Class, Community and Conflict: South African Perspectives* (Johannesburg: Ravan Press, 1987); Lodge, *Black Politics in South Africa since 1945*; Walker, *Women and Resistance in South Africa*.

9 The avid interest in the experiences of African women resulted in works like *Not Either an Experimental Doll* and *Call Me Woman*, which revealed the everyday experiences of African women trapped under the yoke of Apartheid. Marks, Shula (ed.), *Not Either an Experimental Doll: The Separate Worlds of Three South African Women* (Bloomington: Indiana University Press, 1987); Kuzwayo, Ellen, *Call Me Woman* (San Francisco: Aunt Lute Books, 1985).

10 Berger, Iris, *Threads of Solidarity: Women in South African Industry, 1900–1980* (Bloomington and London: Indiana University Press, 1992); Bozzoli, Belinda and Mmantho Nkotsoe, *Women of Phokeng: Consciousness, Life Strategy and Migrancy in South Africa, 1900–1983* (Johannesburg: Ravan Press, 1991); Cock, Jaclyn, *Colonels and Cadres: War and Gender in South Africa* (Cape Town: Oxford University Press, 1991); Walker, Cherryl (ed.), *Women and Gender in Southern Africa to 1945* (Cape Town and London: David Philip and James Currey, 1990); Wells, Julia, *We Now Demand! The History of Women's Resistance to Pass Laws in South Africa* (Johannesburg: Witwatersrand University Press, 1993).

11 Manicom, Linzi, "Rethinking State and Gender in South African History" in *Journal of African History* vol. 33, no. 3 (1992), 441–465; Gordon, Elizabeth Boltson, "The Plight of the Women of Lesotho: Reconsideration with the Decline of Apartheid?" in *Journal of Black Studies* vol. 24, no. 4 (June, 1994), 435–446; McCord, Margaret, *The Calling of Katie Makanya: A Memoir of South Africa* (New York: John Wiley & Sons, Inc., 1995); Walker, Cherryl, "Conceptualizing Motherhood in Twentieth Century South Africa" in *Journal of Southern African Studies* vol. 21, no. 3 (September, 1995), 417–437; Basu, Amrita, *The Challenge of Local Feminisms: Women's Movements in Global Perspective* (Boulder: Westview Press, 1995); Kendall, K. Limakatso (ed.), *Singing Away the*

Hunger: The Autobiography of an African Woman (Bloomington: Indiana University Press, 1997).

12 Hassim, Shireen, *Women's Organizations and Democracy in South Africa: Contesting Authority* (Wisconsin: University of Wisconsin Press, 2006); Seidman, Gay, "'No Freedom without the Women': Mobilization and Gender in South Africa, 1970–1992" in *Signs: Journal of Women in Culture and Society* vol. 18, no. 2 (1993): 291–320.

13 Hassim, *Women's Organizations and Democracy in South Africa*; Gasa, Nomboniso (ed.), *Women in South African History: The Remove Boulders and Cross Rivers* (Pretoria, South Africa: Human Sciences Research Council, 2007); Lee, Rebekah, *African Women and Apartheid: Migration and Settlement in Urban South Africa* (London: I.B. Tauris, 2009).

14 Fields, Sean (ed.), *Lost Communities, Living Memories: Remembering Forced Removals in Cape Town* (Cape Town: David Philip, 2001); Goetz, Anne Marie and Shireen Hassim (eds.), *No Shortcuts to Power: African Women in Politics and Policy Making* (London: Zed Books, 2003); Simons, Ray Alexander and Raymond Suttner (eds.), *All My Life and All My Strength* (Johannesburg: STE Publishers, 2004); Hassim, Shireen, "Nationalism, Feminism and Autonomy: The ANC in Exile and the Question of Women" in *Journal of Southern African Studies* vol. 30, no. 3 (September, 2004), 433–455; Gasa, Nomboniso (ed.), *Women in South African History* (Cape Town: Human Sciences Research Council, 2007); Tripp, Aili, Isabel Casimiro, Joy Kwesiga, and Alice Mungwa (eds.), *African Women's Movements:*

Changing Political Landscapes (Cambridge: Cambridge University Press, 2009).

15 Ngcobo, Lauretta (ed.), *Prodigal Daughters: Stories of South African Women in Exile* (Pietermaritzburg: UKZN Press, 2012); Badat, *The Forgotten People*; Musiiwa, Estella, "Frances Baard's and Helen Joseph's Struggle against Apartheid, 1950–1963: A Comparative Analysis" in *Historia* vol. 57, no. 1 (May, 2012), 66–81; Theron, Jan, *Solidarity Road: The Story of a Trade Union in the Ending of Apartheid* (South Africa: Jacana Media, 2016).

16 Special thanks to Dr. Cathy Frierson at the University of New Hampshire and Dr. Sean Fields at the University of Cape Town for their indispensable consultation on the nature and function of oral histories as a pedagogical tool. Dr. Frierson's most recent book, *Silence Was Salvation: Child Survivors*

of Stalin's Terror and World War II in the Soviet Union (New Haven, CT: Yale University Press, 2015), introduces the experiences of forcibly orphaned, child victims of Stalinist repression in the 1930s and 1940s. Dr. Sean Field's *Lost Communities, Living Memories: Remembering Forced Removals in Cape Town* (Cape Town: David Philip, 2001) has a detailed appendix on oral history projects that offers critical analysis of oral histories as a research method and general guidelines for oral history interviewing. Special thanks, too, to Dr. Florence Bernault at the University of Wisconsin-Madison for an invaluable, graduate seminar in African history in 2004. Dr. Bernault's seminar introduced me to writers, theorists, and intellectual activists like Jan Vansina and Achille Mbembe, and provided one of my first opportunities to engage with histories of the continent, an introduction for which I will be forever grateful.

17 Graduate work at the University of Wisconsin-Madison inspired me to supplement my scholarship with language study, and since 2004 I have participated in domestic and international language programs learning isiXhosa, isiZulu, and SeSotho. Thus, unless otherwise noted, all interviews are author-conducted without the aid of an interpreter or a research assistant.

18 The vast majority of newspaper articles regarding the banning and exile of Elizabeth Mafeking from the 1950s and 1960s refers to Mafeking's youngest child, Uhuru, using both her Christian and family name, but the manuscript will only employ "Uhuru" in subsequent references.

19 Interview, Sophia Khekhemani Mafeking with author, summer 2013, Paarl, South Africa. Original interview conducted in isiXhosa and Sesotho, translated into English.

20 Goode, Richard, *A History of the Food and Canning Workers Union, 1941–1975*. MA Dissertation (University of Cape Town, Cape Town, South Africa, 1986); Lodge, Tom Geoffrey, *Insurrection in South Africa: The Pan-Africanist Congress and the Poqo Movement 1959–1965*. PhD Thesis (University of New York, New York, New York, United States, 1984); Carim, Shirene Fradet and the United Nations Centre against Apartheid, *The Role of Women in the South African Trade Union Movement* (New York: United Nations, 1980); Lodge, *Black Politics in South Africa since 1945*; Walker, Cherryl, *Women and Resistance in South*

Africa (New York: Monthly Review Press, 1982); Iris Berger, *Threads of Solidarity: Women in South African Industry, 1900–1980* (Bloomington and London: Indiana University Press, 1992). The Goode and Lodge MA dissertation and PhD thesis, respectively, offer the type of rich, qualitative detail that provides a thick description of the Food and Canning Workers Trade Union – the preeminent non-racial and militant union birthed in 1941 to address the needs of workers whose labor fed the demand for canned goods during World War II.

21 Berger, Iris, "Gender, Race, and Political Empowerment: South African Canning Workers, 1940–1960" in *Gender & Society* vol. 4, no. 3, Special Issue: Women and Development in the Third World (September, 1990), 406.

22 The status and meaning of "family" within South African history is complex and riddled with overlapping class and racial presumptions, and "The Mafeking Affair" highlighted the instability of this category.

23 Cherryl Walker, Shireen Hassim, Linzi Manicom, Elizabeth Gordon, and Lauretta Ngcobo, all make reference to the politics of intimate relationships in exile, the reserves, and the underground movement, but the reluctance of women to voice those experiences has left that very complicated terrain unexplored. Whether in exile or actively working in the underground, women established relationships with men due to a variety of factors like coercion, necessity, or convenience, and the historical silences surrounding the nature of these relationships have left a noticeable void in a

comprehensive analysis of the lives of women laboring in the underground.

24 I use the term "political refugees" throughout the biography to reference anti-apartheid activists from South Africa who fled the country for neighboring ones due to active government harassment.

25 South African scholars like Saleem Badat and Lauretta Ngcobo have helped to broaden contemporary understandings of previously unexplored aspects of Apartheid by introducing the phenomenon of banning, banishment, and political exile, as categories of historical analysis. Their works bring the forgotten lives of dozens of victims of banning and exile into the light, both men and women who paid the ultimate price for opposing Apartheid. Both *Prodigal Daughters* and *The Forgotten People*

speak directly to the disruption of families, however, it is the experiences of parents, rather than children that is privileged, a distinct departure for this project. Badat, *The Forgotten People*; Ngcobo, Lauretta (ed.), *Prodigal Daughters: Stories of South African Women in Exile* (Pietermaritzburg: UKZN Press, 2012).

26 Badat is quoting Ernest Cole, a photographer who briefly lived amongst a small group of banished individuals in 1964. Badat, *The Forgotten People*, xix.

1

Unbridled Insinuation and Unproven Charges

Banning and the Anatomy of Exile

In 1959, the Paarl Native Commissioner – acting at the behest of the local town council and under police escort – arrived at Elizabeth Mafeking's home to present her with banning orders from the Minister for Bantu Affairs.[1] Mafeking *had* to go. The canning industry in Paarl, in the center of the Boland region known for its rich agriculture and fruit growing, and the "single largest employers of African labor," had been under an unusual amount of pressure to provide more economic security to its largely African workforce.[2] Pressure Mafeking had been helping to exert for more than a decade. She was central to the perception of the Western Areas as "hotbeds of African resistance."[3] She and the protests she engaged in threatened all three of the major industries in the region –

1 Unbridled Insinuation and Unproven Charges

mining, manufacturing, and agriculture – and had created a formidable base of African resistance that necessitated her removal from the Western Cape.[4] She simply *had* to go. Mafeking's firstborn child, then twenty year-old Nozipho "Sophia" Khekhemani remembered the moment as one of disbelief when police arrived at the family home to place Mafeking under house arrest. According to the orders, Mafeking's movements were entirely restricted, and she was not allowed to step foot outside of her home, not even to stand in the front yard or the small garden at the back of the home. Sophia remembers the orders were clear: "she must stay at home, [they said] she can't go nowhere."[5] Sophia understood fully the levels of harassment her mother endured in the name of her activist work – the pair had recently been arrested alongside one another for willfully violating pass laws – but even she could not fathom the idea of banishment for her 41 year-old mother.

Sophia was a young mother herself at the time, and knew first-hand the level of harassment her mother endured because she'd been arrested in October of 1959 alongside her mother for willfully violating pass laws.[6] She was also well-acquainted with her mother's offbeat sense of humor, which manifested itself at the strangest times. Following their release from prison, Mafeking insisted the family take a photo to commemorate the proud occasion. Two weeks later, however, the family's cheerful mood was replaced with one of disbelief when police arrived at the family home to place Mafeking under house arrest. The very next day, Mafeking's supporters – local ANC-leaders, Coloured activists, and even local Muslims – began arriving to find out exactly what the police wanted. When Mafeking showed the group her banning orders, it was agreed that a small party should be dispatched immediately to see Mafeking's proposed place of residence. Within 48 hours ANC-leaders arranged transport to Vryburg and flew to Southey with a small, exploratory group. Three days later, back in Paarl, Mafeking's group of supporters met again to hear ANC Provincial President Oscar Mpetha report on Vryburg. "She can't, and the children won't [go there]. She just can't. We must fight, because she can't go there." The group began to devise a plan, told Mafeking not to worry, and left with a promise to return. Five days later the police

1 Unbridled Insinuation and Unproven Charges

returned in numbers, this time to serve Mafeking with revised orders giving her one week to put her affairs in order and prepare to leave Paarl.

When Mafeking saw the location of her banishment on the form the police handed her was more than 600 miles away in Vryburg, she asked, "What about my kids?" Officials seemed to have planned for this particular contingency in the case of Mafeking, and she was informed her children would be allowed to make the long, one-way journey – which would include an airplane ride across country and an additional helicopter ride to the remote location of Vryburg – with her. Mafeking scoffed at the idea of relocating her eleven children into the wilderness and asked officials what they expected her to do about educating them since there were no African schools within twenty miles. Sophia recalls the police who delivered the banning orders had a ready answer: the government would send a teacher to Vryburg for the express purpose of educating the Mafeking children. Mafeking had very little faith that the government would actually supply her children with a personal tutor during her indefinite time in banishment, insisted they attend a proper

1 Unbridled Insinuation and Unproven Charges

school, and informed officials her children would not be banished along with her. Satisfied they'd made their point and that Mafeking seemed to accept her fate, the police left.

Figure 1.1 The Mafeking family pictured outside their home in Paarl, October 1959. Within days of this photo being taken, Elizabeth Mafeking received banning orders dictating she move more than 600 miles away from her home and family in the Western Cape. [From left to right, back row to front: Mehlo Andrew (13), Nozkhumbuzo Gertrude (19), Ngubenyathi Melford (14), Nozipho Sophie (20), holding her first-born child, Moffat Henry Mditjane, Elizabeth Mafeking (holding baby Uhuru), Atti Stanley (17), Nomahlubi Rhoda (12), Nomonde Mary (4), Nomvula Nominki (18 mos.), Sisinyana Suzan (8), Nomsa Catherine (7).

1 Unbridled Insinuation and Unproven Charges

News Collection ZA (Vault) Hoover Library & Archives, Stanford University. New Age, November 5, 1959

Figure 1.2 The Mafeking home at 34 Barbarossa Street in Paarl, South Africa. This image was taken hours after police served Mafeking with banning orders. A multi-racial crowd of supporters began to gather in front of the Mafeking family home in the days leading up to her escape.

News Collection ZA (Vault) Hoover Library & Archives, Stanford University. New Age, November 5, 1959

Mafeking had not accepted her fate, however, and over the next ten weeks, she and her supporters waged a very public war of conscience against the government dictate of banning, and the intricacies of this protracted

1 Unbridled Insinuation and Unproven Charges

battle – referred to as "The Mafeking Affair" – played out in dozens of articles, interviews, and exposés that eventually filled the pages of newspapers in South Africa, Basutoland, and Great Britain. While Mafeking was ultimately unsuccessful in her bid to have her banning order revoked, her initial struggle to do so offers critical insight into contemporary conversations within the field of South African women's history regarding the personal, cultural, social, and political reconstruction of African "motherhood" under Apartheid. For Mafeking's eleven children, the status and meaning of the word "family" – already under strain in African communities due to Apartheid policies designed to separate husbands working in urban locales from their wives (and subsequently, children) – was further complicated by the politics of exile that defined the next thirty-two years of their mother's life. Media coverage from South Africa during the early weeks of Mafeking's banning introduce her children as unwitting casualties in the government's attack on their mother, and the experiences of Mafeking's children in the wake of her banning provide first-hand insight into the lives of exile's invisible victims.

1 Unbridled Insinuation and Unproven Charges

The Mafeking Affair occurred during a crucial moment of political reordering in South African society when gender and racial oppression were legitimated simultaneously, and this chapter demonstrates that the most valuable lesson the National Party learned in its battle with Elizabeth Mafeking was that in order to secure Apartheid there could be no mercy on native women.

Figure 1.3 This image of the poorly-maintained entrance to the isolated farm of Mafeking's proposed banishment was one of many critics labored to publicize. Prior to Mafeking's banning, the fate of the banned was largely invisible, but Mafeking's plight put a face on the practice and details on its execution.

1 Unbridled Insinuation and Unproven Charges

News Collection ZA (Vault) Hoover Library & Archives, Stanford University. New Age, November 5, 1959

Figure 1.4 These three, isolated shacks were originally constructed to house political exiles, and Elizabeth Mafeking was assigned here to serve out her indefinite banning orders.

News Collection ZA (Vault) Hoover Library & Archives, Stanford University. New Age, November 5, 1959

1 Unbridled Insinuation and Unproven Charges

"The scandal of banishment"

South African Apartheid legislation of the 1950s was not a new phenomenon. Some of the more internationally vilified laws of the decade, including the Group Areas Act, Internal Security Act (Suppression of Communism Act), Population Registration Act, and Bantu Education Act, were merely formalizations of long-standing segregation policies established under both Dutch and British settler rule. Confining Africans to "reserves" that comprised just seven (and eventually only thirteen) percent of the country's available land, prohibiting dissent, racially separating the population, and codifying a wholly inferior education system for non-whites was the glue that held together a white minority population that had historically divided itself along ethnic lines. It was only during the time of Mafeking's very public plight that the world began to understand what Helen Joseph referred to as "the scandal of banishment."[7] Banishment – the policy of removing Africans who opposed government policies from their homes to a remote or abandoned part of the country – was a right the Afrikaner-

1 Unbridled Insinuation and Unproven Charges

led government first gave itself in 1927, then refined through an amendment in 1956. Prior to 1952, however, there were no definitive records of removals, and even then General Hertzog, Minister of Native Affairs, was reluctant to release the names of the 98 individuals banned between January 1948 and December 1958. According to Joseph, Hertzog only supplied a list of names, a list of places where banned individuals came from, and a list of places banned individuals went.

> No details were given of who had come from where, or to where any particular person had been sent, or when, this information was of little value.[8]

It seemed as if the official policy of the Nationalist Government with regards to banned individuals was set: level an unsubstantiated charge, cast an individual into the wilderness, and wait for everyone to forget about them or for the banned to die. For the removed, banishment meant having little to no means of existence, depending upon the charity of other blacks in their general vicinity and laborer's

1 Unbridled Insinuation and Unproven Charges

work if/when available. Resettled on one of three main camps established for the banished in Frenchdale, Driefontein, and Southey – all stark, bare locales in the semi-desert miles from the nearest town – men and women lived in huts that were, according to one deportee, "not fit for human habitation."[9] A significant number of banned elderly (aged 55–75) died in exile due to starvation rather than natural causes.

> Nats Banish Mother of 11 to Semi-Desert N. Cape Area.[10]
> Exiled – for what?[11]
> Bantustan Circus.[12]

When these headlines broke in early November 1959, it seemed truly incomprehensible to rationally minded individuals that it was in the best interest of the general public to separate a mother from eleven children and deport her to an unfamiliar and unwelcoming locale. According to the South African government, Mafeking's "continued presence in Paarl [was] injurious to the peace, order and good administration of the Natives," and no

1 Unbridled Insinuation and Unproven Charges

amount of outside petitioning would alter their decision.[13] At the time of her banning, there were already 80 individuals in exile across the country, but they were all men. While African women had and continued to be displaced by pass laws, Mafeking, alone, stood poised to experience the life of poverty, isolation, and degradation banishment all but assured. Just who was Elizabeth Mafeking, though, and how had a working mother with eleven children risen from the obscurity of the masses to earn the title of "most dangerous threat to native administration?"

Becoming Elizabeth Mafeking

Combining sources from oral histories and government records to newspapers and organizational records provides as comprehensive as possible a look at the professional life of a fascinating woman who was one of the first long-term victims of the Apartheid state. Born in the Tarkastad District in the Cape Province in 1918, Elizabeth Mafeking was the youngest of Andries and Katherine Mofokeng's five

1 Unbridled Insinuation and Unproven Charges

children.[14] Mafeking's parents were of BaSotho origin, but – as most immigrants from the isolated mountain kingdom of Lesotho in the early twentieth century – had been drawn to the prospects of earning a living in the growing, urban metropoles of South Africa before Mafeking's birth.[15]

At that time, Basutoland was an area of approximately 11,000 square miles and was shaped similarly to a slightly irregular, soft-edged rectangle tilted at a 45 degree angle. The long line of the Drakensberg Mountain Range, the eastern portion of the Great Escarpment, extended along the eastern border of the country just to the southern tip of Lesotho – separating the country from the lush, fertile plains of the Natal region further east. Geographically considered the "roof of Southern Africa," Basutoland was situated at a uniformly high altitude with an average ground altitude of 5,000 feet.[16] These altitudes, ironically referred to as "Lowlands," dominated the westernmost portion of the country and accounted for one-third of the land mass. Moving east across Basutoland, these Lowlands quickly gave way to the Maluti Mountains – a "highland" mountain range that was part of the Drakensberg system, which constituted the remaining two-thirds of the country.

The Maluti Mountains are home to Thabana Ntletyana, the highest mountain in Lesotho and the highest peak in Southern Africa, at 11,425 feet.[17] The high-altitude continental climate of Basutoland ensured that summers were hot and winters were cold. It was not uncommon for summer temperatures to reach 95 degrees in the shade during the day, and for temperatures in the winter to drop to 10 degrees at night – cold enough to earn the country the nickname "African Switzerland."[18] Electrical storms and whirlwinds were the only two regularly occurring meteorological natural phenomena – and both could be seen from great distances.[19] While majestic mountain ranges and sweeping landscapes were plentiful, natural resources – such as water – were not. The country relied solely upon ten rivers that were simply too small to meet the needs of its citizens and there were no major industries; thus, hundreds of thousands of BaSotho like Mafeking's parents emigrated in a gamble on a better existence in South Africa.

1 Unbridled Insinuation and Unproven Charges

When her father died the year of her birth, however, Mafeking's mother relocated the family hundreds of miles north to Kimberly, "the city of diamonds," where they settled in Aliwal North and Mafeking joined the household of her 90 year-old grandmother, Martha.[20] The entire family eventually settled in Hugenot in the Cape, and Mafeking attended a school for Coloured children since there were no schools for African children in the immediate area. When Mafeking reached Standard 2, she transferred to an African school in Cape Town until she completed Standard 4, at which time a family crisis precipitated her temporarily leaving school to find work. At the age of 14, Mafeking began selling *amagwinya* at nearby factories to support her family.[21] When the family relocated for the third and final time to Paarl in 1927, Mafeking had the opportunity to attain a Standard 7 education before she finally abandoned her educational pursuits for more practical ones.

For inexperienced, 16 year-old Mafeking, joining the H. Jones & Company canning factory in the city of Paarl in 1934 to clean out the large basins used to sort fruit for canning earned her only a little over three shillings per week.[22] It was a good start, however, the Mafeking family had settled into life as members of the multi-racial community of Paarl, 60 kilometers from the bustling city center of Cape Town, and the non-skilled labor allowed Mafeking to help support her widowed mother. When Mafeking first joined the canning factory in 1934, working conditions were poor. "Virtually all aspects of production were carried out by hand." Canning workers used special knives and spoons to process fruit and manually stirred the caustic chemicals used to dissolve fruit skin.[23] Human skin dissolved too, due to "*vrugte vingers*," a condition suffered by those tasked with working "barefoot on floors wet with acidic fruit juices which blackened the skin and ate into the cuticle, causing swelling and drawing blood."[24] Working women did not have the privilege of set lunch hours, regular breaks, employment benefits, protective clothing, or employment protection for pregnancy and maternity leave.[25] Their employers, however, enjoyed sweeping license over the professional – and even personal – lives of working women. Black-and-white photographs from the factory floor of the H. Jones Canning Factory illustrate the

1 Unbridled Insinuation and Unproven Charges

company's cold efficiency. The first image comes from inside the sorting room, a concrete warehouse approximately half the size of a football field with more than a dozen steel-topped tables, one hundred and sixty feet in length, perfectly spaced one after the other. Each table has fifteen African women – identically clad in sterile, white frocks and matching hair bonnets – standing roughly ten feet apart from one another. On the table in front of each woman are six large basins filled with apricots, and women are busily separating damaged fruit from its sellable counterpart. On both sides of the standing women are crates of un-sorted fruit stacked as high as the table. Another image from the canning section of the H. Jones Canning Factory shows a similarly sized facility with the same long steel-topped tables and uniformed employees, but there are significantly fewer (and lighter-skinned) women performing the marginally more skilled labor of canning, as opposed to the large numbers of African women performing the least-skilled task of sorting.[26] What the images do not show, however, are the actual employment conditions of the hundreds of women photographed hard at work – and the hundreds more *not* pictured.

In 1939, one of South Africa's most widely circulated periodicals, the *Guardian*, ran an exposé on the working conditions of women in the food industry.[27] According to the article, when seasonal work was available, canning workers spent most of their 48-hour work week standing barefoot in water. Employers routinely turned a blind eye to the health and welfare of those on the factory floor. They refused to provide boots or any other protective clothing to guard employees against the stagnant water, dismissed tin-cutting operators unlucky enough to lose fingers while on the job, and fired pregnant workers rather than provide them a legally mandated "confinement allowance."[28] In exchange for long hours spent doing dangerous work on the factory floor, black women in this industry earned roughly $1.50 per week.[29] Liz Abrahams details horrendous working conditions for both the women who worked at the H. Jones Canning Factory and, more shockingly, their very young children. In *Married to the Struggle*, Abrahams recalls memories of her own mother coming home after long days

1 Unbridled Insinuation and Unproven Charges

in the factory to complain about working conditions.[30] Neither workers nor women enjoyed protected rights in the workplace in the early 1940s, and employers took advantage of every opportunity to keep productivity high and costs low. The factory was simply that, a factory. There was no break room, no sitting room, and no coat room. Neither the images nor Abrahams's mother reveal where, how, or if, women working in factories navigated relieving themselves. There was no lunch room either, but working women did not have set lunch hours, so there was no need for such a space. Women were made to "eat their lunch out in the fields" that surrounded the factory, and to use a fruit storage shed as both a cloakroom and holding area for small children. Breastfeeding women necessarily left their small babies out back in the fruit shed for hours at a time until employers decided to grant workers a lunch or tea break long enough to nurse. These particular working mothers were lucky though, because they had somehow managed to keep their jobs.

Employers routinely dismissed both pregnant women and women who were rumored to be pregnant.

1 Unbridled Insinuation and Unproven Charges

Classified as "seasonal" workers as opposed to regular "employees," women could expect to be hired when a harvest came in, then fired for weeks at a time until the next fruit ripened. The growing seasons for apricots, peaches, and pears had just enough length of time between them – two to three weeks during which factory bosses fired women – that seasonal food and canning workers were ineligible for workers benefits like the Unemployment Insurance Act, which stipulated recipients had to be employed for thirteen consecutive weeks to be covered under the plan. It was common practice for working women to accept indignities both great and small, personal and professional. Abrahams recognized her mother's generation of working women in factories accepted these conditions "because they didn't know how to deal with it and had no option because they had to earn wages."[31] For Mafeking and fellow workers classified as unskilled "day work," wages were largely dependent upon employer whim, and daily work hours could easily range from 12 to 18 hours.[32] Getting off work at 1am meant there was no public transport available, forcing women – many with

1 Unbridled Insinuation and Unproven Charges

babies strapped to their backs – to walk home from the factory. When she married in 1938 to Moffat Henry Mditjane – a co-worker employed as a truck driver at the H. Jones Canning Factory and the next year gave birth to her first child, Nozipho "Sophia" Ndiya, Mafeking too strapped her breastfeeding baby to her back for the 3km (2 mile) walk from home to the factory gates.[33]

The long hours and low pay were not enough to convince most women – African or Coloured – working in the H. Jones Canning Factory that union organization could or would fix anything. While this type of attitude amongst workers was typical, Mafeking's response was anything but. Mafeking was moved deeply by the slogan that appeared on most Food and Canning Workers Union (FCWU) literature aimed at building membership: "Their fight is your fight. You must see that they win."[34] Moreover, early concessions from employers impressed the 23 year-old mother who gave birth to her second child – Nozkhumbuzo Gertrude Mditjane – in the closing days of 1940, then immediately joined the loosely formed FCWU, organized by communist and union stalwart Ray Alexander, who had been sent to Paarl by the Communist Party for the express purpose of organizing workers in the food industry.[35]

When the FCWU was officially established in 1941, it was a multi-racial organization with African, Coloured, and European members, tasked with organizing the thousands of non-white workers who comprised the bulk of the food and canning industry in South Africa. Mafeking was no doubt skeptical of the new organization, but her first-hand experiences with the very aims and objectives outlined in the FCWU's constitution as areas for workplace improvement and regulation, were her likely entrée into the politics of union organizing.[36]

When Cecil Capello was elected as the first chairman of the new workers union at H. Jones & Company in 1941 and was summarily fired by employers for that transgression, Mafeking was part of the largely African workforce that took off their working clothes and walked out of the factory in protest. In the ensuing weeks, Mafeking saw first-hand the resolution of Ray Alexander and other leaders of FCWU to both support and develop African workers. When bosses, foremen, and city officials

1 Unbridled Insinuation and Unproven Charges

would not come to the negotiating table with the African labor force, Mafeking saw Alexander advocate for workers directly. When the strike extended from the first into the second, then third week, and workers struggled to feed their families, Mafeking was one of many beneficiaries of funds donated by other unions organized by Alexander herself. When bosses – in a desperate bid to replace the workers – recruited white women from the Afrikaans Christian Women's Association (ACW) to cross strike lines, the young Mafeking no doubt laughed right along with Alexander and the rest of the striking workforce when the ACW women left the factory within hours of arriving because they could not complete the difficult work and "refused to have Coloured workers teach them."[37]

Within the first year of its operation, the new union won its first victory, securing wage increases and sick pay for unskilled workers.[38] In early 1941, Mafeking was a seven-year working veteran of the H. Jones Canning Factory who knew full well the potential power of unions, and joined the FCWU as one of its first shop stewards in the new organization.[39] According to Alexander, workers like

Mafeking had "learnt the power of organization, something no one could take away from them."[40] Within a month, Mafeking established an FCWU branch in her hometown of Paarl, and helped to organize a workers' three-week stay-away.[41] Mafeking led the approximately 400 workers in a strike against canning bosses in Paarl who had previously agreed not to harass strikers, union members, or their leaders, but had only responded with lowered wages and workplace victimization.[42] In the end, workers were able to secure concessions that encouraged them to return to work. Paarl union membership soared, nonetheless, and the strike proved to workers in various industries that the workers union – with more than 3,000 members – was a powerful force for change.[43] In spite of (and perhaps due to) some improvement of labor conditions after the creation of African trade unions in 1941 and their repeated actions, the government still refused to recognize their legality. The FCWU had become so successful in its efforts to secure wage regulation and improved industry conditions that in 1942 the South African Minister of Labor solicited suggestions from the organization regarding the establishment of a potential National Industrial Council.[44] Moreover, the FCWU experienced rapid growth and established branches in Johannesburg, Germiston, Pretoria, Durban, Cape Town, Paarl, Wellington, Worchester, Groot Drakenstein, Stellenbosch, and Wolseley. Hundreds of workers belonging to these branches were employed in industries that touched every segment of South African society – regardless of race, socio-economic level, or even political affiliation. No one was immune from the necessary goods produced by the labor of those employed in the all-encompassing food and canning manufacturing industry. From white housewives of Hillbrow to Coloureds in the Cape, everyone and everything in the country depended upon the labor of those who:

> manufactured, bottled, canned, or packed jam, vegetables, fruit, fish, meat, soups, macaroni, fruit juices, condensed milk, infant and invalid foods, butter, pickles, and sauces, vinegar, condiments, spices, mayonnaise, polony, bacon, jelly, fruit crystals, grape juice, moskonfyt, wine and

1 Unbridled Insinuation and Unproven Charges

> brandy, custard and curry powders, processed products, mincemeat, Christmas puddings, dried and crystallized fruit, dehydrated goods, squashes and cordials, potato chips, weetbix, edible oils and/or food made for animal consumption and the making and processing of cheese.[45]

The union utilized provoking language in its communiques, proclaiming "the Food and Canning Workers' Union has come to stay."[46] It would take more than a decade for the South African government to undertake policies and legislation to decimate the leadership ranks of the FCWU, but for a brief moment in the early years of the union, it appeared as if all things were possible. As the union continued to grow, so too did Mafeking's own family, and just three months after the FCWU submitted its recommendations to the Minister of Labor for more precise job definitions, wage guarantees, and other workplace concerns like payment schedules, overtime, holidays, and working clothes, Mafeking gave birth to her third child – Atti Stanley Mditjane – in April 1942.

1 Unbridled Insinuation and Unproven Charges

Mafeking persisted in her work, and through it slowly began to develop a personal relationship with the well-known Ray Alexander and inspire workers starting out in the union like Liz Abrahams, a new canning factory employee who could not understand why – after seeing her own mother's trials – she needed to join the union.[47] Abrahams knew "in those days the employers and the government were very tough on anyone who tried to organize workers."[48] Organizers encountered difficulties registering new union members due to government surveillance, and they struggled to book meeting halls because hall owners and managers "really didn't like the union."[49] Whereas Abrahams's FCWU branch in Daljosophat struggled to get off the ground, Mafeking's branch in Paarl quickly became a model for successful union organizing. According to Abrahams:

> Paarl had a strong trade union in the community. The community of Paarl was very active, even the trade union. If you were a factory worker, you were a member of the trade union, and at home you were a

member of the community. That really worked. The community also went to the trade union for help and for advice. You could always go and ask them to explain something.[50]

In the early days of the FCWU, the unions in Paarl were particularly strong due in very large part to the purposeful marriage of community and worker. That, and the city's proximity to Cape Town guaranteed that when organizations like the Coloured People's Congress (CPC), the South African Congress of Trade Unions (SACTU), and the Federation of South African Women (FEDSAW) formed and wanted to expand, they all set their sights on Paarl first as a potential and fertile recruiting ground. Abrahams candidly admits "everything you established in Cape Town, you had to establish in Paarl was well."[51] In the Cape Town branch of FEDSAW, trade unions were far more influential than the ANCWL. The demographics of the membership were very different in the Western Cape where Mafeking would eventually be labeled "the most dangerous threat to native administration." The African membership of

1 Unbridled Insinuation and Unproven Charges

FEDSAW was "proportionately smaller" in the Western as opposed to the Eastern Cape, but Mafeking's own family composition, working-class relatability, and factory-based experience in the food canning industry – in particular – posited her as a credible source of the daily struggles against Apartheid for the average worker, regardless of race.[52] Over the course of the next decade, Elizabeth Mafeking labored to build a reputation for Paarl as a hotbed of union organization and expanded her own influence by organizing even further into surrounding communities. While employers instituted a number of policies to keep union organizers and potential members from speaking – like requiring all factory visitors gain permission from management to access the premises – Mafeking and Abrahams found creative ways to circumvent such rules.

Abrahams recalled an evening when she traveled with Mafeking to Tulbagh, a quiet town 60km north of Paarl, to meet with workers recently organized by Mafeking herself. Within a few years of its operation, the FCWU had won enough substantive concessions from employers that they were on the lookout for union organizers, and both

1 Unbridled Insinuation and Unproven Charges

Abrahams and Mafeking were on a very short list of people to watch out for. The evening Abrahams drove to Tulbagh, she and Mafeking decided to hide themselves and the car in the bushes until it was dark enough for them to secret themselves onto the factory grounds. When night fell, the pair exited the vehicle and quietly crept onto the property, quickly making their way to the pre-arranged meeting spot. As they rounded the corner of a building, they ran head-first into a knobkerrie-wielding night foreman who threatened them with violence and demanded the women leave. The night foreman must have contacted the police, because by the time the pair returned to Paarl, they'd already been charged with trespassing and named as defendants in a pending court case. While the women had to retain legal representation and appear in court, the case against Mafeking and Abrahams was eventually withdrawn on a technicality: when the magistrate and prosecutor traveled to the Tulbagh factory to see first-hand where and how the women had allegedly trespassed, "they saw that there was no gate . . . just a fence."[53] The court ruled trespassing could not have occurred because the women never opened a

1 Unbridled Insinuation and Unproven Charges

gate. The Tulbagh incident was one of the first encounters Mafeking had with the judicial system, and subsequent run-ins would not end so providentially.

Elizabeth Mafeking began taking the lead in mobilizing her working-class counterparts and advancing their understanding of radical politics. Like most organized black women in South Africa, she found herself at the center of controversy. When National Party (NP) administrators in the Cape eventually described Elizabeth Mafeking as "the most dangerous threat to native administration" in 1959, it was not wild exaggeration, rather, it was an apt description of her influence within trade union circles in the Cape Province that had been birthed in the 1940s.[54] Membership in the FCWU had almost doubled in less than a decade, from 9,667 members in 1944 to 18,598 by 1951, with the majority of the members coming from the Western Cape, Elizabeth Mafeking's organizational territory.[55]

1 Unbridled Insinuation and Unproven Charges

Figure 1.5 Mafeking pictured at a FCWU meeting in the late 1940s giving the "Afrika" salute.

Courtesy of Sibeko, Archie with Joyce Leeson, Roll of Honour: Western Cape ANC Comrades 1953-1963 (University of the Western Cape, 2008)

1 Unbridled Insinuation and Unproven Charges

Figure 1.6 Mafeking discussing the party newspaper and selling it to workers.

Courtesy of Patel, Yusuf and Philip Hirschsohn, eds., Married to the Struggle: 'Nana' Liz Abrahams Tells her Life Story (University of the Western Cape, 2005)

The attractions of radicalism

Since the late nineteenth century, participation in South African trade unions was restricted to white workers. British immigrants to South Africa organized the first unions, bringing their background of trade union tradition and experience into their organized work. Worker's

1 Unbridled Insinuation and Unproven Charges

organizations met with great hostility from employers and state authorities from the very beginning and well into the first few years of the establishment of the Union of South Africa in 1910. Senate President F. S. Malan admitted, "Parliament had as yet not provided the machinery necessary to deal with industrial disputes, and what was even more ominous, the majority of the members, being totally unacquainted with industrial problems, were unsympathetic towards trade unions and their methods."[56] Even as the government began developing mechanisms for dealing with workers, their unions, and their demands, it was wholly disinclined to entertain the notion of recognizing or negotiating with non-European workers. Early twentieth century conflict between settlers of Afrikaner and English descent, however, created a political space wherein black women could begin to negotiate the conditions and policies that dictated their lives in South Africa. Historian Nomboniso Gasa reintroduces the pass protests of African women in 1913 to South African women's historiography, emphasizing women's political agency and the numerous causes that attracted women to

1 Unbridled Insinuation and Unproven Charges

politics.[57] Successful anti-pass campaigns waged by the Bantu Women's League of South Africa (the forerunner of the ANC-Women's League) in 1918 under the direction of Charlotte Maxeke, were fertile training grounds for African women in protest against state mandates. Widespread protests in South Africa in the 1920s created an opportunity for radical, international political groups to capitalize on the growing political viability of African women.

Women's trade union involvement in the early 1930s served as the catalyst for discussions of gender equality within the larger freedom struggle, and this consolidation of women's political power into local and regional organizations led to the 1935 founding of the National Council for African Women, which was primarily concerned with the economic welfare of women.[58] The extreme poverty of Depression-era South Africa exacerbated the position of the country's black populace, whose deliberate exclusion from a mid-decade economic movement designed to protect Afrikaner interests was the framework of the legal discrimination that would later come to characterize the system of Apartheid. Women

1 Unbridled Insinuation and Unproven Charges

workers of all hues responded to these pressures with an increased level of organization and interaction with the government.

In the 1940s black South Africans formed black trade unions, learned from the mistakes of or affiliated with national organizations like the Industrial and Commercial Workers Union of Africa, the South African Trades and Labor Council, and the South African Congress of Trade Unions (SACTU).[59] The economic stimulant of war resulted in a 60% increase in manufacturing jobs during the same time, with black women, who were new to both the industrial workforce and labor movement, comprising the vast majority of the wartime labor pool. For Malan and his contemporaries, Apartheid was a necessary reaction to a seemingly impossible situation: how best to control frighteningly high numbers of increasingly truculent natives. For the women who flocked to the cities attempting to support themselves and their families, life became a web of new, complicated rules and regulations that often ran directly counter to deeply-held cultural practices. Twice during the inter-war years South Africa had

1 Unbridled Insinuation and Unproven Charges

passed laws that attempted to control the movement of African women to the cities. These efforts sought to direct what was then, in comparison to the veritable flood brought about by wartime manufacturing growth years later, merely a trickle of supposedly surplus persons from the "reserves." By the 1950s, this trickle had become a torrent.

The reaction of the central government to this unwanted influx, often directed at the African population as a whole but most frequently and harshly felt by African women, is well-documented by an extensive scholarship that examines the history of pass protest. Indeed, as Cherryl Walker has observed, "Apartheid as control was most forcibly felt by African women in the form of influx control and the pass laws."[60] These restrictions led to a period of unparalleled political action by African women and "their anti-pass campaign(s) [were some] of the most vociferous and effective protest campaigns of any at the time."[61] The history of pass protest is central to the memory of black women's protest in South Africa in the twentieth century. This narrative, unfortunately, often dominates conversations about women's varied interactions with and responses to state-enforced restrictions on their lives. A host of other issues like voter representation and forced removals, and exposure to international protest movement networks, however, placed African women in opposition to the directives of the South African government – a dangerous place in postwar South Africa – and served as surprising sites of introduction to political activism and interaction with Apartheid policies. This high-time of union activism was, incidentally, the time when Elizabeth Mafeking began her activist career in earnest.

Radicalizing African women

In 1944, the South African Supreme Court ruled that African women in the industrial workforce were employees under the Industrial Conciliation Act and thus deserving of union access and rights. This had little effect on the workings of UP administrators or those who were slowly beginning to be attracted to what would eventually become the National Party (NP), but it made a great impact on African working women. The ruling provided women's protest with new energy, and they pushed to benefit fully from trade union agreements and to further entrench themselves in the everyday workings of their local communities. The industrial organization of Africans reached its peak in 1944, with more than 60 unions in the Transvaal area alone, at a total membership of almost 100,000.[62] Still, without the legal ability to protect the rights of its membership, African trade unions could "hope to exercise only indirect influence on the policies" of the larger trade union movement.[63] The war years and immediate postwar era in South Africa saw women's groups necessarily stepping into the void when government officials and their policies neglected to service the needs of local communities. Women in urban areas formed food committees across racial lines to combat food shortages, further contributing to the perception of the 1940s as a high-time of social activism that was rife with squatter movements, bus boycotts, and the continued agitation of trade unions.

In his discussion of the economic foundations of Apartheid, economist Thomas Hazlett emphasizes that the

1 Unbridled Insinuation and Unproven Charges

pre-1947 efforts of black laborers in South Africa to control, alter, and negotiate terms of employment via collective bargaining – privileges long enjoyed by European laborers – served as a direct challenge to both white workers (against whom they competed for work, but with whom they contentiously aligned under the Communist Party of South Africa (CPSA)) and would-be social engineers. With the help of the Party in South Africa, black workers formed unions in many different trades and used what South African historian Shireen Hassim terms "bread-n-butter issues" to draw African women into its organizational fold.[64] Mid-twentieth century communists knew that most women were "inclined to become active in unions that combine their multifaceted concerns with work, family, and community life."[65] One popular "bread-n-butter" issue taken up by the CPSA on behalf of women was vegetable growing clubs. Billing itself as an "invaluable" service to "people earning low wages," a communist-run vegetable club placed an ad to attract new members. It boasted that members of the club branch in Cape Town recently received "three cabbages, ten squashes, two bunches of carrots, two bunches of turnips and three pounds of peas" for half what the items would have cost through conventional means.[66]

The Party was particularly adept at creating pamphlets and political cartoons that struck at the very heart of issues closest to women. In one wartime pamphlet, a tired, gaunt woman carrying a baby stands outside a store with signs on the window proclaiming there was "No Meat" and "No Butter" inside. Standing in front of the poor woman is an overweight Nazi in full regalia, shaking his fist in the woman's face and spitting as he says, "Why do you expect butter and meat. Don't you know everything is required to make ammunitions so we can get colonies?"[67] At the time, the Communist Party was one of the few international organizations operating in South Africa to cast a spotlight on wartime shortages of goods and products. It was a part of an even smaller circle of groups to actually *implement* substantive programs that directly aided communities *and* overtly linked the struggles black women confronted in their homes on a daily basis to the larger oppression associated with capitalism and institutionalized discrimination.[68]

1 Unbridled Insinuation and Unproven Charges

In 1945, "drastic" cuts in butter rations led to public outrage, with South Africans of all races accusing the government of "playing with health and lives to protect the vested interests of the butter producers."[69] Daily survival issues like this offered the perfect opportunity for organizations like the Communist Party to attract new members, and it targeted its recruiting schemes directly at the most urgent needs of the 250,000 African workers employed in manufacturing.[70] Soaring prices and low availability of fresh vegetables led the Party to establish the Woodstock Vegetable Club in Cape Town, which offered club members significant discounts on fresh produce.[71] Focusing on issues relating to the home – most especially the inability or unwillingness of the government to provide basic foodstuff – allowed the Party to reach countless new members, the majority of whom were poor, black women. Indeed, women's protest of food shortages was a national priority in South Africa in the late 1940s. "Food chaos" was to blame for numerous public food raids in which hundreds of citizens descended upon a location suspected of hoarding goods in search of elusive rations.[72] The situation

1 Unbridled Insinuation and Unproven Charges

was so critical that in 1947 the *Guardian* – a leading South African newspaper – reported that a Cape Town-based Women's Food Committee, representing a multi-racial group of "between twenty and thirty thousand women," had taken it upon itself to monitor the rationing of available foodstuff and maintain order at distribution sites.[73]

By 1947, at the same time women workers found new ways to expand their influence from the political to the social, authorities finagled to rid themselves of certain unions and their leaders once and for all. The Labour Department threatened particular branches of the FCWU with the revocation of their coveted union registration status on the ground that the branches were non-racial – in direct contradiction to government mandates. When faced with no other alternative, the FCWU expelled its African members in 1947 – including Elizabeth Mafeking – who then immediately helped to form the African Food and Canning Workers Union (AFCWU). Despite this technical separation, however, the two unions coordinated their efforts and continued to act as one, and records of both the FCWU and AFCWU attest to the close ties the two

1 Unbridled Insinuation and Unproven Charges

organizations maintained in spite of the government dictate, revealing just how much of a mockery the close relationship between the two organizations made of government dictates for non-racial alliances. By June of 1947 when the AFCWU first organized, it modeled its constitution after that of the FCWU, utilizing verbatim language to signify the alliance between the two unions.[74]

Only four months following the 1948 parliamentary election in South Africa that changed the country's history, the opposition of white unions and the right wing – who felt threatened by black political aspirations – towards the GWU, a multi-racial worker's union, reached a climax. Prime Minister D. F. Malan, who had led his Reunited National Party to victory over the long-standing, left-leaning United Party and its allies, pledged to implement a strict policy of racial separation. White unions and their right-wing allies – emboldened by Malan's supremacist rhetoric and their belief in their own, inherent superiority – determined to take matters into their own hands where non-Europeans unions were concerned. In September of 1948, members of the Blankewerkers Beskermingsbond (White Workers'

1 Unbridled Insinuation and Unproven Charges

Protection League) purposefully disrupted a meeting of the GWU's founding branch at City Hall in Johannesburg.[75] According to Emil Solomon "Solly" Sachs, an anti-apartheid activist and South African trade unionist who was in attendance, an armed mob of "several hundred" broke down the doors and rushed into the hall shouting in Afrikaans, "Today blood must flow!" Sachs contended more than one dozen policeman stood by idly while armed whites indiscriminately assaulted GWU members.[76]

In spite of their efforts and the constant assaults, African unions were not entitled to the right of organizations to register under the Industrial Conciliation Act, which would have added them to the ranks of the more than two hundred registered organizations in South Africa in 1946.[77] In fact, Africans were disqualified from membership in registered unions, and the Labour Department threatened to de-register any organization that admitted African members who did not fall within the strict category of "employees" as defined by the Industrial Conciliation Act. This meant that workers in the typographical, sweet, and canning industries were forced to leave non-racial unions and form independent unions that were largely ignored by the government.

The CPSA estimated that during the early 1940s until the close of the WWII there were more than 80 unregistered African unions with a total membership of more than 150,000. In less than a decade, however, government restrictions and regulations governing African participation in trade unions would dramatically reduce those numbers.[78] As an era, the 1950s was a decade of political activism and agitation in South Africa. There were more than 8 million Africans in the Union in 1951, which comprised approximately 67.5% of the total population, and there were strict methods in place to control the movement of those bodies between urban and supposedly African areas.[79] From the perspective of whites in the Union, the situation was dire. Each year since 1950 it was estimated that an additional 85,000 Africans migrated to urban areas in search of economic opportunities, and that the population density of Africans in urban centers was only to be rivaled by that of African density in the dreaded reserves.[80] Some of the major metropoles had been

1 Unbridled Insinuation and Unproven Charges

deemed to have "reached saturation point," but the bodies kept coming.[81] Apartheid as a formal social and political system was well underway, and the government was making definite steps to extend to African women the pass system it had all but perfected for African men.

Women organized to reject this intrusion into their everyday lives, and often used their positions and experience with trade unions to protest passes, segregation, and educational policy. The civil disobedience of the Defiance Campaigns, the organized precision of the famed Women's March, and the extended support for the exhaustive Treason Trials, were just three of the numerous examples of black responses to increased political harassment during the decade.[82] The political activism of women was an answer to the system of Apartheid, and women like Lilian Ngoyi, Annie Salinga, Viola Hashe, and Elizabeth Mafeking helped to change contemporary ideas regarding the place of African women in local and national protest.[83] The 1950s was also an era of political banning, and during the opening years of the decade numerous organizations and their leaders paid the price for their oppositional politics. The 1950 Suppression of Communism Act formally banned the CPSA, and so broadly defined communism in the process that it provided an effective mechanism by which any individual who determined to affect economic, social, political, or industrial change via "disturbance or disorder" that encouraged "feelings of hostility between the European and non-European races" could be barred from public participation, restricted in their movements, or even imprisoned. Through banning, Apartheid legislation formally brought an end to the political lives of African women's most trusted allies and their organizations in the 1950s with the broad application of the Suppression of Communism Act, forcing many of its anti-apartheid allies underground.[84] What is important to understand – most especially from the perspective of Elizabeth Mafeking's incredibly public experience – is that the relationship of black women to government structures *had* to change dramatically in South Africa the 1950s. In South Africa, at the local and national levels, women's collective voices and protest in the previous decade had

1 Unbridled Insinuation and Unproven Charges

affected changes in the relationship between themselves and Apartheid architects.

Increased opportunities of WWII, followed by heightened postwar oppression, fueled black women's resistance and organizing efforts. The 1943 reformation of the ANC-Women's League as a premier site of social activism and political justice, favorable Supreme Court legislation in 1944 granting African women "employment" status and trade union benefits, and their postwar urban mobilization to address every social issue from food shortages to squatter movements, ran counter to everything Apartheid architects believed defined African women. African women were not superfluous, they were not socially redundant, they were economically viable members of society, and they eagerly used the politics at their disposal as entrées to protest. Passes, education policy, agricultural schemes, taxation, and beer boycotts, were all issues black women championed in their everyday lives, and news of their success caused no small measure of discomfit for government officials. One year after Mafeking welcomed her sixth child, Nomahlubi Rhoda Maranyane,

1 Unbridled Insinuation and Unproven Charges

the National Party ousted the United Party in a 1948 election that represented an historic turning point in South Africa's history.

The early years of Apartheid were the heyday of Mafeking's activist career. In addition to her multiple professional responsibilities, Mafeking's personal responsibilities expanded to include children number seven and eight, Sisinyana Suzan and Nomsa Catherine respectively. Just one year after giving birth to Nomsa Catherine, Mafeking organized her local union to strike against the Coloured Representation Bill, coordinated a strike in Wolsey in the Western Cape for higher wages and better working conditions, protested against the Group Areas Act, and brazenly defied the Native Labour Settlement of Disputes Act.[85] The 1953 Act provided for a separate industrial conciliation mechanism for African workers, but Mafeking, other African union leaders, and their followers had "little faith" in the new Regional Native Labour Committees tasked with settling labor disputes involving Africans. By the end of 1953, there were a little more than two dozen African trade unions with an

1 Unbridled Insinuation and Unproven Charges

estimated total membership of 29,000.[86] In spite of the dwindling numbers, organized women could still feel and exercise the strength of their unions, as evidenced by the small, but significant battles won against employers.[87]

1 Unbridled Insinuation and Unproven Charges

Notes

1 Badat, Saleem, *The Forgotten People: Political Banishment under Apartheid* (Boston: Brill, 2013), 185–186. Badat's comprehensive introduction of the practice of banning during Apartheid offers rich detail on the individuals made victims of state repression, and offers a five-page analysis of the banning of Elizabeth Mafeking.

2 Lodge, Tom Geoffrey, *Insurrection in South Africa: The Pan-Africanist Congress and the Poqo Movement 1959–1965*. PhD Thesis (University of New York, New York, New York, United States, 1984), 265, 269.

3 Lodge, Tom Geoffrey, *Black Politics in South Africa since 1945* (New York: Longman, 1982), 99.

4 Ibid., 110.

1 Unbridled Insinuation and Unproven Charges

5 Interview, Sophia Khekhemani Mafeking with author, summer 2013, Paarl, South Africa. Original interview conducted in isiXhosa and Sesotho, translated into English.

6 Ibid.

7 Joseph, Helen, "The Living Dead" *Africa South: In Exile* vol. 5, no. 4 (July–September, 1961), 17–27.

8 Ibid., 19.

9 Ibid., 25.

10 "Nats. Banish Mother of 11 to Semi-Desert N. Cape Area" *Sunday Times*, November 1, 1959; Helen Joseph Papers. A1985/B8–11. Press Cuttings. Historical Papers Research Archive, The Library, University of the Witwatersrand, Johannesburg. Subsequent references in this chapter from this archival sources will appear as "Historical Papers Research Archive."

1 Unbridled Insinuation and Unproven Charges

---

11 "Exiled: For What?" *Daily Mail*, November 2, 1959; Helen Joseph Papers. A1985/B8–11. Press Cuttings. Historical Papers Research Archive.

12 "Bantustan Circus" *Daily Mail*, November 2, 1959; Helen Joseph Papers. A1985/B8–11. Press Cuttings. Historical Papers Research Archive.

13 The General Conference of the International Labor Organization, Committee on Freedom of Association Report, *The Trade Unions International of Workers of the Food, Tobacco and Beverage Industries and Hotel, Cafe and Restaurant Workers (Trade Department of the World Federation of Trade Unions), the South African Congress of Trade Unions and the World Federation of Trade Unions (Case No. 200)*, June 10, 1959. Text from: *Definitive Report No. 44*, http://webfusion.ilo.org/public/db/standards/nor

mes/libsynd/LSGetParasByCase.cfm?PARA=6349&FILE=200&hdroff=1&DISPLAY=RECOMMENDATION, BACKGROUND (accessed June 17, 2009).

14 According to Elizabeth Mafeking's eighth child, Nomsa Catherine Mafeking, when the Mofokeng family arrived in the Western Cape in the early part of the 1900s, the local Coloured populace found it difficult to properly pronounce the name "Mofokeng," prompting the family to change the spelling of the name on official documents to reflect the local pronunciation and lessen misunderstandings. Throughout the manuscript, I've maintained the correct spelling "Mafeking" unless quoting or citing a source that utilizes one of the many iterations of the surname; Elizabeth Mafekeng (sic) Biography. No date. Federation of South African Women (FEDSAW) 1954–1963

1 Unbridled Insinuation and Unproven Charges

Papers. AD1137-A-Ai-Ai1. Historical Papers Research Archive; "Profile: Elizabeth Mafekeng (sic)," ANC Women's Section Archives, Biographical Profiles, Box 124, Folder 19. Liberation Movement Archives of the National Heritage and Cultural Studies Centre (NAHECS), University of Fort Hare, Alice, South Africa. Subsequent references in this chapter from this archival source will appear as "NAHECS."

15 In the early twentieth century, Basutoland was a "desperately poor country" where half of the economically active men routinely abandoned the country for South African urban centers that offered a chance of cash wages; Lodge, *Black Politics in South Africa since 1945*, 176.

16 Coates, Austin, *Basutoland* (London, United Kingdom: Her Majesty's Stationery Office, 1966), 3.

1 Unbridled Insinuation and Unproven Charges

17 Ibid., 1.

18 The temperature scale used in the text is Fahrenheit; Ibid., 65.

19 Ibid., 1–3.

20 Thompson, Leonard, *A History of South Africa* (Yale: Nota Bene), 110.

21 *Amagwinya* are deep-fried, sweetened dough balls eaten as a small snack, dessert, or side item.

22 H. Jones & Company, an Australian-based company established in the late nineteenth century, made its first entrée into Southern Africa through Rhodesia. In the early 1900s, the company branched out into South Africa; Simons, Ray Alexander and Raymond Suttner (eds.), *All My Life and All My Strength* (Johannesburg: STE Publishers, 2004), 137; Shirene Fradet Carim estimates workers' wages at the canning factory to be "seven shillings and sixpence

1 Unbridled Insinuation and Unproven Charges

per week," but Mafeking's less-skilled work earned much less pay. Carim, Shirene Fradet and the United Nations Centre against Apartheid. *The Role of Women in the South African Trade Union Movement* (New York: United Nations, 1980), 11.

23 Goode, Richard, *A History of the Food and Canning Workers Union, 1941–1975*. MA Dissertation (University of Cape Town, Cape Town, South Africa, 1986), 43–44.

24 *Vrugte vingers* is Afrikaans for "fruit fingers;" Ibid., 46.

25 According to Richard Goode, workers could eat lunch outside when the foreman allowed, and could be called back "when he decided work should resume." Goode, *A History of the Food and Canning Workers Union*, 45.

26 Patel, Yosuf and Philip Hirschsohn (eds.), *Married to the Struggle: 'Nanna' Liz Abrahams Tells Her Life Story*

1 Unbridled Insinuation and Unproven Charges

(Cape Town, South Africa: University of the Western Cape, 2005). Both images appear in chapter two, "Seasonal Work in the Canning Factory."

27 Historian Iris Berger offers a cross-cultural look at women's "high level of involvement" with trade unions and national politics in the mid-twentieth century. While Berger does briefly mention the Communist Party, correctly stating that Party ideology "shaped the AFCWU," she makes no mention of either the rise or fall of the AFCWU's most notorious leader, Elizabeth Mafeking. Berger seems to miss a key opportunity to prove one of her central arguments regarding the importance of local, working-class communities to black women's activism in trade unions. Berger, "Gender, Race, and Political Empowerment," 404–405.

28 Ibid., 403.

29 Accounting for current inflation, Mafeking earned $11 per week; According to the original article, workers earned "12 shilling, 6 pence" for the week. All conversions made using "Old Sterling Currency, £sd," http://anita-calculators.info/html/old_sterling_currency__gbpsd.html, and "The Inflation Calculator," www.westegg.com/inflation/ (both accessed June 8, 2009).

30 Patel and Hirschsohn (eds.), *Married to the Struggle*, 6–7.

31 Ibid., 8.

32 Ibid.

33 Elizabeth Mafeking and Moffat Henry Mditjane married via a traditional ceremony, which included the payment of *lobola* – or a bride price. Mafeking's

1 Unbridled Insinuation and Unproven Charges

daughter, Nomsa Catherine (Mafeking) Mohlete admits "in an ideal situation all [of us] would have used our father's last name," but they did not, and all of Mafeking's children used their mother's maiden name. This is likely the reasoning behind Mafeking's death certificate mistakenly identifying her as "SINGLE: NEVER MARRIED." Nomsa Catherine (Mafeking) Mohlete correspondence with author. Winter 2017.

34 "Paarl Strike: Food Bosses Pay Starvation Wages," meeting announcement, Food and Canning Workers Union, Cape Town, flyer. Communist Party of South Africa, Folder 1, Hoover Institution Library & Archives, Stanford University, Stanford, CA. Subsequent references in this chapter from this archival source will appear as "Hoover Institution Library & Archives."

35 Rachel "Ray" Alexander Simons was a well-known South African communist and trade unionist of Latvian descent with a long history of political involvement and anti-apartheid protest. She was a founding member of the Federation of South African Women (FEDSAW), active in the Garment Workers Union (GWU), a leader with the Congress of South African Trade Unions (SACTU), and helped to draft the 1954 Women's Charter; Simons, *All My Life and All My Strength*, 73.

36 Constitution. No date. Food and Canning Workers Union Papers. AD1175/A1.1 "Constitution." Historical Papers Research Archive.

37 Ibid., 131.

38 Simons and Suttner (eds.), *All My Life and All My Strength*, 118.

1 Unbridled Insinuation and Unproven Charges

39 "Profile: Elizabeth Mafekeng (sic)," ANC Women's Section Archives, Biographical Profiles, Box 124, Folder 19. NAHECS.

40 Simons and Suttner (eds.), *All My Life and All My Strength*, 132.

41 Elizabeth Mafekeng (sic) Biography. No date. Federation of South African Women (FEDSAW) 1954–1963 Papers. AD1137-A-Ai-Ai1. Page 2. Historical Papers Research Archive.

42 "Paarl Strike." Food and Canning Workers' Union. No date. Pamphlet. Hoover Institution Library & Archives.

43 Simons and Suttner (eds.), *All My Life and All My Strength*, 137; Theron, Jan, *Solidarity Road: The Story of a Trade Union in the Ending of Apartheid* (Johannesburg, South Africa: Jacana Media, 2016), 30.

44 Memorandum of proposals submitted by the Joint Conference of Food & Canning Trade Unions to the Conference of Employers and Food and Canning Trade Unions called by the Minister of Labour to Consider the Possibility of Reaching an Agreement between Employers and Employees on Wages and Conditions of Work in the Food & Canning Industry. Food and Canning Workers Union Papers. AH1092 Dba 15–26/Dba 17 "Food and Canning Workers Union (1942–1964)." Historical Papers Research Archive.

45 The only employers spared from the FCWU net were those in the retail meat and dairy trades; Ibid.

46 Ibid.

47 Prior to both Mafeking and Alexander being banned in South Africa, the pair worked closely with one another, at times traveling together to recruit new

union members. The bond they developed while navigating the departure of African workers from the Food and Canning Workers Union (FCWU) into a newly reorganized African Food and Canning Workers Union (AFCWU) in the early 1950s, as Chapter 3 demonstrates, endured for decades in spite of great distance and tragedy.

48 Patel and Hirschsohn (eds.), *Married to the Struggle*, 9.

49 Ibid.

50 Ibid., 10.

51 Ibid., 27.

52 Walker, Cherryl, *Women and Resistance in South Africa* (New York: Monthly Review Press, 1982), 241.

53 Patel and Hirschsohn (eds.), *Married to the Struggle*, 28.

54 Digital Innovation South Africa (DISA), "The Lonely Exile of Elizabeth Mafeking," November 14, 1959, p. 2,

http://www.disa.ukzn.ac.za/index.php?option=com_displaydc&recordID=Ctv2n2359 (accessed March 2007).

55 Food and Canning Workers Union Papers. AD1175/A1.2 "Conferences 1962–1959." Historical Papers Research Archive.

56 Simons, Harold Jack, "Trade Unions" in *Handbook on Race Relations in South Africa* (Cape Town: Oxford University Press, 1949), 158.

57 Gasa, Nomboniso, "'Let Them Build More Goals'" in *Women in South African History* (Pretoria: Human Sciences Research Council, 2007), 129–151.

58 Ibid., 129–151.

59 It was not until the 1995 passage of the Labour Relations Act of 1995 that black trade unionists gained legal recognition under the law.

1 Unbridled Insinuation and Unproven Charges

60 Walker, Cherryl, "Passes for Women after 1948," in *Women and Resistance in South Africa* (New York: Monthly Review Press, 1982), 125.

61 Ibid.

62 Simons, "Trade Unions," 166.

63 Ibid.

64 Hassim, *Women's Organizations and Democracy in South Africa*. In chapter two, "The Emergence of Women as a Political Constituency," Hassim's discussion of "bread-n-butter issues" takes place within the context of the civics movement of the 1980s and references what she calls "people's needs," or the immediate concerns of local communities. The 1980s was a particular era of mass organizing against governmental plans to *reform* rather than abandon the system of Apartheid. Civil disobedience and demonstrations

1 Unbridled Insinuation and Unproven Charges

that supported urban school and consumer boycotts, and trade union movements were common.

65 Berger, Iris, "Gender, Race, and Political Empowerment: South African Canning Workers, 1940–1960" in *Gender & Society* vol. 4, no. 3 (1990), 416.

66 "Join a Vegetable Club" *Guardian*, November 8, 1945. African Studies Library, University of Cape Town, Cape Town, South Africa. Subsequent references in this chapter from this archival source will appear as "African Studies Library, University of Cape Town."

67 "Blackshirts! Greyshirts! Hunger! Slavery! Oppression and War!" No date. Pamphlet. Hoover Institution Library & Archives.

68 "Butterless People Demand Margarine" is a timely example of 1940s wartime shortages that preoccupied the attentions of South African

1 Unbridled Insinuation and Unproven Charges

---

households. The article suggests the shortage was a government conspiracy aimed at deliberately compromising the health and lives of the public to satisfy the greedy corporate interests of butter producers. *Guardian*, November 8, 1945. African Studies Library.

69 "Butterless People Demand Margarine" *Guardian*, November 8, 1945. African Studies Library, University of Cape Town.

70 Lodge, Tom Geoffrey, *Insurrection in South Africa: The Pan-Africanist Congress and the Poqo Movement 1959–1965*. PhD Thesis (University of New York, New York, New York, United States, 1984), 13.

71 "Join a Vegetable Club" *Guardian*, November 8, 1945. African Studies Library, University of Cape Town. It is unclear whether or not this organization was a co-op, or merely one of the many recruiting

1 Unbridled Insinuation and Unproven Charges

vehicles for the Party amongst black South African women.

72 "Food Raids" *Guardian*, January 2, 1947. African Studies Library, University of Cape Town.

73 "Women's Food Committee" *Guardian*, January 2, 1947. African Studies Library, University of Cape Town. Though the *Guardian* was not a Communist newspaper, its staunch opposition to dictatorial government, fascism in Africa, and Apartheid in South Africa, linked the publication with Left-leaning radicalism. Following the 1950 Suppression of Communism Act, however, the *Guardian* necessarily distanced itself from the Communist Party. This disassociation turned out to be a blessing in disguise for the periodical, conversely, because according to one staff writer, the 1950 Act "actually did us a big favor because it meant we

couldn't use the jargon and ever-ready phrases [of communist ideology]." For more on the history of the *Guardian* and its evolutions as the *Clarion*, *People's World*, and *New Age*, see Zug's, James, *Guardian: The History of South Africa's Extraordinary Anti-Apartheid Newspaper* (Michigan State University Press, 2007).

74 African Food and Canning Workers' Union Constitution. Food and Canning Workers Union Papers. AD1175/A1.5 "Central Executive Committee Meetings." Historical Papers Research Archive.

75 Sachs, Emil Solomon, *Garment Workers in Action* (London, United Kingdom: Sachs, 1957).

76 Chapter twenty-five of *Garment Workers in Action*, "A Reichstag Fire Trial Replete with a Van der Lubbe" further details Sachs' personal feelings and revelations about the September 1948 altercation.

1 Unbridled Insinuation and Unproven Charges

Most disturbing to Sachs was the later knowledge that the local railway administration had put a special train at the disposal of the White Workers' Protection League, allowing it to bring white rioters from all over the Rand into Johannesburg to disrupt the GWU general meeting.

77 Simons, "Trade Unions," 165.

78 "They Fight for Trade Union Rights!" Central Committee Communist Party South Africa. 1943. Pamphlet. Hoover Institution Library & Archives.

79 *A Survey of Race Relations in South Africa, 1955–1956* (Johannesburg: South African Institute of Race Relations, 1957), 52.

80 Ibid., 54.

81 Ibid.

82 In 1956, the Apartheid government arrested 156 South Africans – largely the leaders of the African

1 Unbridled Insinuation and Unproven Charges

National Congress (ANC), Congress of Democrats, South African Indian Congress, Colored [sic] People's Congress, and the South African Congress of Trade Unions – and charged the multi-racial group with *"high treason and a countrywide conspiracy to use violence to overthrow the present government and replace it with a communist state."* The Treason Trials were an effort of the Apartheid government to break the leadership backs of national protest organizations. What it revealed, instead, was the multi-racial character of the anti-apartheid movement, and the ridiculous lengths to which architects of Apartheid would go to preserve their system of dominance. After a five-year trial, the accused were found not-guilty.

83 Similar to Elizabeth Mafeking, Viola Hashe is yet another leading activist figure from the mid-

1 Unbridled Insinuation and Unproven Charges

twentieth century whose life and work seems to be largely missing from the historical record, and who deserves more scholarly attention. In the 1950s Hashe was elected to leadership positions in not one, but *two* all-male unions – the South African Clothing Workers' Union and the Dairy Workers Union – and was the first woman named Chairman of the Western Region of the ANC. In 1956 when Hashe received banning orders in the wake of her participation in the famed march on the Union Building in Pretoria, Hashe waged a prolonged protest against the orders until they were ultimately rescinded. Viola Hashe Biography. No date. Federation of South African Women (FEDSAW) 1954–1963 Papers. AD1137-A-Ai-Ai2. Historical Papers Research Archive.

1 Unbridled Insinuation and Unproven Charges

84 The 1950 Suppression of Communism Act declared the Communist Part of South Africa illegal, and banned the publications the government broadly defined as promoting the objectives of communism.

85 "Food and Canning Workers Protest to Ghetto Board" *New Age*, September 22, 1955. News Collection ZA (Vault) Hoover Library & Archives.

86 *A Survey of Race Relations in South Africa, 1958–1959* (Johannesburg: South African Institute of Race Relations, 1960), 218–219.

87 In 1955 AFCWU members at the H. Jones Canning Factory in Johannesburg staged a protest against employers accused of poor treatment and unfair hiring practices. While employers were not legally obligated to negotiate with union members, they were forced to arrive at some understanding in order to keep the factory open. African women

1 Unbridled Insinuation and Unproven Charges

---

workers at the Speedy Products factory in Johannesburg also flexed their organizational muscle in 1955, demanding and securing both a raise for themselves and the reinstatement of two male co-workers who were previously fired by management. "Women Win Their Strike" *New Age*, March 17, 1955. News Collection ZA (Vault) Hoover Library & Archives.

2

Unlikely Alliances

Practical Women and Radical Politics

As their allies took a necessary step backward from their activist work in the mid-1950s, African women took definitive steps forward in their work within trade unions. Even after almost one decade of having worked within trade union circles, Mafeking still doubted herself and what she perceived as the necessary characteristics of a leader.

> I used to think that education [was] the only thing required to change working conditions in the factory, but today I know ... that education is not everything. When I was elected Vice-President of my Union in 1947, I explained my educational standard, because I thought I could not lead workers without education, and I could not get education when I was a child ... I accepted the leadership because I saw that my nation was starving and poverty stricken.[1]

2 Unlikely Alliances

Mafeking clearly subscribed to the conventional notion of leadership equating with a formal education, and having only completed Standard 7, Mafeking felt at a distinct disadvantage. Ironically, it was this lack of a formal education, in conjunction with Mafeking's grasp of SeSotho, isiXhosa, and Afrikaans, that likely made her a more relatable – thus successful – union organizer.

Figure 2.1 Mafeking with Nimrod Sijake (far right), Patrick Molea (with hat) and two other comrades.

Courtesy of Sibeko, Archie with Joyce Leeson, *Roll of Honour: Western Cape ANC Comrades 1953-1963* (University of the Western Cape, 2008)

The mother of six was a member of the AFCWU's Central Executive Committee, routinely attended meetings, nominated and received nominations for leadership positions within the organization, and vigorously recruited new union members up until just before the birth of her seventh child – Sisinyana Suzan Mditjane – in February of 1951.[2] Following her confinement, Mafeking bounced right back into her AFCWU responsibilities, and by January of 1952 participated in the Tenth Annual Conference of the Food and Canning Workers' Union as an invited guest representing the AFCWU.[3] Perhaps the seed for Mafeking's later international travel was sewn at this meeting when she first heard greetings from the Bulgarian Workers Union, the Russian Peoples Republic, and the Food Workers of the U.S.S.R. All three organizations sent their "warmest fraternal greetings" to the FCWU, encouraging it to struggle for the defense of the "economic and social interests" of the workers, which were touted as "vital" not just for South African domestic interests, but "for peace throughout the world."[4] Even giving birth to her eighth child – Nomsa Catherine Mafeking – in November 1952 did not diminish

Mafeking's passion for union organizing, nor did her time in confinement lessen her fascination with the possibilities of aligning with communist-influenced countries. At a March 1953 Central Executive Committee meeting of the AFCWU, in her official capacity as the organization's Vice President, Mafeking used her opening remarks to address "the severe loss to all oppressed and exploited people in the world by the death of the great working man's leader, Marshal J.V. Stalin," and called for one minute of silence before instructing the General Secretary to send letters of condolence to the trade unions of the Soviet Union and Czechoslovakia.[5] Elizabeth Mafeking's long-budding political maturation blossomed during this era, and her actions of defiance against the Apartheid regime reached a definite tipping point when in 1953 Mafeking ended her employment of twenty-one years at the H. Jones Canning Factory in order to devote her full energies to union organizing.

Mafeking was a working member of the Central Executive Committee, and spent the majority of her time in the organizational trenches with her counterparts within

2 Unlikely Alliances

the FCWU to actively recruit new union members and establish new branches of both unions. She began working more closely with seasoned activists and developed a better understanding for the machinery of organization through attending national conferences.[6] The FCWU and the AFCWU flagrantly defied government bans forbidding non-racial organizing, while simultaneously appearing to follow the letter of the law. Mafeking experienced her first real taste of the business of union organizing in 1954, making eight site visits within five months to Malmesbury, Grabouw, Berg River Mouth, Ashton, Mantagu, Mossel Bay, Wolseley, and Tulbagh.[7] She attended almost one dozen executive committee meetings of either the AFCWU as its Vice President or management meetings of the FCWU as a "visitor." While the two organizations could not – technically – have each other's members in the other union, there was nothing keeping the two groups from having major meetings at the same day, time, and place. October 1954 necessitated one such joint meeting when the South African government issued banning orders against Lan, who had long-defied government dictates regarding organizing non-white workers. Mafeking was the first to speak when the meeting convened, stating the banning of Lan, "proves to us more than ever the Government's desire to break our unions," and that it was the duty of all members to fight for the withdrawal of the order. Lan's banning was only the beginning, sadly, and before the year ended, Mafeking assumed even more organizational responsibilities with the banning of AFCWU General Secretary, Oscar Mpetha.[8] Little did Mafeking know, in almost five years, she would be in the same position as Lan.[9]

For the time being, however, Mafeking reveled in the responsibilities of union organizing, which included chairing Executive Committee meetings.[10] In spite of banning orders against Mpetha and Lan, Mafeking continued to make site visits to workers at factories with both activists, and almost doubled her time spent engaged in on-site organizing compared to the previous year.[11] Mafeking shined in the field, drawing workers into the unions with thoughtful responses to their concerns and plain language that demystified politics behind the trade union movement, but she could not escape the tedious,

2 Unlikely Alliances

nuts and bolts of everyday administrative work. Expenditure accounts, subscriptions, donations, petty cash, and even organization stationary, all slowly came under the purview of Mafeking, and her comrades in the AFCWU noticed.[12] The union made clear efforts to grow and consolidate its power in 1955, hoping to capitalize on the steadily increasing number of workers employed in the canning industry. The total number of workers had almost doubled from 9,667 to 18,598 in only seven years. The AFCWU was determined to take advantage of the potential strength in numbers, and the organization was not averse to dropping what it viewed as dead weight in its efforts to do so.[13]

Nine delegates representing five cities – Paarl, Cape Town, St. Helena Bay, Worcester, Port Elizabeth – met for a two-day conference to discuss the direction of the AFCWU, which apparently no longer included leadership under its president, J. Kwinana. AFCWU members elected Mafeking to the position of President, ousting Kwinana, whom they accused of demonstrating "a great lack of interest in the Union work" as was evident by his abysmal record of attendance at Executive Committee meetings in the past year – only three out of eight.[14] Mafeking, on the other hand, rarely missed meetings, attending seven out of eight scheduled meetings in addition to her other well-documented duties. The AFCWU praised Mafeking's efforts, thanked her for her work in both the Paarl branch and "the struggles facing the Head Office" with the systematic dismantling of the leadership through banning.[15] Mafeking tirelessly visited factory workers when Mpetha and Lan were arrested to educate workers on the particulars of the cases, and raised money for her comrades' defense through collections and socials. In the eyes of the AFCWU, Mafeking "set an example . . . of what a fine leader should be," and was unanimously elected President when a motion was made to replace Kwinana.[16] Mafeking wasted no time, and took an incredibly bold, dangerous, and wholly unexpected step to expand the solidarity networks she saw as vital to the success of trade unionism in South Africa.

Whereas in the past she had engaged in protest activities in ways both known (and to some extent, expected) by the NP-led government – African union registration, organizing, pass law defiance – in May of 1955, the 36 year-old mother of eight – who was 6 ½ months pregnant with her ninth child – defied a government ban on her overseas travel and journeyed to the 1955 World Conference of Workers in Sofia, Bulgaria. It was, by no means, an impulsive trip. As a direct result of the influence of the Communist Party in South Africa, global political events of the 1940s – concentration camps, the assassination of Leon Trotsky, the Siege of Leningrad, D-Day, the atomic bombs, German/Japanese surrender, and Churchill's "Iron Curtain" speech – greatly influenced the international linkages and alliances of the FCWU and AFCWU. Since the organizational split of 1947, Mafeking had spent years as an official representative of the AFCWU at FCWU annual conferences hearing fraternal greetings from socialist organizations in Eastern Europe and the Soviet Union. As Vice President of the AFCWU, Elizabeth Mafeking hoped to finally capitalize on the international linkages that had helped to ideologically shape the South African left. Plus, on a more personal note, Mafeking did not entirely believe that concentration camps were real, and she wanted to see them for herself. She had done her best to follow the rules and applied for a travel visa through the proper government channels. When her application was rejected on unspecified grounds, Mafeking refused to allow the dictate to prevent her from representing the Federation of South African Women (FEDSAW), the ANC-Women's League (ANCWL), and the larger anti-apartheid struggle before an international audience. While Mafeking was bound for Warsaw, Poland, a friend of Ray Alexander's was conveniently heading to Berlin with children in tow. Expertly playing off of race presumptions of the era, Alexander and Mafeking devised to dress the latter in the working clothes of the former and effectively disguised Mafeking as nursemaid to the children. Not one alarm was raised, nor were any questions asked when Mafeking – wearing borrowed overalls and a simple cap, likely feigning docility with a lowered head and holding the hands of her "charges" – passed through South African security checkpoints.[17]

Mafeking left the country without a passport to attend not just the international trade union workers

2 Unlikely Alliances

conference in Bulgaria, but to embark upon a weeks-long tour of Europe and Asia as well.[18] Sixty-six countries sent 122 representatives to the conference, but Mafeking was the only black delegate, which afforded her a high level of notoriety wherever she traveled. For three weeks leading up to the conference, Mafeking resided in a Bulgarian rest home, later remarking to reporters that the hospitality showed by her white hosts "overwhelmed" her, ensuring that she would "never forget the welcome ... from the Bulgarian people."[19] Mafeking seemed genuinely stunned by the "joy and friendship the white people received" her with, joking, "I was so happy I forgot I was black."[20]

When the conference began, fellow delegates elected Mafeking to the Executive Committee, and her popularity guaranteed that when she delivered a report on South African racial laws to the body, she did so to a packed house. The attention made Mafeking nervous, and she reported feeling "quite afraid and shivery" upon occasion, but persevered "realizing what an honor it was" for her and those she represented.[21] Mafeking described the painful, almost unbelievable experience of black workers in South

Africa, noting that while there had been *some* improvement of labor condition after the creation of African trade unions in 1941, the government *still* refused to recognize their legality.[22] Mafeking aired South Africa's dirty domestic laundry to an international audience, exposing police brutality, political disfranchisement, economic exploitation, and substandard educational provisions for South Africa's non-European population.

> I was quite afraid and very shivery, but I carried out my duties as best I could, realizing what an honor it was to me and my people ... I told the conference about the different racial laws in South Africa, about the Bantu Education Act, that African trade unions are not recognized by the government ... I told them about the disfranchisement of the Africans, about the threat to the Coloured vote, and how the Coloured people are now fighting side by side with the Africans for the liberation of our country.[23]

2 Unlikely Alliances

Following her presentation, so many delegates surrounded Mafeking, "some kissing [her], some crying, others shaking [her] hands, [and] speaking words of encouragement and support," that it took nearly 30 minutes to bring the proceedings back to some semblance of order. After departing Bulgaria, Mafeking traveled to China where she spent four weeks visiting collective farms. Amazed at both the concept of numerous people rather than individuals owning the land and the fact that farm workers lived in "decent homes," Mafeking saw great potential in advocating just such social and economic restructuring in South Africa. Her travels included a two-week visit to London, a month-long stay in Bulgaria, and a speaking engagement in Poland where she also had the opportunity to visit Auschwitz and attend the Warsaw Youth Festival. According to Mafeking, the levels of camaraderie she witnessed amongst workers, employers, and the postwar Polish state allowed her to "[see] the way in which people should live in the [world]."[24]

> It was at this festival that I really forgot I was black . . . [I saw] that the government was for the workers ... government officials accepted me as a human being and not as an enemy, and welcomed me in a way that could never happen in South Africa.[25]

Being able to greet new acquaintances across the color line as an equal, being welcomed into government offices, and having the opportunity to speak *and* be heard, were no doubt novel experiences for Mafeking. Her amazement continued to grow as her travels resumed after her time in Bulgaria onto Czechoslovakia, China, and the Soviet Union. During her month-long stay in China she witnessed the power of collective farming, and in the Soviet Union was stunned to see the levels of access workers had to officials, spaces to organize, and the freedom to do both. For Mafeking, it was unthinkable "that workers conferences could be held in Parliament Buildings (sic) where the laws of the country were made" without fear of assault, detention, or worse. Mafeking often created a media frenzy in the venues where she spoke. For the first time in her life,

Mafeking realized "that there was an eager desire for knowledge of the struggle of the black people in South Africa," and that black workers, farm laborers, and domestics burdened by the yoke of Apartheid were *not* alone in the world. Mafeking, however, would feel increasingly alone *and* targeted following her return to South Africa.

Invigorated rather than exhausted by her travels and advancing pregnancy, Mafeking immediately returned to her AFCWU duties, and made her first factory site visit within one month of coming back to South Africa.[26] Mafeking's international exploits made her a celebrity to factory workers, who were eager to hear about the world beyond the borders of South Africa. She continued making site visits until two months later when Mafeking gave birth to her ninth child – Nomonde Mary Mditjane. After only three months, Mafeking was back in the field making site visits at a phenomenal pace. In the month of December alone, Mafeking made five factory visits in eight days, traversing from Paarl to Montagu, Ashton, Mossel Bay, East London, and Port Elizabeth.[27] Mafeking's bold defiance of

2 Unlikely Alliances

the law in her recent travels made her story a hot commodity for the trade union movement, but also a ready target for the South African government.

> Figure 2.2 This 1955 headline started a firestorm and contributed to Mafeking being labeled "the most dangerous threat to native administration" in the Western Cape.
>
>
>
> African Studies Library, University of Cape Town, Cape Town, South Africa. New Age, December 8, 1955

When asked about her general impressions of the world outside of South Africa in a fateful 1955 newspaper interview covering her international travel and political work, Mafeking joked with the reporter that, "I was so happy I forgot I was black!"[28] When the story broke,

Mafeking's smiling face appeared in newspapers across the country under a headline taken directly from her jest. For Apartheid officials, whom Mafeking had directly disobeyed by leaving the country without permission, it was no laughing matter. Police surveillance and harassment of Mafeking increased, and on more than one occasion when in the course of her duties Mafeking took food to fellow union members who were incarcerated and awaiting trial for participating in illegal strikes, authorities verbally "heaped abuse" upon her in an effort to publically humiliate the well-respected leader.[29] In spite of her treatment at the hands of government officials, Mafeking served as a defiant example of the amazing potential of the "average" African woman to affect change on both a national and global stage, and members of the AFCWU unanimously re-elected her President of the organization in April of 1956.[30]

Mafeking continued organizing at a breakneck speed – coordinating with the FCWU for meetings and making site visits with ranking members like Liz Abrahams, negotiating new forms of factory work like night shift labor, and offering hands-on assistance to smaller branches struggling to get workers to join the union.[31] As President of the AFCWU, Mafeking worked purposefully to shape the direction of the union, pledging to lead members to experience "freedom in our lifetime."[32]

> Comrades, we have heard fraternal greetings from all over the world, these greetings are from workers of different countries, some from workers who have fought and suffered hardships but have attain[ed] their freedom, some are still struggling under hardships but determined to win their freedom. I have been fortunate to have been in some of these countries and have met some of their leaders. I know exactly what feeling they have, and what sympathetic feeling they have for the South African workers. We can see that we are not alone in our struggle. Our union has suffered a lot, our leaders were banned, imprisoned and are being tried to High Treason. Comrade I ask you not to forget the work done by our leaders and the teachings and not to stop in the struggle to march with all

workers and oppressed people for freedom ... We [are] the workers of the land, we build houses, factories, we produce the machinery and the food, we want peace and freedom to be able to produce the things people need to make life comfortable. We want to be free human beings, we want opportunities for ourselves and our children to do all kinds of work that we are able to do and not because of our color to be deprived of the right to do skilled and semi-skilled work ... [33]

Reaffirming international alliances, combatting government harassment, and educating workers – both to the dignity of their own labors and more formally as a means of developing new leadership – were some of the most critical issues facing the union, and Mafeking displayed a vested interested in each. The AFCWU utilized circular letters, comrade-led study classes, and its journal, Morning Star, to educate new members and budding leaders.[34] Only by knowing the history of the trade union and the working-class movement in South Africa could supposed leaders be "able and ready to give leadership to their fellow workers."[35] Workers, meanwhile, needed to fully understand their centrality to an urbanized civil society and embrace the belief that they deserved to be treated with dignity and respect. Mafeking shared this message widely, making more than one dozen branch visits across the Western Cape, the vast majority of them within three months of having just given birth.[36]

Mafeking spent thousands of hours on the road in 1956 and 1957, visiting established branches of the AFCWU and attempting to organize new ones. There is likely little coincidence that there had been a marked increase in African employment in the canning industry by the end of 1957, with more than 10,000 new workers.[37] As well-versed as she was at recruiting workers and inspiring them to connect their needs *as* workers to the larger political struggles of Africans, Mafeking was less experienced at overseeing the work of other ranking members of the AFCWU, and in 1957, charges of financial mismanagement dominated the meeting agendas of both the FCWU and the AFCWU.[38] Mafeking was never implicated as being responsible for the missing funds, but her re-election as President of the AFCWU for a third term dictated she respond by creating a sub-committee tasked with resolving the issue.[39] The report of the sub-committee was dire: the FCWU had borne the entire financial responsibility of printing the Morning Star for more than one year without the aid of the AFCWU, carried the responsibility for most of the administration costs (rent, telephone, copies, P.O. box rentals, typewriters, and so on), and covered the costs associated with strikes "with the exception of a few donations which came in from AFCWU branches."[40] The AFCWU resolved to pay its debt to the FCWU and Mafeking hoped to move forward from the debacle, but it was not the only financial concern within the AFCWU/FCWU for her. Mafeking struggled to make workers understand that it was their duty to pay their "subs" (union subscriptions), which in turn supported the actual work of the unions, head offices, and the staff that represented workers.[41] Mafeking involved herself with every challenging facet of trade unionism, from the financial to the ideological.

Mafeking knew there was a conspiracy between employers and the South African government to circumvent the work of so-called mixed trade unions, and by 1958 she had proof in the form of revived laws and new policies designed to circumvent the struggle of workers to organize freely. In her opening address at a special conference for branch delegates, Mafeking reviewed the trajectory of the workers' struggle for recognition and the right to organize freely, and she pointed to a conspiracy on the part of the South African government and employers to undermine the trade union movement.[42] In Mafeking's eyes, the Industrial Conciliation Act of 1956 and the Native 1953 Labor Settlement of Disputes Act tested union loyalty by exploiting the racial question: only giving "concessions to certain groups" while simultaneously discriminating against the African worker.[43] What was worse, it worked, and Mafeking openly chastised workers for not fighting jointly against the laws. The glory days of the trade unions were beginning to wane, it seemed. Employers and the government refused to deduct worker membership subscriptions that were the lifeblood of the unions, and according to Mafeking, even "those willing are being forced by the government not to do so." Mass dismissals of "leading committees and shops stewards," stop orders, beggaring the unions, and race-based dispensations were effectively weakening the unions, and Mafeking dedicated the conference to considering the question of how to respond to the situation.

Not only did the Industrial Conciliation Amendment Act and Native Labor Act prohibit "mixed" unions, forbid striking in "essential industries," preserve race-based job classification, and criminalize strikes by Africans, the laws provided a mechanism whereby the government – particularly the Minister of Labour – could and did renege on an agreement regarding wage increases for thousands of unionized workers that were "substantially lower" than in previous agreement.[44] Mafeking was heavily pregnant with her tenth child, but traveled nonetheless to Gouda, Bellville, Worcester, and other union hotspots to hear complaints, explain the Wage Board Recommendations with workers, and to continue to organize new branches in spite of government tactics.[45] Her last recorded factory visit was in April to Tulbagh with Liz Abrahams, approximately one month before the birth of her tenth child – Nomvula Nominki "Minki" Martha Mditjane.[46] Her union work was too valuable to be left in the hands of others, so after only thirty-four days in confinement, Mafeking returned to her duties, addressing the FCWU to discuss the crisis of leadership at a Port Elizabeth branch.[47] Mafeking was tireless in her efforts, and everyone – from the newest union member to the established leadership – was well aware of that fact. According to Rev. W. S. Matholengwe, who opened the 11th Annual National Conference of the AFCWU, "Sister Mafeking" did "great work," "and her reputation among workers" was admirable.[48]

Mafeking was known for her candor, and she did not mince words in her presidential address when she pointed to the mass dismissals of committee members as proof positive that workers were not united and were "therefore unable to protect themselves."[49] Mafeking believed the union needed to intensify its efforts, and that members should not be frightened of government attacks in the form of dismissals, trials for treason, and ironically, banning.

2 Unlikely Alliances

Mafeking redoubled her efforts in 1959, visiting factories and negotiating with bosses in spite of having been dealt a crushing blow with the new Wage Determination No. 179, which set wage rates according to a scale outlined by the Wage Board – rates that were lower than those trade unions and employers previously agreed upon, which were already in effect.[50] Mafeking took to the road to explain the recent developments to branches, visiting factories in Worcester, Wellington, Gouda, Wolseley, and Tulbagh.[51] The AFCWU operated twenty-seven branches of the union across the country by February of 1959, and as President, Mafeking was responsible for notifying branches and the thousands of workers they represented when/if government actions threatened the union.

Mafeking had long recommended to both the FCWU and the AFCWU that their official languages be both English and isiXhosa in an effort to make the work of the unions more accessible to the majority of the African workers it represented, and had even moved in earlier organizational meetings to make it so. It was ultimately decided, however, that consistently reproducing all documents in both languages for all branches was not feasible. As President of the AFCWU, however, Mafeking utilized her discretion to communicate official correspondence in English and isiXhosa when all twenty-seven branches needed to be notified about 288 workers who were arrested and jailed after protesting employers they felt had cheated them out of legitimately earned overtime wages.[52] Individual members and the AFCWU itself were literally under attack. In mid-April of 1959, the AFCWU head office was vandalized by unknown "hooligans" who destroyed office equipment and files, adding yet another concern to Mafeking's already full plate. Mafeking organized boycotts of businesses identified as anti-trade union, advocated for an Unemployment Insurance Fund for African workers, coordinated protests against the Industrial Conciliation Bill and a new University Apartheid Bill, and lobbied government officials to address the woefully out-of-date cost of living allowance.[53]

The pace of Mafeking's work was too much for the activist, who in recent months had realized she was carrying her eleventh child. While the spirit was willing, her body was exhausted, and the eight-month pregnant Mafeking was hospitalized in July of 1959 and placed on complete bed rest. After only a few days in hospital, however, Mafeking penned a hand-written missive to AFCWU leadership informing them that she was with them in spirit. Moreover, she encouraged them to "keep the spirit up of the workers" and sent her "best regards" to African and Coloured union members, most especially those in Port Elizabeth who were suffering the aftereffects of the mass dismissal of its leadership employed in local factories.[54] Mafeking was noticeably absent from the next Central Executive Committee meeting of the AFCWU in the final weeks of her pregnancy, but only three weeks after giving birth to her eleventh child – Uhuru Zikalala Mditjane – Mafeking returned to her union work, chairing the 12th Annual National Conference of the AFCWU.[55] Having been physically indisposed for a number of months, Mafeking "felt obliged" to attend the conference in spite of still being "very weak" from her difficult pregnancy.[56] Mafeking vehemently condemned the banning of the AFCWU General

Secretary, pushing members to recognize the significance of the act of separating people in protest from their leaders.

> It is a challenge to us, which we should be prepared to accept. When one leader is banned two or more leaders should come forward, every [worker] in the factory should be prepared to be a leader . . . the struggle cannot be deterred by banning of leaders.[57]

According to Mafeking, it was a "direct attack" to the Union, and workers needed to recognize and consolidate the power within their own hands. "We as workers in the factories know that without our labor the fruit and vegetables do not get into the cans, and the canned fruit and vegetables will not reach the tables . . . Let us realize what power we have in our hands then the day for freedom will be nearer to you."[58] The strength of the union was obvious, and Mafeking communicated it to workers as plainly as possible. As head of the "sister Union" of the FCWU, Mafeking was a model of organizational devotion. Between August 1958 and May of 1959 just before her hospitalization, Mafeking attended no less than thirty meetings across the country, visiting old and new branches of the FCWU, and encouraging workers "not to be discouraged" by the banning orders imposed on leaders.[59] At home, Mafeking stood boldly in solidarity with the banned President-General of the African National Congress (ANC), Chief Albert Luthuli, and she unrepentantly expressed "full sympathy" with African nationalist movements just beyond the borders of South Africa in Nyasaland and Rhodesia.[60] Mafeking's prominence as the president of the AFCWU and vice president of the ANCWL ensured that when she organized large demonstrations against the distribution of passes to African women, people followed.[61] After one such protest in her hometown of Paarl in October of 1959, authorities arrested Mafeking with nine-week old baby Uhuru strapped to her back, and kept both mother and baby incarcerated for three weeks.

One week after her release from jail, Mafeking received the banishment notice stating she would be sent more than 600 miles away to live in Southey, a desolate area described alternately as a "concentration camp" or

2 Unlikely Alliances

"political detention camp." To add insult to injury, the NP mockingly used Mafeking's own words against her when they issued her banning decree. When Mafeking spoke of the impending banning, she almost could not believe the words she'd only jokingly employed factored into the decision to institute her banning.

> Even though my government say[s] that I visited other countries and forgot that I was black, that (sic) was no reason for my banishment. I do not know whether it is an offense to speak thus, I do not know whether my statement offended the government. I did not mean that I was married to whites. What I saw [while abroad] was that there was no discrimination. There were no signs such as "Europeans only" or "Natives only." Even in hotels there was no discrimination. You are bound to forget that you are black when you arrive at a country where you do not find such signs.[62]

Mafeking maintained she had a right to speak freely, had committed no truly treasonous act, and did not regret having learned first-hand that there was a larger world beyond the borders of South Africa where color seemed largely irrelevant. Clearly, since Mafeking had "been so happy she forgot she was black" while overseas, the NP felt compelled to remind her of her fourth-class status in South Africa, and determined to remove the married mother of eleven from the Western Cape altogether.

Special gifts and attitudes

African female employment in the canning industry was at an all-time high at the end of the 1950s, finally outpacing hiring numbers of their Coloured counterparts, who had outnumbered African women workers by 30% less than a decade earlier.[63] These women joined their voices in protest with thousands of others engaged in anti-apartheid activism across the country. In both the workforce and union representation, women formed the majority.[64] Their participation in trade unions was, as Richard Goode articulates, "shaped by the nature of their incorporation into wage labour (sic) under capitalism," and the perception and nature of their work had drastically changed from previous characterizations which posited African women as an unskilled, "disposable" working population.[65] By 1959, the value of women to the liberation movement had become clear. Chief A. J. Lutuli, exiled President-General of the ANC, praised the extended demonstrations of African women in the Natal Province against Apartheid policies.[66] Welcoming the "special gifts and attitudes" that made women valuable assets to the struggle against racial discrimination, Lutuli actually suggested *men learn from the example of women* in their passionate protest.[67] Positing the failure of men to protest against low wages, influx control regulations, and increased taxation as "shaming," Lutuli attempted to goad men into action by questioning their supposed roles as "protectors and defenders for their family's welfare."[68] Two of Mafeking's daughters – Nomsa Catherine and Nomvula "Nominki" Martha – adamantly profess it was their mother, not their father, who was the protector and defender of the large family's welfare. Their father, Moffat Mditjane, "wasn't into politics at all," Nomsa Catherine remarked off-handedly with a casual wave of her hand.[69] "He let her do what she wanted to do, what she thought was right," Nominki emphasized. "It wasn't like he could have stopped her anyway." Mafeking's meager salaries and allowances earned from her various positions within union leadership circles were the main sources of support within the household, and without both her presence *and* her financial contributions, Moffat Mditjane faced a long, hard road of raising eleven children alone.

The 1958–1959 survey conducted by the South African Institute of Race Relations (SAIRR) showed little improvement in the lives of Africans in the Union, and increased repression of leaders like banned individuals ex-Chief Inkosi Albert John Lutuli and Elizabeth Mafeking.[70] Only one year later, the 1959–1960 survey revealed banning orders no longer just targeted African leaders, rather, general activities and behavior as well – like meeting in public with more than ten people without written permission or attending multi-racial gatherings.[71] For a little more than a decade, Apartheid policies had placed an inordinate amount of emphasis on controlling the movement of black bodies into and out of supposedly "white" spaces – but movement should have been the least of NP worries. Results from the 1961 survey reveal what had to have been frightening census results for the Apartheid regime: in the span of one decade, Africans, Coloureds, and Asians had enjoyed a natural increase *two times* that of whites in the Union.[72]

These census records also give better insight into why NP administrators referred to Mafeking as "the most dangerous threat to native administration." Only one quarter of Africans living in South Africa lived in the Cape, but their closest political allies – so-called Coloureds – densely populated the region at almost 90%. In a very real way, Paarl's reputation as a peaceful, multi-racial community threatened founding precepts of Apartheid that touted separate development as the key to progress. From the perspective of the NP, however, the potential dangers inherent in the breakdown of social stratifications paled in comparison to the threat of political alliances against non-whites in the Cape, where whites were already outnumbered in the main metropolitan areas by their Coloured neighbors.[73] An evident increase in the African population in all of the main metropolitan areas necessitated changed and enhanced tactics to manage their flow into and behavior in urban areas. Mafeking and other banned individuals were simply collateral damage in the futile attempt of a dwindling white population to maintain supremacy indefinitely. The survey also intimates another reason why Mafeking's presence in the Cape was particularly egregious to officials: until her departure, local administrators had been unable to move forward with plans to convert Paarl into a "whites-only" community. Although the report does not specifically mention Mafeking as an impediment to the institution of the policy, it is very telling that the plan stalled for almost six years after its initial advertisement in 1955 – coincidentally enough the very moment Mafeking emerged as a national figure.[74]

Trade unions like the FCWU, the segregated AFCWU, and the Amalgamated Engineering Union (AEU) were three of the first organizations to take an early lead in protesting the banning of Mafeking, requesting reasons for the banning and detailed proof of the government's case against her.[75] Veteran trade unionist Liz Abrahams appealed to the morality of potential supporters while encouraging other unions to support Mafeking. Abrahams implored others to understand:

> Elizabeth has never in her life seen [her banishment location]. She knows nobody there. Elizabeth is a mother of eleven children the youngest a baby of two months old. Her children and husband need her. The Government is breaking up a happy family ... What is Elizabeth's crime? She like thousands of African women all over the country do not want to carry passes ... we cannot allow this inhuman, unjust, heartless act of the Government to pass without protest ... rally to defend her and her babies.[76]

The South African government, however, did not feel obligated to explain or defend its decision to expel and confine this well-known and respected president of the

AFCWU. There were those, nonetheless, whose defense of the government's right to banish Mafeking was downright obtuse. A leading Afrikaner press, *Die Burger*, even went so far as to attack what it perceived as spurious lies in the English press regarding the details of Mafeking's banishment. A political commentator for *Die Burger* condemned the English press for erroneously reporting that Mafeking was being separated from her children. "This is untrue," the correspondent claimed, because "the government is prepared to remove the whole family."[77]

It was Mafeking's recognized level of respectability – a married, working mother with extensive ties in her local community and surrounding areas – that led many whites to begin questioning long-standing ideas about the legitimacy of the Apartheid government. Within religious circles, ordained leaders stood at the vanguard of support for Mafeking. While some, like the Archbishop of Cape Town, Owen McCann, wrote an open letter to the Minister of Bantu Affairs pleading with him not to execute the orders against Mafeking, other religious leaders went much further.[78] Reverend Cecil Wood, a naturalized South African national serving as the Archdeacon of Bloemfontein, wrote to the Dutch Reformed Church (D.R.C.) in 1959 inquiring if there might be any chance of "common action" within religious circles to defend the rights of Mafeking. Rev. Wood's argument detailing why Mafeking should be defended was, ironically, the very proof the government used to justify her persecution: "She is the mother of 11 children, Vice-President of the Women's League of the ANC, and President of the African Food & Canning Workers Union [with a membership of 32,000]."[79] Wood's initial efforts at networking with the D.R.C. were, not surprisingly, unsuccessful. Despite the national and international attention the Mafeking banning had drawn, a D.R.C. representative claimed not to know the particulars of the case, but admitted to having contacted a local Native Commissioner who "assured him that the government had good grounds for their action."[80] These non-specific assurances were apparently more than enough to convince the D.R.C. of the government's case against Mafeking, and Rev. Wood did not miss the opportunity to suggest the D.R.C. might be seen as acquiescing – yet again – to the dictates of the National Party. Unmoved, the D.R.C. representative replied, "his church was used to standing alone and their conscience was clear."[81]

Rev. Woods attempted to appeal to this very conscience, asking whether or not the D.R.C. recognized there were "certain fundamental Christian principles involved" in the case, such as the sanctity of family life. Ultimately, the D.R.C. explained that while it was "deeply concerned about the humane treatment of all people notwithstanding their race or colour," it was not interested in engaging in public agitation against a government the church recognized was in a very difficult position. The D.R.C. did not consider the Mafeking incident "sufficient reason to cast suspicion on the procedure of the government," but assured Rev. Wood that it would speak further with the Minister of Bantu Administration – when it was convenient for all parties to meet, of course.[82] Not all representatives of the D.R.C. were willing to speak. In 1959 when a local newspaper telephoned for his comments on the banishment order, the Moderator of the D.R.C., A. J. Van der Merwe, said that not only did he not have anything to say, he did not want to be called about it again. When the reporter inquired as to whether or not the D.R.C. believed in the sanctity of family life and the home, Van der Merwe replied, "I am going to replace the receiver."[83]

As was the case with most bannings, the government issued a decree without a hearing or concrete reasons for the punishment. This predictable tactic held firm in the Mafeking case. In a letter to the Paarl Native Commissioner, the Minister of Bantu Administration and Development was clear that Mafeking's presence "in, or at any place within easy access of, the district of Paarl was inimical to the peace, order and good government of the Natives in that district."[84] The Minister of Bantu Administration and Development would not, however, elaborate on the specifics of Mafeking's banning, claiming to disclose the information that led the Governor-General to issue the banning order would be a "detriment to the public interest."[85] The magistrate did, however, provide a shockingly broad and vague justification for Mafeking's banning: she "engaged in activities which were detrimental to the Welfare (sic) of the State and by her conduct engendered a spirit of lawlessness and defiance which endangered order and good government of the Natives in the area."[86] Neither the AFCWU nor the AEU, who were in regular contact with the Paarl Native Commissioner, accepted the dictate, sending letters of protest to the High Commissioner of South Africa.

With few exceptions, local and national organizations allied with the anti-apartheid struggle were adamant that Mafeking *not* submit to banning, stressing the extra-legal nature of the order. The National Council of Women in South Africa (NCWSA) had a very different idea of Mafeking's best course of action. Representatives of the Cape Town branch of the NCWSA, a state-wide amalgamation of middle-class white women in South Africa who focused on social rather than political issues, visited the Mafeking family four times in November 1959 hoping to ease Mafeking's transition into banishment. NCWSA members insisted the banning order had to be obeyed and offered to help the family with clothes, food, and medical supplies upon Mafeking's departure. Mafeking was absent from all but one of the NCWSA visits, where she evidently convinced her visitors that she agreed she should "go to Southey quietly and with dignity."[87] NCWSA representatives, who had been so proud of their supposed influence over Mafeking, were shocked to learn of her flight into exile less than one week later. Two NCWSA members of the Cape Town branch were so incensed at the obviously ineffective efforts of their colleagues that they resigned from the organization. In historical retrospect, it is most likely that Mafeking never had any intention of abandoning her family and going to Southey – feigning docility and appearing to agree with the NCWSA was clearly the most efficient way to bring an end to their supercilious visits.

The NP resolved to remove "the most dangerous threat to native administration" from organizational positions of power, the front pages of newspapers, and society at large, and government intolerance of Mafeking's politics and popularity resulted in banning orders that sought to remove the married mother of eleven children not only from her home, and the province in which she lived, but the entire Western Cape as well. South African trade unions, protest organizations, their international allies, and hundreds of Paarl residents collectively denounced Mafeking's banning, and undertook a very public campaign to pressure the government into both explaining and retracting the vague, unspecified charges leveled against their leader.

Notes

1 Elizabeth Mafekeng (sic) Biography. No date. Federation of South African Women (FEDSAW) 1954–1963 Papers. AD1137-A-Ai-Ai1. Page 3. Historical Papers Research Archive, The Library, University of the Witwatersrand, Johannesburg. Subsequent references in this chapter from this archival source will appear as "Historical Papers Research Archive."

2 Minutes of Adjourned Central Executive Committee meeting of the African Food and Canning Workers' Union. July 1, 1951. Food and Canning Workers Union Papers. AD1175/AII "1–7." Historical Papers Research Archive; Minutes of Special Central Executive Committee Meetings of the African Food and Canning Workers' Union. September 30, 1951. Food and Canning Workers Union Papers.

AD1175/A1.5 "Central Executive Committee Meetings." Historical Papers Research Archive; Minutes of Meeting of the Central Executive Committee of the African Food and Canning Workers' Union. December 2, 1951. Food and Canning Workers Union Papers. AD1175/A1.5 "Central Executive Committee Meetings." Historical Papers Research Archive.

3 Minutes of the Tenth Annual Conference of the Food and Canning Workers' Union. January 6, 1952. Food and Canning Workers Union Papers. AD1175/A1.2 "Conferences 1962–1959" (illegible 1962–1959) (sic). Historical Papers Research Archive.

4 Ibid.

5 Minutes of Central Executive Committee Meeting. March 15, 1953. Food and Canning Workers Union Papers.

AD1175/A1.5 "Central Executive Committee Meetings." Historical Papers Research Archive. 6 Minutes of Central Executive Committee Meeting of the African Food and Canning Workers' Union. April 4, 1954. Food and Canning Workers Union Papers. AD1175/A1.5 "Central Executive Committee Meetings." Historical Papers Research Archive; Minutes of Management Committee Meeting of the Food and Canning Workers' Union. May 30, 1954. Food and Canning Workers Union Papers. AD1175/A1.6 "Management Committee 1954–1956." Historical Papers Research Archive; Minutes of Management Committee Meeting of the Food and Canning Workers' Union. July 25, 1954. Food and Canning Workers Union Papers. AD1175/A1.6 "Management Committee 1954–1956." Historical Papers Research Archive; Minutes of 13th Annual

National Conference of the Food and Canning Workers' Union. August 28, 1954. Food and Canning Workers Union Papers. AD1175/A1.2 "Conferences (*illegible* 1962–1959) (sic)." Historical Papers Research Archive.

7 Minutes of Branch Delegates Conference. April 30–May 1, 1955. AD1175/AII "7. Head Office Circulars (a) 1951–1960." Historical Papers Research Archive.

8 Minutes of Central Executive Committee Meeting of the African Food and Canning Workers' Union. October 31, 1954. Food and Canning Workers Union Papers. AD1175/AII "7. Head Office Circulars (a) 1951–1960." Historical Papers Research Archive; Minutes of Central Executive Committee Meeting of the African Food and Canning Workers Union. December 19, 1954. Food and Canning Workers Union Papers. AD1175/A1.5 "Central Executive

Committee Meetings." Historical Papers Research Archive.

9 Minutes of Management Committee Meeting of the Food and Canning Workers' Union. October 31, 1954. Food and Canning Workers Union Papers. AD1175/A1.6 "Management Committee 1954–1956." Historical Papers Research Archive; Minutes of Central Executive Committee Meeting of the African Food and Canning Workers' Union. October 31, 1954. Food and Canning Workers Union Papers. AD1175/AII "7. Head Office Circulars (a) 1951–1960." Historical Papers Research Archive.

10 Minutes of Central Executive Committee Meeting of the African Food and Canning Workers' Union. January 9, 1955. Food and Canning Workers Union Papers. AD1175/A1.5 "Central Executive Committee Meetings." Historical Papers Research Archive.

11 Ibid.

12 Report of the Auditor to the members of the African Food and Canning Workers Union. March 7, 1955. Food and Canning Workers Union Papers. AD1175/AII "7. Head Office Circulars (a) 1951–1960." Historical Papers Research Archive.

13 Report to the Annual National Conference. N.D. Food and Canning Workers Union Papers. AD1175/A1.2 "Conferences (*illegible* 1962–1959) (sic)." Historical Papers Research Archive.

14 Minutes of Branch Delegates Conference. May 1, 1955. Food and Canning Workers Union Papers. AD1175/AII "7. Head Office Circulars (a) 1951–1960." Historical Papers Research Archive.

15 Ibid.

16 Ibid.

17 Simons, Ray Alexander and Raymond Suttner (eds.), *All My Life and All My Strength* (Johannesburg: STE Publishers, 2004), 282.

18 Some scholars erroneously report the length of Mafeking's time in Europe as eighteen months, but the records of the FCWU and AFCWU and the birth schedule of her children confirm the activist spent approximately ten weeks abroad. "I Was So Happy I Forgot I Was Black" *New Age*, December 8, 1955. African Studies Library, University of Cape Town, Cape Town, South Africa. Subsequent references in this chapter from this archival source will appear as "African Studies Library, UCT."; Scanlon, Helen, *Representation and Reality: Portraits of Women's Lives in the Western Cape, 1948–1976* (Pretoria, South Africa: Human Sciences Research Council, 2007), 266. Scanlon is quoting an interview with

Wolfie Kodesh; Simons and Suttner (eds.), *All My Life and All My Strength*, 282.

19 "I Was So Happy I Forgot I Was Black" *New Age*, December 8, 1955. African Studies Library, University of Cape Town.

20 It was evident to Mafeking that her allies were in socialist countries, and her tour of Europe and Asia left her with a life-long enchantment with a radical vision for social change in South Africa.

21 "I Was So Happy I Forgot I Was Black" *New Age*, December 8, 1955. African Studies Library, University of Cape Town.

22 Since the late nineteenth century, participation in South African trade unions was restricted to white workers. In the early twentieth century, black workers recognized the potential trade unions offered to affect substantive change in their social

and economic status. Though black South African formed black trade unions and affiliated with national organizations like the Industrial and Commercial Workers Union of Africa, the South African Trades and Labor Council, and the South African Congress of Trade Unions in the 1940s-1960s, it was not until the 1995 passage of the Labour Relations Act of 1995 that black trade unionists gained legal recognition under the law.

23 "I Was So Happy I Forgot I Was Black" *New Age*, December 8, 1955. African Studies Library, University of Cape Town.

24 Elizabeth Mafekeng (sic) Biography. No date. Federation of South African Women (FEDSAW) 1954–1963 Papers. AD1137-A-Ai-Ai1. Historical Papers Research Archive.

25 Ibid.

26 Report to the Annual National Conference. N.D. Food and Canning Workers Union Papers. AD1175/A1.2 "Conferences (*illegible* 1962–1959) (sic)." Historical Papers Research Archive.

27 Minutes of Management Committee Meeting. April 28, 1956. Food and Canning Workers Union Papers. AD1175/A1.6 "Management Committee 1954–1956." Historical Papers Research Archive.

28 "I Was So Happy I Forgot I Was Black" *New Age*, December 8, 1955. African Studies Library, University of Cape Town.

29 Elizabeth Mafekeng (sic) Biography. No date. Federation of South African Women (FEDSAW) 1954–1963 Papers. AD1137-A-Ai-Ai1. Historical Papers Research Archive.

30 Minutes of the Central Executive Committee Meetings of the African Food and Canning Workers' Union.

April 15, 1956. Food and Canning Workers Union Papers. AD1175/All "1–7." Historical Papers Research Archive.

31 Minutes of Management Committee Meeting of the Food and Canning Workers' Union. June 2, 1956. Food and Canning Workers Union Papers. AD1175/A1.6 "Management Committee 1954–1956." Historical Papers Research Archive; Minutes of Management Committee Meeting of the Food and Canning Workers' Union. July 14, 1956. Food and Canning Workers Union Papers. AD1175/A1.6 "Management Committee 1954–1956." Historical Papers Research Archive; Minutes of Management Committee Meeting of the Food and Canning Workers Union. August 5, 1956. Food and Canning Workers Union Papers. AD1175/A1.6 "Management Committee 1954–1956." Historical

Papers Research Archive; Minutes of the 16th Annual National Conference of the Food & Canning Workers' Union. September 8–9, 1956. Food and Canning Workers Union Papers. AD1175/A1.2 "Conferences (*illegible* 1962–1959) (sic)." Historical Papers Research Archive; Minutes of the 9th Annual Conference of the African Food and Canning Workers' Union. September 8–9, 1956. Food and Canning Workers Union Papers. AD1175/A1.2 "Conferences (*illegible* 1962–1959) (sic)." Historical Papers Research Archive.

32 Minutes of the 9th Annual Conference of the African Food and Canning Workers' Union. September 8–9, 1956. Food and Canning Workers Union Papers. AD1175/A1.2 "Conferences (*illegible* 1962–1959) (sic)." Historical Papers Research Archive.

33 Ibid.

34 Ibid.

35 Ibid.

36 Ibid.

37 Goode, Richard, *A History of the Food and Canning Workers Union, 1941–1975*. MA Dissertation (University of Cape Town, Cape Town, South Africa, 1986), 40.

38 Minutes of Management Committee Meeting of the Food and Canning Workers' Union. May 5, 1957. Food and Canning Workers Union Papers. AD1175/A1.6 "Management Committee 1957–1959." Historical Papers Research Archive; Minutes of Management Committee Meeting of the Food and Canning Workers' Union. July 14, 1957. Food and Canning Workers Union Papers. AD1175/A1.6 "Management Committee 1957–1959." Historical Papers Research Archive; Minutes of Management

Committee Meeting of the Food and Canning Workers' Union. August 11, 1957. Food and Canning Workers Union Papers. AD1175/A1.6 "Management Committee 1957–1959." Historical Papers Research Archive; Minutes of the 16th Annual National Conference of the Food and Canning Workers' Union. September 14–15, 1957. Food and Canning Workers Union Papers. AD1175/A1.6 "Management Committee 1957–1959." Historical Papers Research Archive.

39 Minutes of the 10th Annual National Conference of the African Food and Canning Workers' Union. September 14–15, 1957. Food and Canning Workers Union Papers. AD1175/A1.6 "Management Committee 1957–1959." Historical Papers Research Archive; Minutes of the Management Committee of the Food and Canning

Workers Union. October 6, 1957. Food and Canning Workers Union Papers. AD1175/A1.6 "Management Committee 1957–1959." Historical Papers Research Archive.

40 Minutes of Special Management Committee of the Food and Canning Workers' Union. November 10, 1957. Food and Canning Workers Union Papers. AD1175/A1.6 "Management Committee 1957–1959." Historical Papers Research Archive.

41 Goode, *A History of the Food and Canning Workers Union, 1941–1975*, 162.

42 Minutes of a Special Branch Delegates Conference of the African Food and Canning Workers Union. January 19, 1958. Food and Canning Workers Union Papers. AD1175/AII "7.) Head Office Circulars (a) 1951–1960." Historical Papers Research Archive.

43 Ibid.

44 Minutes of Management Committee Meeting of the Food and Canning Workers' Union. March 1, 1958. Food and Canning Workers Union Papers. AD1175/A1.6 "Management Committee 1957–1959." Historical Papers Research Archive; Minutes of the Central Executive Committee Meetings. March 1, 1958. Food and Canning Workers Union Papers. AD1175/A1.5 "Central Executive Committee Meetings." Historical Papers Research Archive.

45 Minutes of Special Meeting of Branch Representatives and Management Committee of the Food and Canning Workers Union. April 19, 1958. Food and Canning Workers Union Papers. AD1175/A1.6 "Management Committee 1957–1959." Historical Papers Research Archive.

46 Ibid.

47 Minutes of Management Committee Meeting of the Food and Canning Workers' Union. June 15, 1958. Food and Canning Workers Union Papers. AD1175/A1.6 "Management Committee 1957–1959." Historical Papers Research Archive.

48 Minutes of the 11th Annual National Conference of the African Food and Canning Workers' Union. September 14, 1958. Historical Papers Research Archive.

49 Ibid.

50 Minutes of the Central Executive Committee Meeting of the African Food and Canning Workers' Union. January 25, 1959. Food and Canning Workers Union Papers. AD1175/A1.5 "Central Executive Committee Meetings." Historical Papers Research Archive.

51 Ibid.

52 Correspondence from Elizabeth Mafeking to AFCWU Head Office. February 5, 1959. Food and Canning Workers Union Papers. AD1175/AII "8(e) Paarl." Historical Papers Research Archive. The Library.

53 Minutes of the Central Executive Committee Meeting of the African Food and Canning Workers Union. May 18, 1959. Food and Canning Workers Union Papers. AD1175/A1.5 "Central Executive Committee Meetings." Historical Papers Research Archive.

54 Correspondence from Elizabeth Mafeking to AFCWU. July 4, 1959. Food and Canning Workers Union Papers. AD1175/AII "8(e) Paarl." Historical Papers Research Archive.

55 Minutes of the Central Executive Committee Meeting of the African Food and Canning Workers Union. July 22, 1959. Food and Canning Workers Union Papers.

AD1175/A1.5 "Central Executive Committee Meetings." Historical Papers Research Archive; Minutes of the 12th Annual National Conference of the African Food and Canning Workers' Union. September 12–13, 1959. Food and Canning Workers Union Papers. AD1175/A1.5 "Central Executive Committee Meetings." Historical Papers Research Archive.

56 Ibid.

57 Ibid.

58 Ibid.

59 Annual Report of the 19th Annual Conference of the Food and Canning Workers Union. September 12–13, 1959. Food and Canning Workers Union Papers. AD1175/A1.2 "Conferences 1962–1959" (illegible 1962–1959) (sic). Historical Papers Research Archive.

60 Minutes of the 12th Annual National Conference of the African Food and Canning Workers' Union. September 12–13, 1959. Food and Canning Workers Union Papers. AD1175/A1.5 "Central Executive Committee Meetings." Historical Papers Research Archive.

61 Digital Innovation South Africa (DISA), "The Lonely Exile of Elizabeth Mafeking," November 14, 1959, p. 2, http://www.disa.ukzn.ac.za/index.php?option=com_displaydc&recordID=Ctv2n2359 (accessed March 2007).

62 Elizabeth Mafekeng (sic) Biography. No date. Federation of South African Women (FEDSAW) 1954–1963 Papers. AD1137-A-Ai-Ai1. Pages 4–5. Historical Papers Research Archive.

63 Goode, *A History of the Food and Canning Workers Union, 1941–1975*, 41.

64 Ibid., 47.

65 Ibid.

66 "The African Women's Demonstrations in Natal," 1959, Conferences, Box 68, Folder 2. NAHECS.

67 Ibid., 21.

68 Ibid., 23; This law, in combination with the 1961 transformation of the Union to *Republic* of South Africa, greatly stifled, but did not destroy the efforts of the Women's League to gain full citizenship rights in the face of Apartheid. National Party legislative tactics determined to close the window of opportunity on the free and open exchange of ideas, tactics, strategies, and aid, between black protest organizations like the ANCWL and the global community, but inadvertently triggered a tidal wave of interest and assistance from international organizations.

69 Interview, Nomsa Catherine Mafeking with author, summer 2013. Mbekweni, Western Cape, South Africa.

70 *A Survey of Race Relations in South Africa, 1958–1959* (Johannesburg: South African Institute of Race Relations, 1960), 13–14, 39, 225.

71 *A Survey of Race Relations in South Africa, 1959–1960* (Johannesburg: South African Institute of Race Relations, 1961).

72 *A Survey of Race Relations in South Africa, 1960* (Johannesburg: South African Institute of Race Relations, 1960), 82.

73 Ibid., 83.

74 Ibid., 173; Within two years of her escape to Basutoland, the vast majority of Paarl had been rezoned, allocated to whites, and Africans and

Coloureds were pushed just outside of the city into a new township, Mbekweni.

75 Correspondence from African Food and Canning Workers' Union to The Acting General Secretary of the South African Trade Union Council, 14 December 1959; (AH1426 TUSCA: Trade Unionism; File (Cd. 3.1); Historical Papers Research Archive.

76 Correspondence from Food & Canning Workers' Union to Garment Workers' Union, 30 October 1959; (AH1092: Individual Unions File (Dba17); Historical Papers Research Archive.

77 "Words Fail Us!" *New Age*, November 12, 1959; News Collection ZA (Vault) Hoover Library & Archives.

78 "Moarchbishopo McCann le Mrs. E. Mafekeng[sic]" *Moeletsi oa BaSotho* [Lesotho], November 28, 1959, 12. Print. Thomas Mofolo Library. Archives, Records Management, Museum and

Documentation Division. National University of Lesotho. Roma, Lesotho. Newspaper Collection (accessed July 2015).

79 Diary entry, AB1420 Canon Cecil Thomas Wood Papers 1902–1980 (A4.2); Historical Papers Research Archive.

80 Ibid.

81 Ibid.

82 Ibid.

83 *New Age*, "DRC: No Comment," November 5, 1959. Hoover Institution Library & Archives.

84 Correspondence from The Minister of Bantu Administration and Development to Paarl Native Commissioner, 4 December 1959; (AH1426 TUSCA: Trade Unionism; File (Cd. 3.1); Historical Papers Research Archive.

85 Ibid.

86 Ibid.

87 Statement by Mrs. V.C. Davie – Chairman of the Cape Town Branch of the N.C.W., January 1960; (AD843/RJ SAIRR: Justice G4-G5, Box 129 (File 1). Historical Papers Research Archive.

3

"God Made Liz Abrahams"

Family, Community, and Leaving Everything Behind

Mafeking's original banning order from October 1959 stipulated she and her children would go to Southey. This order was replaced days later by another with the altered condition that she go alone. Additionally, the South African government granted Mafeking one week's grace "to organize her affairs" before leaving her home of 32 years, stipulated a small government allowance "for her needs" during confinement, and gave the activist the *option* of taking her nursing infant into exile with her.[1] Mafeking's ten other children would be left in the care of their father, who faced having to support the family without the trade union salary of his wife, which accounted for approximately 60% of the monthly household income.[2] According to her banishment orders, Mafeking would receive only one-tenth her full-time salary "for her needs" in exile. Whether or not

3 "God Made Liz Abrahams"

she could or would continue to contribute to her family in Paarl was of no importance to the government. Indeed, very little about Mafeking's personal life was of consequence to public officials. Even when faced with negative reports of Mafeking's plight in foreign presses and pressure from international organizations to rescind the banishment order, South African officials were resolute in their justifications regarding Mafeking's treatment. According to the government, Mafeking's "continued presence in Paarl [was] injurious to the peace, order and good administration of the Natives," and no amount of outside petitioning would alter their decision.[3]

Mafeking's supporters persisted, and in early November just before her banning orders went into effect, SACTU formally requested the International Labor Organization (ILO) intervene on Mafeking's behalf. The appeal contended "the real reason for the [sic] Government's action is Mrs. Mafeking's persevering struggle for better living conditions for cannery workers."[4] The committee's report reveals a complicated lobbying effort on the part of SACTU and the ILO that included numerous written complaints requesting government response "as a matter of urgency."[5] Despite the ILO appeal, the South African government remained unmoved. After the Director-General of the ILO sent two letters to South African officials in November and December of 1959 regarding Mafeking, the government waited until February of 1960 – almost 3 full months – to respond. Government officials insisted that the banning was for "reasons completely unrelated to Mrs. Mafeking's trade union activities." It could not, however, "precisely and with sufficient detail" specify for the ILO the supposed non-political activities that led to Mafeking's removal order. Technically, the government did not *have* to respond to the ILO appeal, it merely deigned to do so. Section 5(1) (b) of the Native Administration Act (No. 38 of 1927) gave the South African government *carte blanche* to order any person or persons to relocate to a location selected by officials, for a duration selected by officials. Said officials only cared if the presence of the removed "in their home area gave rise to dissension and was, consequently, detrimental to good government," not if their actions were

3 "God Made Liz Abrahams"

popular abroad.[6] The government's long-awaited response, however, was irrelevant. By the time the missive reached the ILO, Elizabeth Mafeking had taken matters into her own hands.

In a ruse so elaborate as to impress even the most experienced Hollywood directors, Mafeking's comrades devised a plan to smuggle the highly visible leader out of the country. One week before Mafeking was scheduled for removal, she made a public appearance to bid a sad farewell to her supporters.

> I think everybody is upset today in this country. But I personally am not upset about my going, because I think that we mothers feel what the pass laws and other oppressive laws mean to us. We mothers are the people who gave birth to children and we are the people who suffer most from the laws of the Nationalist Government. We must stand together and unite to fight for freedom.[7]

Mafeking couched her stance against Apartheid policies in the protection of motherhood. Her appeal to mothers

3 "God Made Liz Abrahams"

challenged the perceptions of African women as so-called superfluous appendages with little or no function in the economy of the white ruling class. By means of their own interpretation of the place of women in "traditional" African society – perpetual minors subject to the authority of men and lacking in parental rights – white social engineers endeavored to create a docile, subservient labor reserve of African women. The source of Mafeking's guilt was clear: she'd engaged African women in a range of organization work that frequently resulted in a heightened, mainstream awareness of issues specific to them and their needs as contributing members of society. This was the true, unarticulated reason behind Mafeking's branding as "detrimental to good native administration."[8] With no options and no legal course of appeal, in one final act of defiance, Elizabeth Mafeking eluded her escort on the day her banning went into effect and fled the country for a life in exile.

3 "God Made Liz Abrahams"

Skipping the country

The police maintained a constant presence outside the Mafeking home once the second banning orders were issued, but at the end of the workday the Friday before they went into effect, the majority of police left for the weekend. As the working day ended and people got off work, a multi-racial crowd of community members began to grow in front of the Mafeking home, and they began to sing. Recently relieved officers were called *back* to Paarl, and they returned to the Mafeking home as the sun began to set, incensed to see such a large gathering. One officer entered the Mafeking home, spotted Mafeking and demanded to know "what those people wanted." Mafeking feigned innocence and assured the officer that the people had only come to wish her farewell. The next evening around 9pm, police again entered the Mafeking home, this time walking straight past her protesting family to Mafeking's bedroom. When officers opened cabinet drawers and wardrobe they saw all of Mafeking's clothes, shoes, and personal possessions still neatly lined up. While Mafeking was

3 "God Made Liz Abrahams"

actually next door at the neighbor's house planning her next move, her family told police she was using the public toilets, an excuse the authorities accepted then left. About one hour later, Mafeking sent for her children. There had been a clandestine meeting at the neighbor's home wherein Mpheta and other comrades of Mafeking proposed an immediate plan of action. Sophia remembered overhearing bits and pieces of conversations about a potential escape as she and her siblings were fetched by other neighbors and taken to their mother.

> They arrived late and they said, "Rokie, you must just pack some old clothes. Just wear anything, but you must not look smart, because [the police] will see that you are Rokie."

Mafeking was known as a "modern" woman of the 1950s who always wore colorful frocks and tasteful jewelry. Ironically enough, today seventy-one year-old Nopumelelo Hani, a former Executive Mayor of the Stellenbosch Winelands District, and a current Western Cape Executive

3 "God Made Liz Abrahams"

of the ANC, remembers her first interaction with Elizabeth Mafeking just months before the activist's banning *because of* her stylish form of dress. In 1959, Hani was just 13 years-old and a classmate of Mafeking's fourth eldest child, Ngubenyathi "Nyati" Melford, when Mafeking visited the Standard 2 classroom. Hani recalled the excitement in the air when the glamorous "Mme. Fix" (*May-Feex*) – as many called Mafeking due to her outspoken promises to "Fix up!" any obstacle in her path – walked through the door:

> She looked smart. *Very*, very smart! Her hair was pulled back, and she wore a small hat that covered her head. She wore a green, two-piece suit with a skirt, and the jacket had shiny buttons running down the front.

Hani's description of Mafeking's presence as "smart" – or very neat and stylish – was one local police were just as familiar with. As Hani described and police were aware of, Mafeking stood out amongst the crowds of women with whom she worked, and so in the days after her banning orders were served, police payed close attention to any

3 "God Made Liz Abrahams"

well-dressed African woman walking into and out of the Mafeking home. As Sophia recalled, altering her mother's appearance seemed important to *some* plan to which she was not yet privy. Sophia remembered a neighbor coming to fetch all of the children (except for the infant, Uhuru, who was asleep at home) and escorting them to a pre-arranged spot in the row of public toilets. Sophia has never forgotten her mother's terse words:

> *Into endini bizela yona ndiyahamba*
> *namhlanje. Andiyazi apho ndiyakhona . . .*
> *ndicela nihlale kakuhle.*
> The reason I called for all of you [is to say] I
> am leaving today. I don't know where I'm
> going . . . please stay well.

With little time to spare before she had to depart, Mafeking then turned to Sophia – whom she affectionately called "Khekhe" – and asked her to look after nine of her siblings; Uhuru was coming with her, Mafeking simply would not be parted from her nursing infant. Mafeking payed close attention to the earlier advice of her comrades regarding

3 "God Made Liz Abrahams"

her dress, and Sophia recalled when they returned home there was complete silence as her mother removed her customary hat to plait her thick hair in braids running the length of her scalp, redressed herself and baby Uhuru in simple, borrowed clothes, packed a solitary suitcase, and sat down to wait. Within the next hour, Mafeking's ANC comrades arrived "and they took her." Sophia was in shock. With their mother gone and no plan for the immediate future, it seemed as if Sophia now had to figure out how to take care of her nine siblings in the absence of their mother. The task was much easier than Sophia imagined though, because while Mafeking was absent, her comrades were not. Sophia sighed when she recounted the weeks immediately following Mafeking's escape:

> *Akhonto besinida thina pha because abantu bebesiza day and night . . . amakhalad asi phatele ifish, asiphatele iinyama, asiphathele ntoni . . . nabantu nje.*
> There was nothing we needed because people came day and night . . . the Coloured people brought us fish, meat, and everything . . . everybody did that.

3 "God Made Liz Abrahams"

Sophia remembered having the full support of a multi-racial community of activists, local leaders, and beloved friends of the family. When Semkane returned to the Mafeking home in Paarl after having successfully spirited Mafeking into Lesotho, he pulled Sophia aside and told her not to worry, the people would look after her and the rest of Mafeking's children. Local Coloureds, business owners, elders, and "even the Boers who had shops" began bringing provisions like jam, butter, and bread to the Mafeking household in Paarl. Just north of the city was Huguenot, a multi-racial enclave comprised predominantly of Coloured families and what was left of their African neighbors who hadn't yet been forced to relocate even further north to the resettlement township of Mbekweni. After years of working with the FCWU, AFCWU, and their executive leadership, the city developed a reputation upon which it prided itself: a community of workers who had learned the "meaning of brotherhood." Indeed, multiple communities worked together to provide for the Mafeking children in the days immediately following their mother's departure, but Sophia remembered one person in particular from Huguenot as

3 "God Made Liz Abrahams"

having offered everything she had in her time, efforts, and energy: Liz Abrahams.

> *uThixo wenza uba uAbrahams. Abrahams was like a mother to us, inene andifuni xoka . . . she was better than [some of mother's family] to us . . . everything besiyifuna ku Abrahams, we got.*
>
> God made [Liz] Abrahams. Abrahams was like a mother to us, truly I don't want to lie . . . she was better than [some of mother's family] to us . . . everything we needed from Abrahams, we got.

Sophia lovingly recalls Abrahams being "like a mother" to her and her siblings. Abrahams began arriving at the Mafeking home early in the morning before the children went to school to prepare breakfast for them. Once she and Sophia had gotten the younger children off to school, Abrahams would stay to help Sophia with household chores until around 1pm, when she would return home to check on her own family. Abrahams always returned in the evenings to cook supper for Mafeking's children. The actions of Abrahams and others proved to Sophia that everyone really did understand how difficult it was to lose one's mother to Apartheid and that "they cared for the family, they cared very much for us." This calm was disrupted in short order, however, by both the South African police who began harassing the Mafeking children, and Mafeking herself, who was determined to hold her family together – one way or another.

Peace in Paarl, disturbing details

The government's efforts to remove Mafeking from Paarl were far more disruptive than her presence, and the violence that ensued belied the notion of the so-called peace, order, and good administration her absence was supposed to ensure. Mafeking's banning was not passively accepted by the members of her community, who responded to her banishment-turned-escape with petitions, demonstrations, and – when those avenues were exhausted – violence.[9] *New Age*, an English-language periodical with extensive readership in black, white, Indian, and Coloured homes in South Africa, reported that thousands of people across the nation were working to – as a November 5, 1959 headline stated – "Save Elizabeth Mafeking from Exile!"[10] Readers were outraged to learn the details of Mafeking's banning, which included relocating from her home in Paarl to "three huts in the wilderness" that were specifically built for political exiles. *New Age* took particular care to document what Mafeking's new life might look like, photographing everything from the desolate entrance to the countryside where Mafeking was to be banished, to the actual structure in which she'd be forced to live indefinitely. Michael D. C. De Wet Nel, Minister of Bantu Administration and Development, initially thought to send Mafeking to Driefontein, but a local official informed him, "Driefontein is a terrible place. It's right in the Kalahari."[11] Officials ultimately chose a location named Southey – but it was hardly any better. Everyone knew what Elizabeth Mafeking faced, and no one could believe it would actually come to pass for the mother of eleven.

Editorial and political cartoons were rather effective in showcasing the absurdity of the banishment and

3 "God Made Liz Abrahams"

castigating major players. One particularly adroit artist illustrated a simple scene where a lone Elizabeth Mafeking, single suitcase in hand, stands under a hot sun in the middle of an arid wasteland named Southey, next to a growing cactus labeled "New Africa." Zooming past her on a train labeled "Banishment Express" is Minister De Wet Nel, who is shouting out the window while pointing at the small cactus, "I told them this wasn't a desert. Something is growing right there next to you!"[12] While it was not quite a desert, Southey *was* a sparsely populated trust farm of the Bantu Administration and Development office. The nearest school or store was approximately three miles away, the nearest clinic 15 miles away, and there was no transportation available. The government had a clear and effective plan in place:

> [Exiles] are sent to areas where they are not known, where the language of the people is strange to them, and where the Government feels it will be impossible for them to undertake any form of opposition. Mostly the detention places are sparsely populated

and poorly cultivated so that it is practically impossible for the exiles to make a living there.[13]

This disturbing plan of purposefully inflicting emotional and psychological harm on individuals had been incredibly effective with the eighty African men officially banished (or living in exile due to banning orders) prior to Mafeking's struggles. Mafeking's gender would not earn her any special treatment or considerations. In an interview with a reporter from the London *Daily Herald*, the would-be Native Commissioner of Mafeking in Vryburg detailed what would be her new, daily life in the dusty, largely uninhabited wilderness of Southey. The proper management of Mafeking's "welfare" on the Native Trust Farm she'd call home indefinitely included two sparsely furnished rooms, a monthly allowance of £1 "for her needs," and the inability to leave her new home/area without express permission from Minister De Wet Nel himself.[14]

3 "God Made Liz Abrahams"

Figure 3.1 A *New Age* political cartoon satirizes Mafeking's proposed banning to Vryburg in Southey. In the original caption, Minister De Wet Nel shouts, "See! I told them it wasn't a desert. There's something growing right next to you!" as he zooms by on the appropriately-named Banishment Express.

News Collection ZA (Vault) Hoover Library & Archives, Stanford University. New Age, November 5, 1959

3 "God Made Liz Abrahams"

Perhaps most egregiously, the only vocational opportunity available to Mafeking would be as a domestic servant in one of the homes of a local white farmer. Damned and doomed for an indefinite period of time, Mafeking would be isolated without chance of appeal, penniless, trial-less, and utterly hopeless. The *New Age* had every faith this could not be the case, though, making a chillingly foreboding statement regarding the possible fallout of Mafeking's banning. "The Government and the canning bosses will reap a bitter harvest from this banishment order. The people of this country will not take this sort of thing lying down."[15] The very peace in Paarl officials claimed could only be realized with the removal of Elizabeth Mafeking was, ironically, only truly disturbed when the government attempted to forcibly remove Mafeking from her home.

On Monday, November 1, 1959, eight days before the banning order went into effect, they began to arrive. Friends, neighbors, and eventually the whole community trickled onto the Mafeking property – at first just manageable groups of people standing around in front of the family home discussing the particulars of the case. Four

3 "God Made Liz Abrahams"

days later, the trickle of bodies amassed enough of a crowd to warrant coverage in a local newspaper. By Friday, reports of the multi-racial crowd of workers gathered outside the white, terraced cottage of the Mafeking family at No. 64 Barbarossa Street had garnered national interest. Documents from the ANCWL archives suggest that the gathering crowd was not spontaneous, rather it was a coordinated effort on the part of the FCWU, AFCWU, ANC, Congress of Democrats, and Coloured People's Congress to "guard [Mafeking's] house day and night" in an effort to prevent her removal.[16] "Over a thousand people" gathered over the weekend, with only one incident of note: "a [white] traffic cop tried to drive through the crowd; they lifted him on his bicycle and placed him quietly but firmly on the ground in the next road. He drove away without a backward glance."[17]

When the press arrived Monday morning to cover events leading up to the banishment orders going into effect that afternoon, "there were roughly three thousand people waiting."[18] Groups of people in the watchful and suspicious crowd sang protest songs and hymns, while the

3 "God Made Liz Abrahams"

press interviewed some of Mafeking's weeping family members – Mafeking herself was not present. One angry voice outside shouted, "They'll get her over our dead bodies!" and everyone speculated what would happen when the police arrived at 4pm to take Mafeking away. In the meanwhile, no one had seen Mafeking, and neither the press nor the police could answer a recurrent question circulating in the crowd: "Where is Mrs. Mafeking?" Just before 4pm, Mafeking's police escort arrived, but seeing the large crowd in front did not approach the house. By nightfall – after children had returned home from school and adults from work – the crowd swelled exponentially, spilling over into adjacent streets. What sparked the conflict remains unknown, but the facts associated with the subsequent riot are clear:

> Suddenly there were police, screams, batons, bullets, stones hurtling into windows. "Kill Verwoerd! Kill De Wet Nel! Kill the police!" was heard about the tumult.[19]

3 "God Made Liz Abrahams"

Over the course of the next three hours, heavily armed police and their reinforcements engaged in open battle with enraged demonstrators. Cars were overturned, shops destroyed, and white bystanders were attacked by stone-wielding assailants. It wasn't until 12:30am that the Deputy Commissioner of Police for the Western Cape, Col. I.P.S. Terblanche could proclaim the situation was under control. Eyewitness reports later stated the first shots "were fired by 'nervous whites,'" but Terblanche maintained the police had been fired upon *first* and merely returned fire. Ultimately, ten individuals ended up in the hospital, several with gunshot wounds, of which one man later died.[20]

The next evening, Paarl, the supposed "Pearl of the Cape" bore more resemblance to a military base than the conscience-cushioning community white officials and citizens in the Cape had long pointed to as an example of success. Armored cars, larger reinforcements, and armed police patrolled the oak-lined streets. If a small crowd did not move quickly enough when instructed by officers in armored vehicles, "twelve policemen with batons and rubber hoses leapt out of the armoured (sic) car and tore

3 "God Made Liz Abrahams"

into [it]."[21] International news affiliates picked up the story, and in the United States the *New York Times* reported a mob of "thousands of screaming Africans" stoning cars, setting fire to local white businesses, and rioting over the banishment of Mafeking.[22] Police forces chased men, women, and children indiscriminately through the streets of Paarl, and the second night of bloody violence in the area had locals lamenting the fact that there *had been* peace in Paarl – until Minister De Wet Nel served Mafeking with banishment orders. In seeming direct response to the unfounded charges against Mafeking, the front page of *New Age* proclaimed "peace, order, and good government in Paarl have been disturbed by the Nationalists. Not by Elizabeth Mafekeng (sic)."[23] Despite what government officials claimed, the violence in Paarl was not caused by "Coloured (sic) hooligans" or outside agitators, rather, it was symptomatic of the underlying sense of grievance and frustration among the masses against the intransigent and inhuman policies of the Apartheid government.[24]

Figure 3.2 The morning Mafeking's banning went into effect, hundreds of supporters filled her front yard in a show of solidarity for the married mother of eleven. Hours after this image was taken as night descended on Paarl, police forces, enraged that they'd not been able to take Mafeking into custody at the appointed time, returned to Paarl en masse and opened fire. What then ensued was a two-day riot that left one dead and police casting the blame on so-called "Coloured hooligans."

News Collection ZA (Vault) Hoover Library & Archives, Stanford University. New Age, November 12, 1959

3 "God Made Liz Abrahams"

Wednesday, November 11, three days after Mafeking's banning orders had gone into effect and following two nights of rioting, local reporters began to speculate that Mafeking had fled the country. Police in South Africa, meanwhile, began a campaign of harassment against Mafeking's children with a disturbing and violent altercation just days following her escape. Three days after Mafeking's disappearance – but before anyone knew she'd fled to Basutoland – police "banged on the door of the Mafeking home at 2 o'clock" in the morning, demanding Mafeking's three eldest children had to come with them.[25] Police pulled Sophia, fourteen year-old Melford, and thirteen year-old Mehlo from bed, reportedly kicking one of the children awake, dragged them outside in the middle of the night to question them, and left the home with two of the boys when it was discovered the eldest Mafeking son, 17 year-old Atti, was at work. The next day police picked up Atti on his way home from his job on third shift and interrogated him in an effort to connect him to specific acts of violence that occurred during the worst of the rioting just a few days earlier. Luckily, the white employer of

3 "God Made Liz Abrahams"

Mafeking's son verified he'd been working night shifts the evenings of the riots, which left police with no other alternative than to release him. The personal indignities the Mafeking children suffered in the days immediately following their mother's departure were analogous to feelings expressed by community members, who were incensed that police placed the blame for the riots on "Coloured hooligans" and refused to accept any responsibility in the two nights of violence.

When word of Mafeking's safe crossing into the British Protectorate of Basutoland (present day Lesotho) reached Paarl, crowds of demonstrators rejoiced while embarrassed police forces – still searching for Mafeking in Paarl – recalled officers. How had Elizabeth Mafeking managed to take everyone by surprise? In spite of the all-night vigils held by gathering demonstrators and constant police surveillance in the days leading up to her banishment, just before the midnight deadline of her banishment orders Mafeking secreted herself and her youngest child, three-month old baby Uhuru, away in what her husband would later tell reporters was an effort "to avoid bloodshed."[26] With assurances from her own mother and a legion of neighbors that they would take care of the family while she was away, Mafeking left behind a loving husband, ten children, and an elderly father-in-law for a life of self-imposed exile in Lesotho.

While Sophia was not privy to the exact details of her mother's departure, she vaguely recalled hearing about a plan to secret Mafeking across South Africa and into Lesotho using a series of cars and drivers who exchanged custody of Mafeking and baby Uhuru until the pair reached Lesotho. It wasn't until days later that Sophia knew for sure her mother and little sister arrived safely at their destination.

> *Kuthiwa she's in BaSotholand now and they can do nothing. Abakwazi ukumthotsharisha okanye bathini!*
> They said she's in BaSotholand now and they can do nothing. They cannot torture her or anything!

3 "God Made Liz Abrahams"

Sophia was overjoyed to know her mother managed to elude South African authorities and whatever special punishments they would have likely inflicted upon Mafeking if she'd been intercepted. Mafeking had, however, just leapt from the proverbial frying pan into the fire, because driving non-stop from the Cape across the desert of the Karoo to find refuge at a small church mission in Maseru, Basutoland, was the easy part. In exile, Elizabeth Mafeking the refugee would have to survive.

3 "God Made Liz Abrahams"

Figure 3.3 Supporters were delighted to learn Mafeking and baby Uhuru had evaded Security Forces and escaped to Basutoland. This image was taken in Maseru, Lesotho, just hours after Mafeking's arrival. Members of the BCP surround Mafeking.

News Collection ZA (Vault) Hoover Library & Archives, Stanford University. New Age, December 3, 1959

"Broken families and bewildered children"

In 1960 an anonymous correspondent writing from exile in Swaziland described the struggles faced by recent fellow exiles – all victims of the first South African "State of Emergency" declared just a few weeks earlier.[27] Regardless of color, education, or vocation, refugees living in Basutoland, Swaziland, and Bechuanaland (now Republic of Botswana), during the opening years of the decade faced many of the same trails: a dangerous journey towards the unknown, anxiety over abandoned lives and commitments, and in the case of Elizabeth Mafeking's exile in Lesotho, "broken families and bewildered children."[28] While the correspondent guiltily admits white refugees fared better than their black counterparts because "white skins and income still remain the open sesame to comfort," the interminable time of exile spawned a sadly predictable flow to one's life: a constant hunt for lodgings, a meal, or non-existent employment.[29] To add insult to injury, refugees routinely faced the criticism of locals, many of whom did not hesitate to offer a steady "stream of provocation and insult," which vacillated between suggesting refugees were cowards who fled from a good fight, or were an unwelcome drain on the country's already limited resources.[30] *The Swaziland Chronicle*, a popular weekly newspaper, announced, "There are too many refugees in Swaziland. The Passover is over – time some of them passed back."[31] Although the Protectorates were independent of South Africa, the heavy economic links between the countries often blurred that line, and refugees lived with the anxiety (and often rumors) of extradition. According to the anonymous correspondent, Basutoland, Swaziland, and Bechuanaland, were the "children of a broken marriage" between the custodial parent Great Britain and the belligerent father of South Africa.[32] The constant uncertainty of their lives, in addition to the personal and interpersonal trials of exile, meant there was no safety from the influence and reach of Nationalist injustice.

There are no firm statistics regarding the numbers of refugees who fled South Africa for supposedly greener

3 "God Made Liz Abrahams"

political pastures abroad in the opening decade of the country's State of Emergency. In the case of Basutoland, however, both the numbers of exiles and their respective positions within the anti-apartheid struggle were of enough import to warrant continued surveillance beyond the borders of the Union. In this regard, Elizabeth Mafeking was likely one of the most monitored African women on the continent in the late 1950s. It is not surprising that both South African and local Basutoland officials had a vested interest in the Mafeking affair, but recently unclassified records from The National Archives reveal British officials also kept themselves well-informed of events in the rapidly decolonizing nation. Elizabeth Mafeking's decision to seek refuge in Basutoland was not a *fait accompli*, and in fact, the activist likely never knew how frequently she was the topic of official conversation or how close (and how frequently) she came to expulsion.

In 1993 and 2012, respectively, officials declassified two files containing more than 300 documents from former colonial administration records and a postwar Commonwealth Relations Office which provide an

3 "God Made Liz Abrahams"

important source for understanding the complex web of political influence and reluctance that motivated the British government's part in Mafeking's ability to maintain her refugee status and evade deportation back to South Africa. The Secretary of State for Commonwealth Relations (Commonwealth Relations Office) was an officer of the British Cabinet who oversaw British relations with members of the Commonwealth of Nations – fifty-three member states comprised primarily of territories of the former British Empire. The Commonwealth Relations Office relied upon an intricate bureaucratic system of local and regional officials dispersed across both Basutoland and South Africa, but were overseen by national agents based in Pretoria and Cape Town. The future of Basutoland, in particular, was of great importance to the British government due to the small country's physical relationship and dependence upon South Africa. While most of the concerns of the British government with regards to Basutoland revolved around constitutional developments in the 1950s and the legislative election in 1960, Nationalist Party politics in South Africa during the same period could not be ignored and the substantial body of reports, media materials, and classified communiques within the records in this regard cannot be ignored. Following WWII, the British government felt it would be possible to incorporate Basutoland into South Africa once the smaller country achieved independence from the British Empire. This position, however, became less and less plausible after the 1948 election in South Africa when the nation declared itself a republic and dozens of refugees began seeking shelter from Apartheid in the territory.

3 "God Made Liz Abrahams"

Figure 3.4 Newspapers featured Mafeking and baby Uhuru in special interest stories during their first few months of exile. This image was the first taken during the course of an interview with a Soto-language newspaper.

Courtesy of Thomas Mofolo Library. Archives, Records Management, Museum and Documentation Division. National University of Lesotho. Roma, Lesotho. Newspaper Collection. Leselinyana, p. 9, Pherekhong (January) 1960

3 "God Made Liz Abrahams"

Elizabeth Mafeking was one of dozens of politics refugees who fled South Africa for freedom in Basutoland during Apartheid. For the first three years of her residence in the British High Protectorate, the activist was at the center of conversations within the Commonwealth Relations Office – most particularly as they related to the political work of refugees that threatened diplomatic ties with South Africa. Careful examination of recently declassified administrative records reveal the ways in which refugees in Basutoland – Mafeking in particular – shaped the country's policy with regards to immigration standards. More importantly, they offer rare insight into the machinations of the British government in a recently postwar world. It is ironic that in her efforts to escape the political harassment and persecution of *one* government, Elizabeth Mafeking unwittingly placed herself directly in the crosshairs of *three* nations, and each had very different ideas on the subject of her new residency.

3 "God Made Liz Abrahams"

"Ke Senatla Sa Mosali"

When Elizabeth Mafeking arrived in Basutoland in 1959, the small, mountainous country, roughly the size of Belgium, was a land of stark contradictions. Geographically speaking, the tiny nation was viewed as an "island of freedom" by opponents of Apartheid in South Africa, but it was completely surrounded by the Republic. Basutoland was on track to become the political Cinderella of the decolonizing colonial world in Southern Africa, but it was an economic blight in modern African eyes. BaSotho citizens felt intensely proud of their homeland's rich historical and cultural traditions, but thousands necessarily flooded across the border into the hostile territory of South Africa to escape crushing levels of poverty.[33] Thousands more, however, could only see the beauty and freedom that seemed unique to Lesotho. Mpho 'M'atsepo Nthunya recalled Lesotho in the mid-1950s as a land where the grandeur of the "mountains, the sky, the space, [and] no crowding," were only eclipsed by the lack of Boer policemen with their "white, white skin and red eyes like white rats"

3 "God Made Liz Abrahams"

who killed blacks out of hatred.[34] In spite of these paradoxes, Basutoland was Mafeking's only real option of escape, and she necessarily made the decision to retreat to a country struggling with poverty, internal and external political crises, and a growing refugee population.

While stunning in its topography, Basutoland was not the most geographically hospitable locale. Politically, however, for a brief moment in Elizabeth Mafeking's exile, the country was much more welcoming. Crossing the border in 1959 was easy enough for Mafeking and her escorts – prior to 1962 there were no permanent South African/Basutoland border posts.[35] Getting *to* the border of Basutoland from Paarl, however, was a challenge unto itself. Basutoland lay almost 800 miles east of Paarl, and reaching the destination required traversing the "incredible emptiness and flatness" of the Cape Province and the western part of the Free State that lay just beyond it. For Mafeking, there was only one way into Basutoland – a girder bridge over the Caledon River, which created a natural border along the northwest perimeter of the country – and travelers could and did cross from South

3 "God Made Liz Abrahams"

Africa into Basutoland at will. With no discernable difference in the landscape to mark a difference between the territories of South Africa and Basutoland, locals relied upon a simple understanding of public works and knowledge of the local topography: when the tarred highway "disintegrate[ed] into a dirt track," and flat-topped mountains dominated the landscape, you knew you were in Basutoland.[36] Entrants then walked or drove under a "ceremonial entrance arch with its splendid slogan, *Kena ka Khotso* – Enter in Peace," and were greeted by the sight of the Union Jack billowing in the wind high atop a flagpole.[37] Once safely in exile, Mafeking granted an exclusive interview to C. M. Seipobi, a reporter for a national Basutoland newspaper *Leselinyana*.

3 "God Made Liz Abrahams"

Figure 3.5 Mafeking's dramatic escape to Lesotho made her and baby Uhuru famous. Newspapers vied for the opportunity to interview the activist, who was the first African woman to choose self-exile over banishment.

News Collection ZA (Vault) Hoover Library & Archives, Stanford University. *Fighting Talk*, vol. 13, no. 9, December 1959

3 "God Made Liz Abrahams"

In a featurette entitled *"Tseo Mrs. Mafekeng [sic] a'li boletseng ho rona,"* or "Things Mrs. Mafekeng [sic] Told Us," she spoke candidly of her persecution in South Africa, and provided titillating details of her harrowing, high-speed escape to Basutoland.[38] Today, the drive from Paarl to Lesotho can be completed in twelve hours via the N1, a well-maintained national highway that extends the entire distance between the two countries. For Mafeking and her compatriots in 1959, however, the drive took considerably longer and occurred under much less hospitable road conditions. When first leaving the outskirts of Paarl heading east into the South African interior, Mafeking recalled, *"Ba khannile koloi eo ka matla a makatsang,"* (they drove the car at an alarming speed), making her fear on more than one occasion the vehicle would overturn. They drove east the entire day, first towards the rising sun, then away from it as it set behind them. Night had long descended as the group reached the eastern outskirts of the Free State, and a flat tire forced the convoy to make its first, extended stop in the day-long drive. Anxious, wary of being caught, but too exhausted to repair the flat tire, the group decided to push

3 "God Made Liz Abrahams"

the car into the bushes where they slept for the night. When they awoke in the morning, they quickly fixed the flat, got back on the road, and in short order *"ba kena Lesotho ka khotso"* (they entered Lesotho in peace). In the photograph that accompanies the article, Mafeking – safely ensconced at an unidentified location in Basutoland – holds two-month old Uhuru in her arms. The caption above the photograph reads, *"Mrs. Elizabeth Mafekeng [sic], ke senatla sa mosali"* (she is a superwoman).

Public opinion was on Mafeking's side in 1959 when she first arrived in the country seeking asylum. Simultaneous administrative and communication issues between the South African Police and Basutoland officials resulted in Mafeking's smooth transition into Basutoland, and once inside the territory Mafeking was no longer subject to the laws of the Republic, rather, to the dictates of a colonial administration on its way out. The Commonwealth Relations Office wasn't quite out of the country yet, however, and it determined to ensure future political alliances were not ruined by the presence, protest, and work of refugees. While the rest of the world pleaded with British leaders to preserve the sanctity of the concept of refuge, British officials engaged in secret – and morally questionable – conversations aimed at undermining the civic freedoms of political refugees during the first three years of Mafeking's exile in Basutoland.

Within weeks of arriving in Basutoland, Mafeking began making regular appearances as an invited guest at political rallies organized by the Basutoland Congress Party (BCP). January 1–3, 1960, Mafeking attended a BCP rally in Maseru where she shared the stage with Ntsu Mokhehle and Lilian Ngoyi. Ngoyi was President of the ANCWL, and Mokhehle was the head of the BCP and a rising political star many speculated would play a significant role in the post-independence political reorganization of Lesotho.[39] Mafeking addressed a crowd of more than two hundred, many of whom openly wept as she described her persecution at the hands of the NP in South Africa. When Ngoyi addressed the crowd holding Uhuru Mafeking in her arms and Mokhehle announced a BCP-organized fund to aid Mafeking and other political refugees, it seemed the

3 "God Made Liz Abrahams"

struggles of the BaSotho people and blacks in South Africa were the same.

Figure 3.6 Mafeking and her infant, Uhuru, were instant celebrities upon arrival in Lesotho, and frequently found themselves in the pages of local newspapers.

News Collection ZA (Vault) Hoover Library & Archives, Stanford University. New Age, November 12, 1959

3 "God Made Liz Abrahams"

Figure 3.7 Lilian Ngoyi holds baby Uhuru aloft during a speech in Basutoland.

News Collection ZA (Vault) Hoover Library & Archives, Stanford University. New Age, January 4, 1960

3 "God Made Liz Abrahams"

Figure 3.8 Mafeking speaking to a crowd at a BCP rally about the evils of Apartheid in South Africa.

Courtesy of Thomas Mofolo Library. Archives, Records Management, Museum and Documentation Division. National University of Lesotho. Roma, Lesotho. Lentsoe la Basotho, August 13, 1960

Figure 3.9 Mafeking and baby Uhuru at their first BCP rally in Lesotho where they shared the stage with party leader Ntsu Mokhehle. In later years, Mokhehle condemned Mafeking and other political refugees in Lesotho.

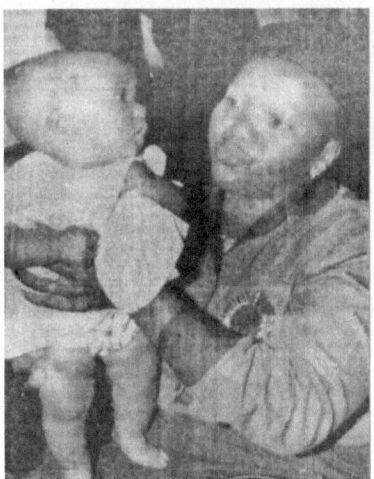

Courtesy of Thomas Mofolo Library. Archives, Records Management, Museum and Documentation Division. National University of Lesotho. Roma, Lesotho. The African Echo, January 16, 1960

3 "God Made Liz Abrahams"

On both sides of the border there were too few job opportunities for blacks, and the few, coveted government positions that existed consistently went to whites. Mokhehle announced a charitable fund that had been established to aid refugees, and even went so far as to proclaim "Basutoland is now the Jerusalem for all African refugees and all are welcome in Basutoland."[40] Mafeking took those words to heart, and made very public plans to establish a home in Maseru and to apply for a permanent residence permit in Basutoland. The country allowed visitors the right to remain in the country for 90 days, at which time they either needed to return to their country of origin or apply for a residence permit. Mafeking, who was still enjoying the honeymoon period of her exile in Basutoland, could "see no reason why [she] should not get one."[41] Within a month, however, the march of African independence – in both Basutoland and across the Continent as a whole – and associated pressures began to change the national narrative regarding the so-called welcome of political refugees in Basutoland.

3 "God Made Liz Abrahams"

A banished mother in Basutoland

British officials in Basutoland knew from monitoring the South African media that there was "a mass meeting" in Cape Town of more than 500 people from four national organizations protesting the banning of one Mrs. Elizabeth Mafeking.[42] Within days of the first murmurs of controversy, the South African media confirmed Mafeking had evaded the Secret Police when her banning order went into effect and speculated she'd escaped to Basutoland, "quite likely . . . living quietly with friends waiting until the uproar arising from the banishment order served on her" died down.[43] In the past, the "common practice" involving wanted South Africans crossing into the High Commission territories was a simple matter: "the [local Basutoland police] would co-operate with the South African police and put the person back over the border into Union territory."[44] Mafeking's celebrity, BaSotho origins, and Basutoland's slow march to independence, however, seemed to ensure that it would be "extremely unlikely" those same types of dirty tricks would be employed against Mafeking.[45] As if to

3 "God Made Liz Abrahams"

foreshadow what was to come, *The Star* even insinuated that if Mafeking were to decide she wanted her children to live with her in Basutoland, with the permission of the High Commission authorities, it should be her right.

Though public opinion may have been on Mafeking's side, political alliances were not. In a secret communique from the Resident Commissioner in Maseru to the High Commissioner in Pretoria, Basutoland police had "no knowledge [whatsoever of] her whereabouts," but had already notified all of the district commissioners of Mafeking's impending arrival.[46] Basutoland police presumed Mafeking "might conceal herself . . . for some time" and requested clear instruction from Pretoria officials. Basutoland police were prepared "to take no further action" until they learned of the specific banning orders served on Mafeking, and specifically asked what – if anything – they should do "if any approach is made by Union authorities under [the] Fugitive Offenders Act" to apprehend Mafeking.

While Basutoland police may not have immediately known Mafeking's whereabouts, records indicate South

3 "God Made Liz Abrahams"

African police may have known exactly where the activist was. Notes from a secret interview with the Acting Commissioner of Police in Maseru reveal South African police *knew* about Mafeking's plan to escape to Basutoland, and even provided Basutoland police with the name of Mafeking's getaway driver, a detailed description of the car inclusive of the license plate, and the approximate time of the small party's departure from Paarl in the early morning hours of November 9.[47] The records indicate *what* information was available to police forces on both sides of the border, but not *when* – timely miscommunications that aided in Mafeking's successful escape. The very next day, *The Friend* confirmed Mafeking's arrival in Basutoland, and credited her uneventful crossing into the territory to particularly good timing. Her banning order did not go into effect until 9:00am, and Mafeking and her party crossed at 7:26am.[48] Technically, at the time of her crossing, "she had not committed any offence in view of the date of her banishment order," and was not in contradiction of any law inside the country of South Africa, so she was allowed to enter.[49] The High Commissioner in Pretoria immediately

3 "God Made Liz Abrahams"

contacted the Resident Commissioners of both Maseru and Mafeteng to outline the official position of their office, and by proxy, the British government:

> Should [Elizabeth Mafeking] enter [the] territory and Union police demand her surrender it is important that provisions of Fugitive Offenders Act should be scrupulously followed ... no, repeat no action to declare her a prohibited immigrant should be taken without reference to this office.[50]

The High Commissioner would not prohibit Mafeking from entering the territory, but the office also would not protect the activist from the South African government if the Union decided to take custody of her. The High Commissioner was clear: until Mafeking broke a law or South Africa decided to arrest her, Basutoland officials were to stand down. Meanwhile, British officials closely monitored what the media knew: there were now warrants out for Mafeking's arrest in South Africa, Mafeking was in Basutoland rumored to be headed towards Roma, and no one could seem to

3 "God Made Liz Abrahams"

confirm her whereabouts.[51] This, however, was not the case for British officials working in conjunction with Basutoland police. Not only did British officials know exactly where Mafeking and her infant child were, but they *purposefully misled the press* – whom they described as being "hot on [the] trail seeking confirmation" of Mafeking's presence in the territory – when their office was questioned by the press about what its official response would be to the controversy.[52] The Resident Commissioner confirmed for the High Commissioner that a vehicle matching the description of the one carrying Mafeking across the border had been tracked through the streets of Maseru to Roma Village, some 27km away. Given the building resentment and organized strength of the youth movement within African activist circles in South Africa, British officials closely monitored developments on African college campuses, and the communique to the High Commissioner was clear to point out that while the car went to Roma, which was the home of the nation's only institution for higher learning, Mafeking was "NOT REPEAT NOT [connected to the] UNIVERSITY."[53] While the woman in the vehicle was strongly suspected of being Mafeking, Basutoland police could not be 100% certain in their report – a fact they blamed on the South African police for failing to pass on pertinent information about the car and woman in question in a timely manner.[54] Within days of Mafeking's arrival, the High Commissioner in Pretoria submitted a report to the Secretary of State for Commonwealth Relations in London wherein he described for the home office the "unusual degree of indignation in Opposition (sic) circles" to the banning of Mafeking, which even he had to remark was "by no means unique."[55] This internal document of the British government noted it was, however, the first time an order of this nature had ever been executed against a woman who just happened to have eleven children.

Elizabeth Mafeking only entered Basutoland because she believed residing under the authority of the High Commission Territory was the only way to combat the power the Apartheid government sought to exercise over her life. It was not simply happenstance that she arrived in Basutoland without incident. South African police failed to coordinate with Basutoland officials, which resulted in

3 "God Made Liz Abrahams"

Mafeking's safe entry and a missed opportunity for South African officials who were left with egg on their faces. The day after her arrival, competing headlines declared Mafeking was "afraid" that action would be taken against her.[56] Rumors swirled furiously in the media that Mafeking was a "needle in a Basutoland haystack" who would not be found unless she wanted to be found.[57] Others reported that hiding was unnecessary, since Minister De Wet Nel himself allegedly declared "if [Mafeking] is found to be outside the Union, no further steps will be taken against her by his department."[58] News of the Mafeking Affair had, embarrassingly enough, reached the hallowed halls of Parliament when the Minister of State for Commonwealth Relations had to answer difficult questions posed in the House of Commons. British politicos from the Labour Party wanted to know what arrangements – if any – were in place for individuals entering the High Commission Territories in order to escape prosecution in South Africa.[59] Maseru's Resident Commissioner assured officials in Pretoria that there were regular meetings between South African Police from Bloemfontein and Basutoland police in Maseru

3 "God Made Liz Abrahams"

regarding Mafeking's entry into the country. Basutoland police claimed to be unable to confirm Mafeking's presence due to the lack of information supplied by South African police. According to Basutoland officials, too little information trickled in too late for their forces to offer any type of real assistance to the Union.[60]

Figure 3.10 Mafeking eluded authorities to the delight of her supporters, and to the frustration of Apartheid leaders desirous of making an example out of the activist. NP leadership was privately enraged that Mafeking had managed to escape "justice," but publically maintained an air of indifference. In the original caption, Verwoerd and De Wet Nel (pictured right) discuss the case with two political consultants--vultures--who mock recent statements made by authorities in the press regarding their feelings about Mafeking's escape: "What do you mean the British government can have Mrs. Mafekeng (sic)? This is a fine time to become humanitarian."

Courtesy of Patel, Yusuf and Philip Hirschsohn, eds., *Married to the Struggle: 'Nana' Liz Abrahams Tells her Life Story* (University of the Western Cape, 2005

3 "God Made Liz Abrahams"

For its part, the Union seemed not to care in the least about Mafeking's flight, even if (and most likely because) her escape was an official embarrassment. Prime Minister Verwoerd proclaimed the "British can have [the] whole family," and even offered to pay the transport costs of the Mafeking clan if it would ensure that "Native[s] who come to live in White areas . . . behave in such a manner . . . as to maintain peace and good order."[61] Verwoerd felt his position was sound: banishment orders existed to protect white areas. In the case of Mafeking in particular, Verwoerd professed to not understand the outcry over potentially separating Mafeking from her children via banishment when she willingly "left them behind when she went on a visit behind the Iron Curtain" years earlier.[62] The difference between temporary versus permanent separation was, clearly for Verwoerd, inconsequential. What was imperative for the larger Nationalist Party, however, was consolidating South Africa's power in the region and securing its borders.

While its leadership feigned indifference at Mafeking's escape, rank-and-file members of the NP were

3 "God Made Liz Abrahams"

furious that she had managed to evade arrest in Cape Town and escape to the British Protectorates. Delegates attending the Cape Congress of the Nationalist Party had private conversations wherein they demanded that incorporation of the Protectorates "should be renewed or that the Government (sic) should consider establishing immigration posts at the borders" of the three Protectorates.[63] Mafeking's escape to Basutoland was the third time that year when a so-called criminal fled South Africa for either Bechuanaland, Swaziland, or Basutoland to evade capture, and Nationalists blamed the British government for passively facilitating the escapes. British officials, themselves, were under an inordinate amount of pressure at home from the reigning, conservative leadership of the Labour Party and the international allies of Mafeking's many activist organizations. The London-based Trades Union Congress (TUC) issued a statement through the office of its General Council that "protest[ed] strongly" against the NP government's behavior, Mafeking's banishment, and the "vague assertions made by the South African Government" (sic) regarding her

3 "God Made Liz Abrahams"

supposed wrongdoings.[64] Mafeking was primarily concerned with staying beyond the reach of South African authorities, and she knew full well that Basutoland police were often complicit in returning South African refugees to the waiting hands of Apartheid. Mafeking likely never imagined she might need to fear the British government – which was supposedly de-investing in its colonial territories, most specifically in Basutoland with democratic elections on the immediate horizon.

3 "God Made Liz Abrahams"

Notes

1 Digital Innovation South Africa (DISA), "The Lonely Exile of Elizabeth Mafekeng," November 14, 1959, 2. www.disa.ukzn.ac.za/index.php?option=com_displaydc&recordID=Ctv2n2359 (accessed March 2007).

2 Financially speaking, by 1959, Elizabeth Mafeking had come a long way from her first food canning job in 1934 that had paid only $.75 cents per week. At the time of her banishment, Mafeking earned £5 per week as a full-time trade union worker, roughly $12USD per week. Her husband's earnings of £4 per week (approximately $9.60 USD) meant the thirteen-person Mafeking family relied upon a monthly income of $86.40. Upon banishment, however, Mafeking would only receive £2 ($4.80 USD) *per month*! Even *if* Mafeking could have

continued to contribute to her family's financial well-being (assuming she did not need every penny of the monthly $4.80 to survive in isolation), reducing the family's earnings by 50% would have made survival seem impossible.

3 The General Conference of the International Labor Organization, Committee on Freedom of Association Report, *The Trade Unions International of Workers of the Food, Tobacco and Beverage Industries and Hotel, Cafe and Restaurant Workers (Trade Department of the World Federation of Trade Unions), the South African Congress of Trade Unions and the World Federation of Trade Unions (Case No. 200)*, June 10, 1959. Text from: *Definitive Report No. 44,* http://webfusion.ilo.org/public/db/standards/normes/libsynd/LSGetParasByCase.cfm?PARA=6349&F

ILE=200&hdroff=1&DISPLAY=RECOMMENDATION, BACKGROUND (accessed June 17, 2009).

4 Ibid.

5 Ibid.

6 Scanlon, Helen, *Representation and Reality: Portraits of Women's Lives in the Western Cape, 1948–1976* (Pretoria, South Africa: Human Sciences Research Council, 2007), 191; quoting document from South African Institute of Race Relations.

7 *New Age*, November 12, 1959 (African Studies Library, University of Cape Town, Cape Town, South Africa).

8 Berger, Iris, "Gender, Race, and Political Empowerment: South African Canning Workers, 1940–1960" in *Gender & Society* vol. 4, no. 3 (1990), 400; The 1930s was a decade of unparalleled change and ideological expansion for the Communist Party. Such previously under-considered themes as race,

class, and gender, were no longer dismissed as divisive or counterproductive to working class struggles. These issues (and defining the Party's stance on them) became central to ideological discourses of the Left.

9 Badat, Saleem, *The Forgotten People: Political Banishment under Apartheid* (Boston: Brill, 2013). Chapter 8 of *Forgotten People* illustrates the varied ways in which families and supporters of banned individuals challenged the orders. Unfortunately, the vast majority of these "meetings, demonstrations, boycotts, petitions and statements of protest" came to naught after 1956, because by that time there had been three (3) successful court challenges to banning, which resulted in a series of amendments that "brought

an end to all possible legal opposition to banishment in South Africa." 244, 250.

10 *New Age*, "Save Elizabeth Mafeking from Exile!," November 5, 1959. Hoover Institution Library & Archives, Stanford University, Stanford, CA. Subsequent references in this chapter from this archival source will appear as "Hoover Institution Library & Archives."

11 Ibid.

12 "Untitled Cartoon" *New Age*, November 5, 1959. Hoover Institution Library & Archives.

13 "Over 80 Already in Exile" *New Age*, November 5, 1959. Hoover Institution Library & Archives.

14 Blumberg, Myrna, "The Mafekeng Affair" in *Africa South: In Exile* vol. 4, no. 3 (April–June, 1960), 39–46. Hoover Institution Library & Archives.

3 "God Made Liz Abrahams"

15 *New Age*, "Save Elizabeth Mafeking from Exile!," November 5, 1959. Hoover Institution Library & Archives.

16 "Profile: Elizabeth Mafekeng (sic)," ANC Women's Section Archives, Biographical Profiles, Box 124, Folder 19. Liberation Movement Archives of the National Heritage and Cultural Studies Centre (NAHECS), University of Fort Hare, Alice, South Africa. Subsequent reference in this chapter to this archival source will appear as "NAHECS."

17 "The Mafekeng Affair," 42.

18 Ibid.

19 Ibid., 43.

20 "New Riots in South Africa" *New York Times*, November 11, 1959 (ProQuest Historical Newspapers: The New York Times (1851–2008), 8.

21 Ibid.

22 Ibid.

23 "We Will Never Stop Saying 'Africa Must Come Back': Elizabeth Mafekeng's Farewell Message" New Age, November 12, 1959, 1.

24 "The Mafekeng Affair," 44–45.

25 "3 Mafekeng [sic] Children Questioned by Police" in New Age vol. 6, no. 4 (November 19, 1959). News Collection ZA (Vault) Hoover Library & Archives; Nominki Mafeking interview.

26 Ibid.

27 Anonymous Correspondent, "Diary from Refugee" in Africa South: In Exile vol. 5, no. 1 (October–December, 1960), 31–40. Hoover Institution Library & Archives.

28 Ibid., 33.

29 Ibid.

30 Ibid., 35.

31 Ibid.

32 Ibid., 40.

33 Halpern, Jack, Basutoland, Bechuanaland, and Swaziland London, United Kingdom: Penguin, 1965), 65, 135.

34 Nthunya, Mpho 'Matsepo, Singing Away the Hunger, Limakatso Kendall, ed., (Pietermaritzburg, South Africa: University of Natal Press, 1996), 59, 37.

35 In response to the ever-increasing refugee population, however, by 1965 there were almost two dozen border posts established on the borders of Basutoland.

36 Coates, Austin, Basutoland (London, United Kingdom: Her Majesty's Stationery Office, 1966), 4, 3.

37 Halpern, Basutoland, Bechuanaland, and Swaziland, 136.

3 "God Made Liz Abrahams"

---

38 Seipobi, C. M., "Tseo Mrs. Mafekeng [sic] a'li boletseng ho rona" Leselinyana [Lesotho], January 9, 1960, 6. Print. Thomas Mofolo Library. Archives, Records Management, Museum and Documentation Division. National University of Lesotho. Roma, Lesotho. Newspaper Collection (accessed July 2015). Subsequent references in this chapter from this archival source will appear as "Archives, Records Management, Museum and Documentation Division, NUL."

39 "Ntsu O Bua Sebokeng" The African Echo [Lesotho], January 16, 1960, 12. Archives, Records Management, Museum and Documentation Division, NUL.

40 Halpern, Basutoland, Bechuanaland, and Swaziland, 161.

41 "Mrs. Mafeking Is to Apply for a Residence Permit" The African Echo [Lesotho], January 30, 1960, 9. Archives, Records Management, Museum and Documentation Division, NUL.

42 "Big Cape Protest Over Banning" The Friend, November 9, 1959. The National Archives (TNA): FCO 141/479: Basutoland: Flight of Mrs. Elizabeth Mafekeng (sic), South African Trade Unionist, to Basutoland; Application and Residence. (1) Declassified 2012. Subsequent references from this archival source will appear as "TNA: FCO 141/479: Basutoland."

43 "Mafekeng (sic) Is Thought to Be in Basutoland" The Star, November 11, 1959. TNA: FCO 141/479: Basutoland. (4).

44 Ibid.

3 "God Made Liz Abrahams"

45 "Elizabeth Mafekeng (sic) Is in Basutoland" The Star, November 11, 1959. TNA: FCO 141/479: Basutoland. (4).

46 Correspondence from Resident Commissioner (Maseru) to D. H. C. (High Commissioner for the United Kingdom, Pretoria), November 11, 1959. TNA: FCO 141/479: Basutoland. (2).

47 "Interview with Mr. Baartman," November 11, 1959. TNA: FCO 141/479: Basutoland. (3).

48 Ibid.

49 "Mrs. Mafekeng (sic) Is Found: Exiled Mother Is in Basutoland" The Friend, November 12, 1959. TNA: FCO 141/479: Basutoland. (5).

50 Correspondence from D. H. C. (Pretoria) to Resident Commissioner (Mafeking) and Resident Commissioner (Maseru) November 11, 1959. TNA: FCO 141/479: Basutoland. (6).

3 "God Made Liz Abrahams"

51 "She Is in Basutoland: But Where?" The Friend, November 12, 1959. TNA: FCO 141/479: Basutoland. (5); "STOP PRESS" The Friend, November 12, 1959. TNA: FCO 141/479: Basutoland. (5).

52 Correspondence from Resident Commissioner (Maseru) to D. H. C. (Pretoria) November 12, 1959. TNA: FCO 141/479: Basutoland. (8).

53 Ibid.

54 Ibid.

55 Telegram from High Commissioner for the United Kingdom (Pretoria) to Secretary of State for Commonwealth Relations (London) November 12, 1959. TNA: FCO 141/479: Basutoland.

56 "Mrs. Mafekeng (sic) Is Afraid, They Say" The Friend, November 13, 1959. TNA: FCO 141/479: Basutoland. (12).

3 "God Made Liz Abrahams"

57 Ibid.

58 "The Story of the Paarl Escape: No Action, Says Nel" The Friend, November 13, 1959. TNA: FCO 141/479: Basutoland (11).

59 Ibid.

60 Correspondence from Resident Commissioner (Maseru) to D. H. C. (Pretoria) November 13, 1959. TNA: FCO 141/479: Basutoland. (9).

61 "Mrs. Mafekeng (sic) Seeks Refuge in Mission" The Star, November 14, 1959. TNA: FCO 141/479: Basutoland. (11)

62 Ibid.

63 "Nats. (sic) Upset by Escapes to the Protectorates" Sunday Times, November 15, 1959. TNA: FCO 141/479: Basutoland. (16).

64 Press release. "General Council Statement." Trades Union Congress, Press and Publications

3 "God Made Liz Abrahams"

Department. November 18, 1959. TNA: FCO 141/479: Basutoland. (124C); "Unions Hit at Ban on Mrs. Mafekeng (sic)" The Friend, November 19, 1959. TNA: FCO 141/479: Basutoland. (20).

4

A Dangerous Embarrassment

The Refugee Problem in Basutoland

Elizabeth Mafeking overestimated the supposed generosity of the British government and entered the territory thinking it a promised land, rather than the lion's den it turned out to be. London was keenly interested in Elizabeth Mafeking's presence in the territory. Communicating with the High Commissioner in Pretoria and both Resident Commissioners in Maseru and Mafeteng simultaneously, Asst. Under-Secretary G. B. Shannon communicated the official position of the government to the Mafeking Affair:

> If Mrs. Mafekeng (sic) applies for a residence permit, her application will of course have to be considered by the Board in accordance with the Proclamation, and the Secretary of State would be reluctant to lay down in advance what decision should best be reached: in any case, as I understand the

4 A Dangerous Embarrassment

Proclamations, the decision rests with the BaSotho majority. But, if your information is that Mrs. Mafekeng (sic) is a Communist, the Secretary of State would not be happy with a proposal to let her stay in Basutoland. Presumably the only way of putting, or keeping, her out would be for the Board to refuse her application, or for the Resident Commissioner to deem her presence to be, or to be likely to be, prejudicial to the peace, order and good government of Basutoland. If either course has to be taken, the former would be preferable. The latter course would be certain to have sharp political repercussions here.[1]

4 A Dangerous Embarrassment

Figure 4.1 Mafeking's first application for a residency permit in Lesotho made headlines with a confident Mafeking declaring, "I see no reason why I should not get it!"

Courtesy of Thomas Mofolo Library. Archives, Records Management, Museum and Documentation Division. National University of Lesotho. Roma, Lesotho. Newspaper Collection. The African Echo, January 30, 1960

Under the 1958 Entry and Residence Proclamation of Basutoland, non-residents had 90 days to declare their intent to remain in the territory beyond the three courtesy months. Mafeking had only been in the country for less than

4 A Dangerous Embarrassment

one month, but with few alternatives, it was generally accepted that she would – at some point – submit an application for residency. In the spirit of fair play, the Commonwealth Relations Office was, "of course," prepared to consider a duly submitted application. It was even magnanimous enough to wait until *after* Mafeking submitted an application to determine "what decision should best be reached." It was also helpful enough to suggest the most effective way of ensuring Mafeking would not be welcomed in the territory: find evidence "that Mrs. Mafekeng (sic) is a Communist."

To the British government, despite the focus of the media and sympathizers in the international community the plight of Elizabeth Mafeking was not a moral issue, rather, one of potential political liability. Mafeking fled to Basutoland just as deep political rivalries were beginning to form in the tiny country in the years before the pre-independence general election of 1965, and the British government had no intention of ceding a former colony to the influence of Communism. While Elizabeth Mafeking worked with and knew communists in South Africa, she was

4 A Dangerous Embarrassment

never an official member of the SACP, which was incredibly fortunate for her since it would have spelled disaster for the activist in Basutoland. Failing to find the stain of Communism on her political reputation, the Commonwealth Relations Office could only devise of two potential ways to keep Mafeking out of Basutoland: first, outright refuse to accept whatever application she submitted to the Entry and Residence Proclamation Board, or second, use language eerily similar to the Apartheid dictates that drove Mafeking from her family and home in Paarl in the first place.

Faced with that kind of decision, even the Under-Secretary recognized there would be "sharp political repercussions" in London if the Commonwealth Relations Office appeared to simply parrot the South African government, and conceded it might just be easier to reject the application.[2] In the early weeks of Mafeking's flight to Basutoland, *any* decision for the British government was a difficult one considering its sources. The Commonwealth Relations Office in London relied upon intelligence from its own agents who, in turn, depended heavily upon

4 A Dangerous Embarrassment

information culled from their contacts with the SAP and Basutoland police. South African forces were consistently reluctant and tardy in supplying their British and Basutoland contacts with crucial information on Mafeking, and Basutoland officials claimed that even one month after Mafeking's arrival in the country that although there was "little doubt" the woman they'd been following was Elizabeth Mafeking, they still could not positively identify her.[3] This seems highly improbable given the fact that Mafeking announced her arrival in Basutoland in the New Year with a much-publicized bang. Drum magazine published a three-page featurette on Mafeking's flight from South Africa, calling the story the "newspaper scoop of the year."[4] British officials in Basutoland learned about the more intimate details of Mafeking's journey into Basutoland for the first time, and even heard from Mafeking herself when questioned about her intent to return to South Africa.

4 A Dangerous Embarrassment

> Of course [I will return to the Union]. And as soon as possible. But what makes me afraid sometimes is that I don't know when that day will be.[5]

Images of Mafeking cradling her three month-old daughter, Uhuru, accompany the story. The images of Mafeking shading her baby on a hot day, gently holding her on the couch, and balancing Uhuru on her hip as the pair walk to a nearby store to listen to the radio, were no doubt a very pointed mockery of the bullying might of Apartheid against a defenseless mother. Stories relevant to the Mafeking affair filtered in from sources both abroad and back home.

Within the course of a week, *The Star* published a series of articles that were of great concern to members of the High Commissioner's Office in Pretoria and its agents in Basutoland. Protests had erupted in the U.K. in response to Mafeking's plight and the perceived inaction of British officials to respond appropriately. Picketers blocked the entrance of South Africa House, the diplomatic mission from South Africa to the UK, carrying placards that demanded Mafeking be allowed to return home. The multi-

4 A Dangerous Embarrassment

racial, multi-national crowd also called for a general boycott of South African goods as they took their protest from the steps of the South Africa House and paraded around the perimeter of the building.[6] Supporting Mafeking seemed to be all the international rage, as the newspaper later reported BCP leadership's promise to "give political asylum to people like Mrs. Mafekeng (sic)" and even extend material support like "a house of her own" to accommodate her.[7] With so much outspoken support from inside and outside of the UK, but so little from British officials themselves, it was clear Prime Minister Harold Macmillan would have some very tough questions to answer when he arrived in South Africa for a scheduled state visit. Macmillan was a major proponent of decolonization, and had seen both Ghana and the Federation of Malaya gain independence and join the Commonwealth of Nations during his tenure as P.M., but Mafeking's evasion of banishment created a "tricky situation" for the British administration, which had to make a decision about her residency that could have serious future political consequences for both Basutoland and South Africa.[8]

4 A Dangerous Embarrassment

Macmillan just happened to be coming to South Africa at the same time the immigration board in Basutoland met to consider applications, and the High Commissioner feared "the issue might prove embarrassing to" the Prime Minister upon arrival in Pretoria.[9] The P.M. might have found it difficult to respond in a way that did not create diplomatic tensions between the South African and British governments, but documents suggest his agents were not above betraying the confidence of individuals, Mafeking and her allies in particular.

> **Message for Mrs. Mafekeng (sic) from the "Tribune"**
>
> In a letter to the Resident Commissioner, the Deputy High Commissioner states as follows:-
>
>> I enclose a message for Mrs. Mafekeng (sic) from the Tribune which we have been asked to forward to her. The Special Branch will no doubt

4 A Dangerous Embarrassment

know what to do. I should be interested to hear the outcome in due course!

2. The message is enclosed in a sealed envelope as received. Will you please inform me what action you consider should be taken; you will, no doubt, wish to examine the contents of the message.[10]

This communique – twice marked and underlined "secret" – addressed to the Commissioner of Police in Maseru reveal a wealth of knowledge regarding the true level of collusion and betrayal British authorities were willing to engage in where Elizabeth Mafeking was concerned. Basutoland police were clearly informed of and had access to internal conversations within the Commonwealth Relations Office, even more shocking, British officials willingly relinquished a confidential document knowing it would be opened before it reached Mafeking. The editors of the *Tribune* clearly misplaced their trust in the Deputy High Commissioner (D.H.C.) when they

4 A Dangerous Embarrassment

asked him to use the authority of his office to relay a message to Mafeking. It is highly likely that Mafeking received the no-longer-secret message from the *Tribune*, but entirely probable she never knew her eyes weren't the only ones to see it. Weeks later in a month-end missive from the Maseru office to the D.H.C. in Cape Town, high-ranking officials scribbled hand-written notes to one another at the bottom of the two-page telex message that spoke directly to the issue of Mafeking's letter from the *Tribune*:

> Please check verbally that the letter mentioned can be conveyed to the addressee without any hint that it has been opened.
> I spoke to [the contact] and he is able to act accordingly.[11]

British authorities knew they did not have a majority on the immigration board that would oversee Mafeking's eventual application, and feared declaring her a "prohibited immigrant" – thus eliminating her ability to apply for residency – in advance of her submitting an application

4 A Dangerous Embarrassment

would influence the upcoming elections in the favor of the Basutoland Congress Party (BCP). Ntsu Mokhehle, president of the BCP, very vocally proclaimed Mafeking was under protection of the party and would have its unwavering support as long as she remained in Basutoland.[12] The BCP was in the midst of making a strong bid for support in the Basutoland elections, and its opposition to the principle of chieftainship in a post-colonial Africa threatened long-standing relationships between local leaders and the UK. Clearly, officials were willing to use whatever means at their disposal – even coordinated duplicity – to improve their chances of ending the Mafeking saga and restoring proper political order.[13] British officials *had* to do something, because it was clear to them that South African officials had washed their hands of Mafeking. A hand-written report from an unidentified individual within the office of the Resident Commissioner in Maseru verified that "the problem of Mrs. Mafekeng (sic)" could have been averted altogether if the Union had simply exercised its right to extradite her.[14] The High Commissioner was fully prepared to allow extradition law to "take its course," but the Union

4 A Dangerous Embarrassment

failed to invoke its rights and, in the words of the unnamed agent, "seem[ed] content to allow Mrs. Mafekeng (sic) to stay in Basutoland."

For the remainder of January 1960, British officials in London, South Africa, and Basutoland were preoccupied primarily with confirming Basutoland Intelligence Reports that included pertinent information about Mafeking and brainstorming politically correct ways to prevent Mafeking from remaining in the territory.[15] Mafeking's presence in Basutoland had a direct impact on the lives of dozens of political refugees taking shelter inside the tiny nation in that British officials ultimately decided to contact *all* refugees – those they deemed to be in Basutoland "without authority" – to pointedly remind them of the provisions of the Entry and Residence Proclamation.[16] Wanted individuals who had been able to remain largely incognito in the territory for "several months" were put on notice that their time in the country was finite, and officials even reached out to hotel proprietors asking they make note of "guests staying for more than three months." Mafeking's presence also influenced a specific codicil authorities included in

4 A Dangerous Embarrassment

residency permits issued in 1960. Thanks to her close ties to the BCP and fears of what her political influence could mean for upcoming elections, "a condition was contained in all permits issued to persons who are given asylum in Basutoland that they should not engage in politics." The immediate problems with this rider were two-fold for British authorities: first, they were unsure if they could "sell" the idea of a residency restriction to local control boards, and second, they had no idea how to enforce the condition.

In the case of Mafeking, officials were clear that it was very likely she would receive a temporary permit and they were determined to curb her political activities as much as possible. According to one official, once a permit was issued it would be much more difficult for British authorities "to get rid of her, without raising [a] political storm." When Elizabeth Mafeking fled Paarl in November 1959, she necessarily left ten of her eleven children behind and only took her two month-old infant into exile with her. Records from the Commonwealth Relations Office, however, reveal that by June of 1960, some of Mafeking's children had been able to join her in Basutoland, as the activist had included their names on her residence application.[17] Indeed, Mafeking's decision to raise her children in exile most likely saved her life, because following their relocation from Paarl to Lesotho, documents now available at the National Archives in the UK attest to the fact that while British officials in London may have wanted Mafeking out of the territory desperately, their agents on the ground in Southern Africa – those in Basutoland in particular – were, due to the presence of her children, increasingly unwilling to use legalese as a method of disqualifying Mafeking from the protection of a residence permit.

Left behind

In spite of everything everyone had done in November of 1959 to support the Mafeking children after their mother left, Sophia – the eldest – remained heartbroken. She had not even begun to deal with her hatred of the machinery of Apartheid and its architects – particularly Minister De Wet

4 A Dangerous Embarrassment

Nel – when she was dealt another blow. Only five months after her mother's departure, Liz Abrahams arrived at the house one morning and informed Sophia that the children were leaving. "Khekhe, you must put aside the children's clothes, everything, because they are going to [Basutoland]."[18] Sophia could not help but notice Abrahams had said *the children* were going to Basutoland, and asked about a passport for herself. Abrahams had the sad duty of informing Sophia that while she could escort the children to their mother, Sophia would have to return to Paarl because otherwise her father would be left alone with the two eldest sons, Atti and Mehlo, who were "useless" when it came to cooking, cleaning, and maintaining a home. Sophia packed the children's belongings and waited for their ANC escorts to arrive. "The ANC people prepared for us, and they came to look after us. We had a nice trip to Lesotho, and we arrived there to find her waiting, looking for us."[19] Mafeking excitedly hugged each of her children, whom she'd not seen in five months, and thanked her comrades for delivering them to her safely. The moment was bittersweet for Sophia, however, who had only minutes to be with her mother before she had to return to South Africa with her escorts.

Sophia was saddened to see her family spilt, but did not resent the decision for her to remain in Paarl. As the eldest daughter of a traditional African family, Sophia was expected to perform a number of familial duties associated with aiding her mother in running an effective household. Sophia would have been both a second mother to her younger siblings and her mother's trusted right hand, and as such, she alone would have been recognized as being both trained and competent enough to maintain the family home in Mafeking's absence. Meanwhile in Basotuland, given the introduction of Mafeking's children into the residency saga months earlier, by October of 1960 officials finally decided on a course of action that coerced Mafeking's compliance. The District Control Board approved Mafeking's application for permanent residence, but with the stipulation that the activist sign a document presented to her on government letterhead that read:

4 A Dangerous Embarrassment

> I, Mrs. Elizabeth Mditjana, known as Mrs. Mafekeng (sic), hereby voluntarily undertake not to interfere in any way, now, or in the future, in the affairs of the Union of South Africa, and in particular political or trade union affairs, nor to embarrass in any way the Basutoland Government (sic) in its relations with the Union Government (sic), nor to abuse the hospitality extended me by the BaSotho nation.[20]

Under duress, with no alternatives, permanent residency at stake, and eight children to feed, Elizabeth Mafeking effectively signed away her rights to freely participate in international political processes important to the UK, and provided the BaSotho government with a convenient (and broad) means to find future cause against her. Perhaps because she recognized the crafty language of the pledge, Mafeking – who just happened to be wearing her new BCP membership badge – specifically "inquired if this [represented] any objection to her engaging in Basutoland politics," to which the DC replied no.[21] While this technically

4 A Dangerous Embarrassment

meant that Mafeking could be involved in politics in Basutoland, it did not necessarily mean that her presence in that arena would be welcome.

The Basutoland Paramount Chief, King Moshoeshoe II, contacted the Resident Commissioner in Maseru in early November with his concerns regarding Mafeking's recently granted residence permit.[22] King Moshoeshoe II described Basutoland as a nation that would "always sympathize with any African who desert[ed] the Union" for whatever reason, but in the case of Mafeking felt "some definite arrangements [had to] be made with regard to people of this type."[23] King Moshoeshoe II urged caution in continuing to allow "these refugees" to reside in Basutoland without adopting precautionary measures to protect the nation against the actions of future residents. Too late, the King suggested the District Control Board only grant temporary rather than permanent residence to Mafeking and other residents because he knew "it would be easy to take any actions on these [individuals] when necessary." Quite frankly, the King stated, "it is easier to repatriate a temporary resident than a permanent one."[24] From the perspective of British authorities, it is unfortunate that they did not attempt to include King Moshoeshoe II in their conspiracy to oust Mafeking from Basutoland earlier, because by March of 1961 even the Paramount Chief wanted the activist gone.[25]

The plight of refugees

Basutoland was no political utopia for exiles. On the contrary, life in Basutoland could be even more difficult for political exiles, who had to contend with not only local police, but British officials and South African Security Branch officers, as well. Being a single mother with an infant in exile could have been a never-ending series of tragedies that resulted in her untimely death. For Elizabeth Mafeking, however, this particular trial of exile was more easily navigated due to her extensive political and social connections. In the early months of her self-imposed exile, she'd been able to maintain working relationships and friendships with high-ranking politicians and activists, and had frequently appeared in local newspapers with them while in the course of their duties.

Figure 4.2 The early years of her banning had little effect on Mafeking's activist spirit, and she routinely participated in local politics. In this image, Mafeking (center) joins a group of BCP members in a demonstration in front of the offices of the District Commissioner at Mafeteng. On her left is Mrs. Masibane Mokate, president of the BCP-Women's League, and beside her is Mrs. L. K. Maphathe, BCP-Women's League Secretary of Foreign Affairs.

News Collection ZA (Vault) Hoover Library & Archives, Stanford University. New Age, November 22, 1960

In the summer of 1960, *Leselinyana* reported on the spring journey of Mrs. N. S. Maphathe to Copenhagen, Denmark to participate in the Women's International Democratic

Federation's (WIDF) annual conference.[26] Women of the Basutoland Congress Party elected Maphathe to represent their voices at the event. In the photograph that accompanies the article, Maphathe is seen departing her home in Mafeteng to catch her flight at the airport. To her right is an opened car door, and immediately to her left is Elizabeth Mafeking. The women, both dressed in their Sunday finest, are presumably discussing Mahpathe's upcoming journey, as Mafeking's insights would have been valuable to Maphathe, who recognized the importance of Mafeking's previous experiences with international activist work and organizational representation. In the photograph, it appears as if Maphathe is consulting a short list and Mafeking is gesturing as if to emphasize a point. Given her past experience with the International Worker's Convention in Bulgaria six years earlier, Mafeking knew a topic of discussion at the 1960 WIDF conference would be Apartheid in South Africa. She likely would have wanted to apprise Maphathe of some of the questions, issues, and concerns she encountered in her own travels. The women's likely preparation made an impact at the conference. As the

4 A Dangerous Embarrassment

article reports, Apartheid policies and effects in Southern Africa would be a central topic for discussion in the delegate working committees, and as the only woman from Lesotho, Maphathe's words were sure to carry special weight.

Figure 4.3 Mafeking and Mrs. N. S. Maphathe conferring prior to Maphathe's departure to Copenhagen, Denmark to participate in the Women's International Democratic Federation's (WIDF) annual conference.

Courtesy of Thomas Mofolo Library. Archives, Records Management, Museum and Documentation Division. National University of Lesotho. Roma, Lesotho. *Leselinyana*, p. 9, Phupu (July) 1960

The image of Mafeking in the Lesotho media was clear: here was an authentic and trusted ally in the struggle against racialized oppressions. This image was bolstered even more

4 A Dangerous Embarrassment

just one month later in August of 1960 when the front page of *Lentsoe la BaSotho* featured a ½ page photograph of Mafeking addressing a crowd at a BCP rally in her new hometown of Mafeteng.[27] Mafeking's right arm is outstretched, with her palm up and fingers reaching towards the crowd imploringly. With a furrowed brow she "narrated a sad story" about the cruel truths of living under Apartheid in South Africa. The crowd was shocked to learn that Apartheid policies "attacked even in the night while [people] are in bed," leaving children to awaken to a missing parent. The crowd listened in disbelief as Mafeking described the fear and frenzy that accompanied the late night police raids as so great that adult men would forget they were naked in bed and run into the streets to present documents for inspection.

When she discussed the details of her flight from South Africa to Lesotho, Mafeking no doubt recounted how South African police dragged three of her children out of their beds to interrogate them in the middle of the night. Mafeking adamantly defended her children's innocence to the audience, making it clear they knew nothing about her escape and insisted they could not "tell whether [she] went out through the door or the window." A local chief, Mofumahali 'Mamohlalefi, cried during Mafeking's account of life for blacks in South Africa, and the ways in which mothers, fathers, and children suffered.

The initial outpouring of support for Mafeking's plight in Basutoland came from numerous sources, both individual and collective. Old school friends in the community of Mafeteng offered Mafeking and her infant daughter a home shortly after they'd established asylum, and more than 3,000 supporters attended a conference organized by the Basutoland Congress Party (BCP) – a left-wing, pan-Africanist political party founded just eight years earlier – to hear both Mafeking and National President of the African National Congress Women's League, Lilian Ngoyi, speak.[28] One front page account in mid-January showed an image of Ngoyi holding Mafeking's by then three-month-old daughter, Uhuru.[29]

In her capacity as national president of both the ANCWL and FEDSAW, Ngoyi capitalized on the opportunity to confirm the shared, ideological struggles between black

4 A Dangerous Embarrassment

South African women suffering the yoke of Apartheid and the women of Basutoland who faced the uncertainty of so-called self-government.[30] Ngoyi buttressed her emphatic plea for Basutoland women to ally more closely with their South African counterparts by holding Mafeking's infant aloft while stating, "As mothers we must struggle together to build a decent future for our children."[31] Everyone in attendance knew full well the plight of Elizabeth Mafeking, knew of the impossible decision she'd made to escape with one child but leave ten others, a husband, and aging grandmother behind. When Ngoyi yielded the floor to Mafeking and the exiled activist began to detail her banishment in South Africa and subsequent relocation in Basutoland, "people at the conference wept openly." Ngoyi asked for the entire nation of Basutoland to aid Mafeking and her family as the activist transitioned into life in "the Jerusalem of African refugees." The very public call for support did not translate into substantive support, however, which placed Mafeking in the unenviable position of attempting to track down resources on her own.

4 A Dangerous Embarrassment

Weeks after the Basutoland conference, Mafeking wrote to friends in the Cape Town office of the South African Institute for Race Relations (SAIRR), who she'd learned through following the press were soliciting for donations in her name:

> I have been wondering what I could do to get in touch with you since I left Cape Town but as I followed all the press statement I've find [sic] in one of the papers that your organization were also collecting some stuff from some of your members for me, I would very much like you to send it along to me if there could be such a chance.[32]

Mafeking gently reminded her "friends" that the situation for political exiles in Basutoland was difficult. While she reported being "in good health with [her] dear baby," AFCWU records show the organization was well aware that "comrade E. Mafeking was starving and having financial difficulties in Basutoland."[33] Mafeking would have been devastated to know the truth: the FCWU and AFCWU had actually established a trust fund to assist the activist and her family while in exile, but out of more than twenty branches nationwide, "only Paarl Branch had collected this money" and made a contribution.[34] Mafeking desperately needed that financial support for food, clothing, and shelter, because the activist had made the decision to reunite her family in exile – despite the challenges. In her efforts to piece back together that which was broken, Mafeking arrived upon the most imperfect of compromises: five months after she fled to Basutoland, allies in South Africa secreted Mafeking's next seven, youngest children out of the Western Cape and into Basutoland, leaving her husband and three eldest children behind.[35]

A child of exile

Just one month before Mafeking's allies smuggled her children out of South Africa in April of 1960, the Apartheid government initiated a key instrument in its battle to neutralize political dissent within the country – the State of Emergency (SOE). The first decade of Apartheid faced

4 A Dangerous Embarrassment

exceptional internal revolts, and immediately following the Sharpeville Massacre – where South African police opened fire on a group of unarmed African protestors in a small township – the government declared the first Emergency. The so-called Emergency targeted individuals and organizations alike, and in an effort to consolidate white minority rule, Apartheid architects systematically instituted measures to invalidate African political groups and detain thousands of political activists in an effort to consolidate white minority rule.

Under these conditions and facing the threat of banning himself, Puleng Malawa's ANC-aligned father made the difficult decision to abandon South Africa for a life in exile in Basutoland. As the eldest of seven children, Malawa's mother sent her to Basutoland in advance of the rest of the family because she wanted Malawa to enroll in the local school system as a positive example for the rest of her siblings.[36] In Basutoland, Malawa shared the same school district as the Mafeking children – but not the convenience. Unfortunately, the family Malawa initially lived with in Basutoland was more than 100km away from

4 A Dangerous Embarrassment

the school, so during her second year in the country her mother determined Malawa's chances at earning a quality education might be increased by sending her to stay with the Mafeking family. For young Malawa, the prospect of going to live with such an infamous figure was almost overwhelming.

> I used to listen to elderly people talking about the movement . . . I would pick up here and there and some of the things would stick in my head up to now from that early age. So I knew there was this lady called Mrs. Elizabeth Mafeking . . . and how she skipped the country. I knew it before we went to Lesotho . . . I knew there was this lady there but I never even thought I'd one day meet her.

As a young child of 10, Malawa had been fascinated by the tale of Mafeking's dramatic escape from South Africa, and recalled one of the oft-recited explanations of how Mafeking was able to pull off such a feat:

4 A Dangerous Embarrassment

> I heard that [Mrs. Mafeking] was like a modern lady, always dressed smartly. So [her comrades] dressed her in Xhosa tradition . . . with the long dress and big *doke* on her head, a pipe in her mouth, and a baby on her back. She looked very traditional. Then she walked out [of her home], she just walked right by [the Secret Police], even the people [who knew her] didn't notice her! She just left normally, and then there was a car waiting for her somewhere.

After years of hearing this and similarly dramatic tales, Malawa never imagined she'd one day meet the very woman everyone talked about in hushed tones, much less become a member of her family. Moving into the home of a well-known political activist wasn't nearly as daunting to 13 year-old Malawa as the prospect of living in a home with eight other children. Malawa went from being the eldest of seven children in her family's household, to the middle of nine children in a family of strangers. She transitioned seamlessly into the Mafeking home, however, and quickly realized what it meant to *live* with the Mafekings.

4 A Dangerous Embarrassment

> I didn't feel like a[n] extended member of the family. I actually felt like a family member. I was very comfortable there. She was my real mother, her children were my brothers and sisters, so there was no separation of saying, "This one is an outsider," or whatever.

Mafeking's public persona in Lesotho was carefully crafted to depict her as a model of activists in exile. She was family-orientated, industrious, committed to helping people in her local community, and well-connected across racial barriers. Moreover, she kept the political company of well-known radicals like Brian and Sonia Bunting, exiled communists from South Africa who in 1961 passed through Lesotho on their way to self-imposed exile in London and enjoyed a highly publicized meal with both Mafeking and fellow communist, John Motloheloa.[37] The initial celebrity Mafeking enjoyed during the first few years of exile began to wane, however, as Basutoland pushed closer and closer to both independence and an essential political relationship with the Republic of South Africa. Quite frankly, the feasting

4 A Dangerous Embarrassment

days were over, and the next few years in exile were ones of famine – felt most particularly by the children Mafeking struggled to support.

One of Uhuru's earliest memories of life in Basutoland was of a crushing hunger that – by the age of three – she was slowly learning to ignore. With so many mouths in the house to feed and so little financial support available, Uhuru remembers *pap*, or mieliepap, being the single constant in the diet of her youth. While pap is a very important, inexpensive, staple food readily available and consumed in traditional African households throughout Southern Africa, it is *not* a comprehensive source of nutrition meant for long-term sustenance. The mealie porridge, however, did take away hunger, so with no livestock or even bread to eat, Uhuru and her siblings made the best of the heaping bowl of pap they received twice per day. Uhuru shook her head in amazement at the recollection, "there would be no meat, no vegetables, no *nothing*! Just pap." On rare occasions, she would follow her older sisters around the corner of their L-shaped home in Mafeteng to the spot where their mother stored empty

4 A Dangerous Embarrassment

plastic jugs that had once contained cooking oil. Uhuru lifted her hands high above her head as she described what happened next:

> We would turn those containers upside-down and *shake, shake, SHAKE* them until just a few drops of oil would drip onto the pap in our bowls. Just that little bit of *nothing* was a real treat.

The constant sense of hunger that defined her toddler years lessened noticeably after 1962, when Uhuru's mother made a fateful decision to stand in solidarity with other South African exiles who wrote an open letter to the Secretary of State for Commonwealth Relations in London regarding the treatment of refugees in Basutoland.[38] The move left Mafeking vulnerable to political attack, but inspired a new, professional relationship with Gilbert Hani, a fellow ANC comrade recently exiled himself.

A group of fifteen exiles – including Hani and Mafeking – exposed what they felt was an increasing level of harassment at the hands of the Basutoland police and a

4 A Dangerous Embarrassment

rapidly disintegrating relationship with their allies in the BCP. Raids, interrogations, and eventually the rejection of applications for indefinite or permanent residence were of particular concern to the small group which represented a much larger exile population. Mafeking's own Permanent Residence Certificate, first granted in 1960 just months after her arrival in Basutoland, "[had] been withdrawn . . . without any reason being shown." Mafeking was one of many who were reclassified by the Basutoland government as "prohibited entrants," and she was given a single opportunity to appear before the Appeal Board in Maseru to plead her case. Molefi and other exiles urged British officials to use their influence on the Central Control Board, the governing body of residence permits, in the hopes of prohibiting it from expelling the newly classified "prohibited entrants" from Basutoland.

In response to the allegations of unfair treatment, the president of the BCP, Ntsu Mokhehle, a former comrade and friend of Elizabeth Mafeking, published Molefi's letter in a BCP publication along with a personal reply wherein Mokhehle claimed unnamed refugees were simply the

4 A Dangerous Embarrassment

"mischievous" pawns of whites. Mokhehle further asserted that the BCP had always "welcomed and looked after refugees in Basutoland," but that the recent actions of some – which included ending distorted reports to the press and levelling malicious attacks at the BCP – revealed their refugee friends as "ignorant" due to a lack of understanding how the Basutoland constitution worked. With particular regard to Mafeking's residency status, Mokhehle insisted her original permit was only temporary and as such, only covered a two-year stay in Basutoland. Mokhehle explained that Mafeking would, indeed receive her permit in due time, suggesting patience was needed. Mokhehle reminded Molefi that a touch of understanding was necessary as well. Refugees had to understand that the BCP would not associate with "the imperialist British in their acts to support the apartheid (sic) Republic of South Africa against" them, but exiles had a responsibility to "cooperate genuinely" with both the BCP and the Basutoland government.

A short time later, Mokhehle made much less diplomatic statements regarding his feelings towards the refugee population in Basutoland. Whereas eighteen months earlier he'd appeared on stage with Elizabeth Mafeking and her child, urging the crowd to support a fund set up for the family, by 1962 Mokhehle reversed his position on support of political refugees in the country, claiming to "hate these so-called freedom fighters" whom he characterized as "cowards."[39] Shockingly, he even "denounced Mrs. Mafekeng [sic] by name as an infiltrator and saboteur who was trying to organize Communist cells in Basutoland to take over the BCP." Mokhehle's smear campaign against Mafeking and high-ranking members of the ANC in exile instigated a bitter response from the underground Nelson Mandela, who accused Mokhehle of being "a renegade and traitor" who only made such brash and slanderous statements for the benefit of the South African government.[40] When the bottom fell out of her working relationship with the BCP and there were no more speaking engagements or political rallies, Mafeking struggled to feed her children. At one point, the activist was reduced to returning to the streets to make and sell *amagwenya* along the roadside in a makeshift stall to

4 A Dangerous Embarrassment

support her family as she had as a teenager decades ago. Uhuru recalled thinking it was a "treat" when her mother brought home the unsold *amagwenya*. She also remembered thinking it was much less of a treat when the only *amagwenya* that came home were the ones used for display that had sat out in the sun all day and been exposed to the elements.

> Along the roadside cars and people pass, so whatever dust, dirt, or whatever comes by, it would settle on the *amagwenya*. She did not waste food, and we had to eat whatever was left over for a meal at the end of the day. You would just brush off whatever or whatever, and eat it.

In mid-1962 Helen Joseph traveled to Basutoland to visit Mafeking and was shocked at the toll less than three years in exile had taken on her friend. According to Joseph, Mafeking had already been "reduced to real privation," and given the political climate in Basutoland at the time, Joseph could not imagine a feasible solution to Mafeking's problems.[41] Indeed, Mafeking was in a desperate situation, and her life in exile had come to mirror that of the vast majority of women in the territory who lived their lives in despair, anxiously awaiting the most nominal of remittances. In her conversations regarding the erosion of family relationships under the conditions of migration in Lesotho in the 1970s, historian Elizabeth Gordon provides details of the decades-long pattern of endemic poverty for women in the country – conditions Mafeking was largely able to avoid upon arrival in Basutoland due to her political notoriety, yet now faced in the wake of a failed alliance and financial betrayal. While Mafeking was not the wife of a migrant worker, Gordon's study offers a useful glimpse into the realities of single motherhood in Lesotho and the subsequent strain under which Mafeking suffered. Specifically, Gordon points to deteriorating economic conditions, emotional and psychological stress, and "marital dissolution" as insurmountable realities facing women left behind in the territory.[42] There was a decided lack of resources or industry in the country that forced "40% to 50% of Basotho men [to] work as migrants in South

4 A Dangerous Embarrassment

Africa," leaving scores of women completely dependent upon financial support from absentee husbands and fathers.[43]

Though Mafeking had not been "left behind," her situation was just as – if not more dire than – the wives of migrants. Mafeking was an urbanized, proletarianized woman who had to negotiate an entirely new social identity in a country were the only "opportunity" for women seemed to be complete dependence on a man.[44] Her husband was not an absentee migrant worker, rather, a politically divorced partner whose meager income was committed to maintaining the family home and supporting three of the elder children back home in Paarl: Nozipho Sophia Ndiya (20), Atti Stanley (17 ½), and Ngubenyathi Melford (14). Moreover, Mafeking had eight other children who were now solely dependent upon her for their own survival in exile: Nozkhumbuzo Gertrude (19), Mehlo Andrew (13), Nomahlubi Rhoda (12), Sisinyana Suzan (8), Nomsa Catherine (7), Nomonde Mary (4), Nomvula Martha (18 mos.), and Uhuru (2 ½ mos.). As fate would have it, however, an unexpected relationship between Mafeking and Hani had begun to develop while working alongside one another propagating for the rights of refugees, and the relationship was – in many respects – yet another saving grace for Mafeking in exile.

Ntate Hani

Elizabeth Mafeking's relationship with Gilbert Hani emerged through a complicated understanding of family that pays attention to overlapping meanings, common cultural influences, and societal pressures among African women under attack from Apartheid.[45] Both activists were very well known in the community of exiles in Basutoland, both had families back in South Africa that were broken without them, and both were married to spouses anxiously awaiting their return. Mafeking also had nine children watching her every move, and endeavored to craft a relationship with Hani – whom the children had begun called *Ntate* Hani – that allowed her children to understand and respect the role he played in their lives.[46] Mafeking had firm ideas and rules for her budding relationship with Hani.

4 A Dangerous Embarrassment

Nomsa Catherine and Uhuru explained their mother's first stipulation:

> We had our house in Mafeteng, you see, and just a ways away Ntate Hani had his house. They were both married and it would not have been right [to live together], but he was always there. He lived *right* there.

Mafeking's relationship with Hani was hard work, but it allowed her to transcend the worst of the trials of exile discussed in earlier chapters. With nine mouths to feed, Mafeking could not afford to sit around and wait for well-meaning comrades and organizations in South Africa to forward her material support in Basutoland, and when she recognized a kindred, entrepreneurial spirit in Hani, the pair decided to open a series of small businesses – the first of which were a butchery and adjacent restaurant where Mafeking worked in the kitchen as the lone cook serving local Basotho fare. Mafeking's then 14 year-old foster daughter, Puleng Malawa, asserts Mafeking "was a business woman" at heart who frequently involved the

4 A Dangerous Embarrassment

children in every aspect of the businesses. Malawa recalled waking before school at 4 o'clock in the morning alongside the Mafeking girls her age to go to the restaurant and help prepare the dough for *amagwenya*.[47] After school, Malawa and the other children often reported to the butcher shop, where their primary responsibility was to clean the sheep heads used in the restaurant next door. On any given day Mafeking would even task any or all of the children to deliver plates of food to the indigent – which coincidentally included other exiles who were neither as industrious nor as fortunate as Mafeking.

Mafeking's relationship with Hani provided a vital, emotional connection both activists needed to endure the trials of exile, and over the decades they were able to rely upon each other for this very intimate and much-needed support. It also created even more responsibilities for a woman already taxed beyond measure. Having insisted upon two separate households at the beginning of their relationship meant Mafeking was now responsible for either completing the daily cooking and cleaning in both homes herself, or for inspecting work she'd assigned to her

4 A Dangerous Embarrassment

daughters living in exile. Catherine Nomsa vividly recalled how exacting her mother's cleaning standards were, and how her siblings in exile would scramble to make sure "every single thing was in its place" when their mother came home at the end of her day.

> One of the younger ones would spot her coming up the path and say, "She's coming! She's coming!" and we would run. She would come in, and sit in her chair. She could see the entire house from that chair. She would sit in that chair, cross her arms, and slowly look at every little thing. She could tell if anything was out of place, and you did not want anything to be out of place. Yho!

Mafeking managed her household of nine with a firm hand, and demanded the same level of attention was paid to Ntate Hani's home when she tasked her daughters or even Malawa with completing chores there. Malawa insisted that during her years in the Mafeking household so little distinction was made between her and Mafeking's own children that when discipline needed to be meted out,

4 A Dangerous Embarrassment

Malawa was sure to receive her fair share. Malawa recalled a recurring incident involving boys and teenage flirting with great amusement. As high school students, rather than go home or to the butchery directly after school, Malawa and some of the elder Mafeking girls would lag behind in an effort to spend time with their respective crushes. Most of the time the girls could get away with their innocent flirtations and eventually make their way home within what they imagined was a respectable timeframe. Other times, however, their efforts at subterfuge were ruined by an unlikely source – little sister Catherine Nomsa!

> When she [saw] us with boyfriends she would go running home and tell [Mrs. Mafeking]! [Mrs. Mafeking] would come out looking for us and we would just disperse quickly. When we got home we would get some beatings and some talks.

Malawa's use of the word "beating" is not to be understood literally, rather, in a more broad cultural context that refers to a variety of disciplinary tactics that included but were not

4 A Dangerous Embarrassment

limited to a simple spanking, hand swats, or in the most dire of circumstances, a hiding with *induku* – a thin piece of wood or branch that had either fallen from or been cut deliberately from a tree. In fact, Malawa recalled with great fondness this time and others that Mafeking disciplined her alongside the activist's own children. According to Malawa, it reminded her that she was no mere guest, rather a treasured child in the family who needed the same boundaries, protections, and lessons imparted upon her as Mafeking's birth children. One of the few lessons Malawa simply could not appreciate, however, were the responsibilities associated with Sunday lunches – primarily, the required use of cutlery. Malawa readily admits she "hated Sunday lunches," because it was the one day each week Mafeking insisted the entire family sit at a precisely decorated dinner table for a family meal and use an entire set of cutlery – not just the single, customary spoon routinely used for meals.

4 A Dangerous Embarrassment

> I wasn't used to using a fork and knife. I never used a fork and knife and [all of the other] children were very good in using a fork and knife ... so I found myself also having to use a fork and knife, and when I wanted to use a spoon [Mrs. Mafeking] would forbid me! I never used to enjoy my meals because I couldn't get any food into my mouth.[48]

Mafeking's diligent labors to impart notions of ladylike propriety and personal responsibility were, for Malawa, just as important as the work ethic she cultivated in the Mafeking home. From the perspective of a child, Malawa was amazed at the seemingly limitless energy Mafeking poured into the children, Hani, and their business ventures. The retrospect of adulthood, however, allowed Malawa to put into perspective some of the things she witnessed in the Mafeking household as she more fully understood what it must have meant for Mafeking to bear such great personal responsibility while enduring very public political attacks from former allies like Ntsu Mokhehle and the very real

4 A Dangerous Embarrassment

threat of deportation to South Africa, all the while feeling deeply betrayed that former comrades were depriving her and her children of funds being collected in their name.

> She started taking drinks, you know, and she actually took them frequently because of the frustration. I wouldn't say she enjoyed taking the drinks, because I don't remember her sitting with friends and enjoying a drink ... and I always say if you drink alone it means there's something wrong.

Everywhere Mafeking turned in Basutoland, responsibility loomed, and despite her small business ventures, Mafeking still earned less money than she had in South Africa as a unionized worker and organizer for the ANCWL and AFCWU. Isolated in exile and bearing the awesome responsibility of providing for nine children amidst the harsh backdrop of rural living in Basutoland, Elizabeth Mafeking lived in a state of constant dismay that she worked hard to hide from the children who looked to her for support. Even with (and likely also because of) Hani in

4 A Dangerous Embarrassment

her life, and the relative aid it offered, Mafeking was wracked with grief over the state of her life, and felt deep guilt over her relationship with Hani – guilt that only increased three years later in 1965 when her husband back in Paarl, Moffat, died of complications due to diabetes. Today, Mafeking's eldest daughter, Sophia Khekhemane, is grateful for the complex web of cultural expectations that prevented her from joining her mother and siblings in exile, because when her father was first diagnosed with diabetes in mid-1964 things had already progressed too far and he required constant care. Sophia did her best, but in early 1965 Mditjane's health rapidly declined. Sophia admitted her father to hospital for treatment, but after a brief stay he passed away. Sophia's eyes welled with tears as she recounted her father's funeral service. "No one came. Not Mama, none of the children. No one. Just me, Atti, and Mehlo."

Coincidentally, immediately after the death of her husband, the NP officially rescinded Mafeking's banning orders, which ostensibly gave her the opportunity to fulfill her promise to her children that they would return home.

4 A Dangerous Embarrassment

Today, Mafeking's youngest child, Uhuru, candidly rejected the idea this represented a chance to return to the Union-turned-Republic in 1965, saying, "By then, everyone knew better than to believe that lie." Rescinded banning orders often tricked banned individuals into returning home, thereby exposing themselves to capture and forced deportation – often times in the middle of important events like weddings and funerals. The orders rescinding Mafeking's banishment, however, did not abide by any such pretense. According to Prime Minister Vorster in a correspondence to Acting State President Jozua Francois Naude:

> daar tans genoegsame meer toepaslike wetgewing bestaan om teen die verwyderde op te tree indien sy na die Republiek sou terugkeer.[49]
> *. . . there is enough appropriate legislation that exists to deal with the remote if she returns to the Republic . . .*

4 A Dangerous Embarrassment

Clearly, the NP felt it had numerous, potential legislative tricks up its sleeve to subdue Mafeking if she ever attempted to return home to South Africa. Neither Mafeking nor the children she'd managed to have smuggled out of the country dared to believe the threadbare lie and attend Mditjane's funeral – in spite of the coincidentally timed lifting of Mafeking's banishment order – and Sophia had only the support of her brothers Atti and Mehlo the day they laid their father to rest. Mafeking's drinking problem began to spiral slowly out of control following Mditjane's death, and even baby Uhuru – now thirteen years-old – was subject to the intense judging, scrutiny, and unpredictable rages that emerged as a consequence of her mother's growing drinking problem.

> She would get angry. Very, very angry, if she sent you to the bottle store and you came back empty-handed. When we walked past Ntate Hani's house, he would call us over to him, question us, then take the money he knew she had given us for alcohol. He knew she drank, but that was all he could do, take

4 A Dangerous Embarrassment

the money. When we returned home with no money and no alcohol... yho! It was bad. Very, very bad.

By the late 1960s, drinking had become Mafeking's primary coping mechanism in exile, and she readily turned to the bottle to deal with feelings of powerlessness in her situation. It was clear to everyone by 1967 that political exiles in Lesotho realized they no longer had an activist, intellectual home in the Kingdom of Lesotho. Many pleaded to leave the country, and asked the Deputy Prime Minister, Chief L.S. Masirebane, to lobby the South African government on their behalf.[50] Refugees wanted Masirebane to negotiate for permission for them "to cross South Africa unimpeded" if they wanted to leave or were ordered out by officials. Prime Minister Jonathan vowed to "have no mercy" on exiles who engaged in politics in Lesotho or violated the terms of their asylum, and the repeated media threats, covert arrests and repatriations, and government offer to airlift refugees over South Africa to the "Black North," was evidence of the country's exasperation with the alien population.[51] Unsurprisingly, few refugees seriously considered the offer of safe, government-assisted repatriation. South African authorities routinely kidnapped political refugees from international locations of exile, and years earlier in 1963 had been suspected of detonating an explosive on an aircraft chartered to transport political refugees from Bechuanaland to Tanganyika.[52] Mafeking was no fool, and determined to take her best chance at survival in Basutoland. When business ventures with Hani failed and began again, and where and when her own intuition, work ethic, and determination weren't enough to feed her children, Mafeking unashamedly reached out to rely upon the generosity of others.

Love, Your Elizabeth

Elizabeth Mafeking had a number of allies during her exile, but few offered the same level of long-term mental, emotional – and at times financial – support as Ray Alexander. Prior to both Mafeking and Alexander being

4 A Dangerous Embarrassment

banned in South Africa, the pair worked closely with one another, at times traveling together to recruit new union members. The bond they developed while navigating the departure of African workers from the FCWU into a newly reorganized AFCWU in the early 1950s endured – in spite of bannings, distance, and tragedy – for decades. Elizabeth Mafeking worked. She labored diligently to support both her children and those entrusted to her care while in exile, and those efforts came at great personal cost. Frustration, solitude, fear, and loneliness (in spite of being surrounded by the majority of her children) all plagued Mafeking, and a sizeable collection of personal correspondence exchanged over the course of twenty years between the activist and her dear friend – also in exile – reveal how Ray Alexander provided much-needed support during the toughest of times in Basutoland.[53] The letters exchanged between Alexander and the Mafeking family also bring to light a unique perspective on exile: that of its unintended victims, children. While the vast majority of the letters this chapter analyzes were exchanged between the two friends, almost two dozen letters in the collection were written to

4 A Dangerous Embarrassment

Alexander by Mafeking's children. These letters, in particular, provide heartbreaking insight into the phenomenon of children struggling with exile.

One of Mafeking's first letters to Alexander in mid-September 1968 expressed the former's anxiety over a recent radio address she'd heard at a local store in Mafeteng. According to the report, all South African refugees were being expelled from Basutoland at the end of the month, and the government was in the process of preparing official notices for that purpose. Mafeking – who'd weathered the storm of the District Control Board years earlier to gain permanent resident status – was at a loss to figure out how to navigate this new challenge. It had been years since she'd entered the territory, and the notoriety and support she'd initially enjoyed had largely waned by the time Basutoland gained its independence in 1966. More than anything, Mafeking was tired of struggling against forces that never seemed to tire of struggling with her. She confided in Alexander that she was resolved "to leave the country with the children to one of the African states who will [accept] me."[54] She finished the

4 A Dangerous Embarrassment

correspondence with the same valediction she would use over the course of the next twenty years, "Love, Your Elizabeth."[55]

Mafeking did not respond to Alexander's reply to her first letter for a number of months, prompting Alexander to gently chastise her friend when the pair next spoke.[56] According to Mafeking, she had a really good excuse for the delay: four of the activists' girls had passed their final exams, and Mafeking had been busy "trying means and ways to [get] them accomodations (sic) at their different [boarding] schools."[57] Mafeking's youngest, the infant she'd fled to Basutoland with, was now ten years-old, enrolled in Standard 4, and hoping to follow in the footsteps of her sisters. Graduating had not been an easy task for the Mafeking girls, and their mother admitted "they did go very slow ... because of the language" difference, but they succeeded in spite of the linguistic barrier and she was proud they were moving forward with their lives. Moving forward, however, was expensive, and Mafeking needed help.

4 A Dangerous Embarrassment

Notes

1 Correspondence from Commonwealth Relations Office (London) marked "Mrs. Mafekeng" (sic) December 2, 1959. TNA: FCO 141/479: Basutoland. Subsequent references from this archival source will appear as "TNA: FCO 141/479: Basutoland."

2 Ibid.

3 Correspondence from Acting Commissioner of Police (Maseru) to Government Secretary (Maseru) marked "Mrs. Elizabeth Mafekeng" (sic) December 5, 1959. TNA: FCO 141/479: Basutoland. (24).

4 Hitchcock, Bob, "Newspaper Scoop of the Year: Mrs. Mafekeng (sic) Talks to Drum" in Drum, January 1960 (East Africa February 1960), 21–23. TNA: FCO 141/479: Basutoland. (35).

5 Ibid.

4 A Dangerous Embarrassment

6 "'Traitor,' Labour (sic) M.P. Told" Star, January 2, 1960. TNA: FCO 141/479: Basutoland.

7 "Mrs. Mafekeng (sic) in Maseru" The Star, January 5, 1960. TNA: FCO 141/479: Basutoland.

8 "Problem for Macmillan: Mrs. Mafekeng (sic)" The Star, January 6, 1960. TNA: FCO 141/479: Basutoland.

9 Correspondence from High Commissioner's Office (Pretoria) to Resident Commissioner (Maseru) January 9, 1960. TNA: FCO 141/479: Basutoland. (40).

10 Correspondence from D.H.T. to Commissioner of Police (Maseru) January 8, 1960. TNA: FCO 141/479: Basutoland. (38).

11 Correspondence from Resident Commissioner (Maseru) to D. H. C. (Cape Town) to January 26, 1960. TNA: FCO 141/479: Basutoland. (46, 47, 48).

12 Unknown. TNA: FCO 141/479: Basutoland. (45).

4 A Dangerous Embarrassment

---

13 Correspondence from D. H. C. (Pretoria) to Resident Commissioner (Maseru) January 9, 1960. TNA: FCO 141/479: Basutoland. (40).

14 Notes. Author unknown. January 10, 1960. TNA: FCO 141/479: Basutoland. (42).

15 Correspondence from Commonwealth Relations Office (London) to T. V. Scrivenor (sic) January 11, 1960. TNA: FCO 141/479: Basutoland. (45B); Correspondence from High Commissioner's Office (Cape Town) to Commonwealth Relations Office (London) January 21, 1960. TNA: FCO 141/479: Basutoland. (45A); Correspondence from High Commissioner's Office (Cape Town) to A. G. T. Chaplin (Maseru) January 21, 1960. TNA: FCO 141/479: Basutoland. (45).

4 A Dangerous Embarrassment

16 Correspondence from Resident Commissioner (Maseru) to Deputy High Commissioner (Cape Town) January 26, 1960. TNA: FCO 141/479: Basutoland. (46).

17 Correspondence from High Commissioner (Pretoria) to Resident Commissioner (Maseru) June 30, 1960. TNA: FCO 141/479: Basutoland. (71)..

18 Interview, Sophia Khekhemani Mafeking with author, summer 2013, Paarl, South Africa. Original interview conducted in isiXhosa and Sesotho, translated into English.

19 Sophia reluctantly recalled one of the less joyful moments associated with her first trip to Lesotho. Upon arrival in Lesotho she realized that some of the children's clothes were missing, presumably stolen by local guides.

20 Untitled. Elizabeth Mafeking's non-politics pledge. October 26, 1960. TNA: FCO 141/479: Basutoland.

(89A); "Mditjane" was Mafeking's married name, the surname of her husband, Moffat Henry Mditjana. According to Nomsa Catherine Mafeking, "Mditjane" is the paternal family surname, but Mafeking retained her surname, and her children were referred to accordingly.

21 Correspondence from District Commissioner (Mafeteng) to Government Secretary (Maseru) October 27, 1960. TNA: FCO 141/479: Basutoland. (87).

22 "Moshoeshoe" is pronounced moe-SCHWAY-schway.

23 Correspondence from Paramount Chief, Motlotlehi Moshoeshoe II (Basutoland) to Resident Commissioner (Maseru) November 7, 1960. TNA: FCO 141/479: Basutoland. (90).

24 Ibid.

4 A Dangerous Embarrassment

25 Tom Lodge wonderfully outlines and articulates the unique "problems and difficulties" associated with the politics of exile in the early 1960s, but clearly has a very masculine understanding of exile, most especially those subject to the dictates of the South African government. His conversations on foreign missions and military training programs, the internal leadership of the ANC during the Rivonia trial, the youth exodus in the wake of the Soweto uprising, and the sabotage campaigns of the 1980s all occur from a very masculinized perspective. Elizabeth Mafeking was already in exile in Basutoland in 1960 when the ANC sent its deputy president-general, Oliver Tambo to Bechuanaland and eventually London in the hopes of garnering international support against Apartheid. The ANC established multiple guerilla training camps in

Tanzania in 1963 following the establishment of the Organization of African unity (OAU), and as this chapter will demonstrate, Elizabeth Mafeking served as a vital, material link to insurgents making their way out of South Africa and into the underground movement.

26 "Mrs. Maphathe o bile China le U.S.S.R." Leselinyana [Lesotho], July 9, 1960, 3.

27 "Mrs. Mafekeng (sic) O Bua Phuthehong" Lentsoe la BaSotho [Lesotho], August 13, 1960, 1.

28 Gqabi, Joe, "3,000 At Basutoland Conference: Audience Weeps as Mrs. Mafekeng [sic] Speaks" in New Age vol. 6, no. 12 (January 7, 1960); News Collection ZA (Vault) Hoover Library & Archives, Stanford University. Subsequent references from this archival source will appear as "Hoover Library & Archives."

29 "Basutoland Elections Next Week: Wide Support for Congress Party, New Age vol. 6, no. 13 (January 14, 1960). News Collection ZA (Vault) Hoover Library & Archives.

30 "3,000 At Basutoland Conference" New Age, January 7, 1960.

31 Ibid.

32 Correspondence from Elizabeth Mafeking to unknown, January 19, 1960, SAIRR: Justice, AD843/RJ G4-G5 Box 129 (File 1); Historical Papers Research Archive, University of the Witwatersrand, Johannesburg, South Africa. Subsequent references from this archival source will appear as "Historical Papers Research Archive."

33 Minutes of the Adjourned Management Committee Meeting of the African Food and Canning Workers' Union. August 4, 1962. Food and Canning Workers

Union Papers. AD1175/A1. Management Committee (1957–1959). Historical Papers Research Archive.

34 Annual Report, 20th Annual Conference, September 24 and 25, 1960. Food and Canning Workers Union Papers. AD1175/A1.2. Conferences (1962–1959). Historical Papers Research Archive; Minutes of Management Committee Meeting of the Food and Canning Workers' Union, October 27, 1962. Food and Canning Workers Union Papers. AD1175/A1.4. National Executive Committee. Historical Papers Research Archive.

35 "Fugitive's Family Joins Her" New York Times, April 21, 1960; ProQuest Historical Newspapers: The New York Times (1851–2008). This article erroneously reports Mafeking was joined in Basutoland by all ten of the children who remained in South Africa

following their mother's escape. The surviving Mafeking children, however, confirm only eight (8) of the children followed Mafeking into exile. (Summer 2013).

36 Molaoa was only the first of many youths – children of the banned, exiles, and political refugees themselves – who passed through the doors of the Mafeking home in Basutoland/Lesotho. Mafeking's actions were well-known within refugee circles, and as Chapter 4 will demonstrate, her decision to make her home a safe-haven for dispossessed youths following the 1976 Soweto Uprising created a pipeline from South Africa for refugees bound for insurgency training camps in Angola, Libya, and Tanzania.

37 Notes from private collection of David Ambrose. Provided to author. August 2015.

38 Letter from Joe Molefi to the Secretary of State for Commonwealth Relations and the Basutoland Congress Party. Basutoland Congress Party. Makatolle International vol. 2, no. 3–4 (March–April, 1962). (Cairo, Basutoland Congress Party External Mission); Private collection of David Ambrose.

39 Halpern, Jack, Basutoland, Bechuanaland, and Swaziland (London, United Kingdom: Penguin, 1965), 161–162.

40 Ibid., 162.

41 Badat, Saleem, The Forgotten People: Political Banishment under Apartheid (Boston: Brill, 2013), 189.

42 Ibid., 444.

43 Gordon, Elizabeth Boltson, "The Plight of the Women of Lesotho: Reconsideration with the Decline of

Apartheid?" in Journal of Black Studies vol. 24, no. 4 (June, 1994), 435, 437.

44 Gordon reports ninety percent of the 524 wives interviewed for her study "reported complete reliance on remittances" from absentee husbands. Gordon, "The Plight of Women in Lesotho," 437.

45 At this juncture I would like to thank the Mafeking family for allowing me to bring the relationship between their mother and Gilbert Hani to light. Culturally speaking, it is considered disrespectful to voice such private matters, and the fact that both activists still have living family members greatly complicates the telling of this aspect of Mafeking's life in exile. This discussion is vital, however, in that is speaks directly to scholarly conversations surrounding the personal lives of female exiles and political refugees. In a word, Mafeking was lucky to

have found Hani (and vice versa), because he allowed her to avoid having to experience the demeaning interactions untold numbers of women who labored in the underground simply refuse to speak about. Mafeking's surviving children adamantly stress their deep love and respect for the role Gilbert Hani played in their lives, and for the decades of support he offered them and their mother. They are grateful to umndeni wakwaHani for its understanding of the hardships their loved ones faced which led them to one another, and cherish the unique bond their families share to this day.

46 The word "Ntate" in Sesotho is similar to "Baba" in isiZulu, which both mean "father" and operate to recognize a wide spectrum of natural and extended family. "Ntate" is a respectful way of referring to

one's own father, specifically, but also elder men in general. It is similar to the Western concept of employing "sir," which is ironic given the fact that you would not use either the isiZulu or SeSotho word for "sir." In both languages, both words are used to reference a leader or ruler of a people or clan. Referring to an elder man in Lesotho or South Africa using either of these words who is *not* a leader or ruler of a people or clan generally elicits an indulgent smile and a gentle laugh.

47 A traditional South African bread that is deep-fried and served with savory or sweet fillings and known colloquially as a 'fat cake.'

48 Despite her frustrations as a child with the weekly meal, Molaoa acknowledges Mafeking's efforts at cultivating table manners were not in vain. "Struggling with the fork and knife was a good

education, [and] I think of her all the time. I think of her because I know I am perfect in using a fork and knife because of her."

49 "Minuut No. 1513" Correspondence from Prime Minister B.J. Vorster to Acting State President Jozua Francois Naude, September 7, 1967 (N108/7/43); National Archives of South Africa – Pretoria. Document in Afrikaans, translated by author.

50 "Refugees Plea by Lesotho" The Star [Johannesburg], January 12, 1967 in Information Services.

51 Ibid.; "After the Struggle, a Cry for HELP: The Trick Refugees" The Post [Johannesburg], January 13, 1967 in Information Services; Cohen, Ralph, "Leabua Gives Warning to Refugees" Rand Daily Mail [Johannesburg], January 16, 1967 in Information Services; "Lesotho Tougher to Aliens"

4 A Dangerous Embarrassment

The Star [Johannesburg], February 6, 1967 in *Information Services*; "Only 15 Want to Fly Out: Few Refugees Take Lesotho Offer" *The Star* [Johannesburg], February 20, 1967 in *Information Services*; "Lesotho Refugees Can Go" *The Star* [Johannesburg], May 3, 1967 in *Information Services*.

52 United Nations Security Council, "Report of the Special Committee on the Policies of Apartheid of the Government of the Republic of South Africa," (1964), 148–149.

53 Ray Alexander was first presented with banning orders from the South African government in 1953. This was the first in a series of bannings for both Alexander and her husband, Jack. Eventually, the pair fled the country in 1965 to live in self-imposed exile in Lusaka, Zambia, until the early 1990s when

they briefly returned to South Africa after the fall of Apartheid.

54 Letter from Elizabeth Mafeking to Ray Alexander. September 18, 1968. Ray Alexander Collection: General Correspondence (Box 21). Special Collections, University of Cape Town, South Africa. Subsequent references in this chapter from this archival source will appear as "Alexander Papers: Special Collections, UCT."

55 Ibid.

56 Several letters between Alexander and members of the Mafeking family suggest the mail was either sluggish, lost, or stolen in transit. Just as Alexander chastises Mafeking for a slow reply, so too does Nomsa Mafeking say something to Alexander in 1970 about ignoring "several" correspondence.

4 A Dangerous Embarrassment

---

57 Letter from Elizabeth Mafeking to Ray Alexander. February 10, 1968. Alexander Papers: Special Collections, University of Cape Town.

5

"One day we are going home"

Survival, Identity, and the Return of Elizabeth Mafeking

> Ray, you know up to now as I am writing you this letter I haven't pay (sic) a cent for their books as I've only promised to the teachers that the money is coming. Of course I had appealed to some of my old friends although I don't think that I will be successful. Anyhow, I hope for the best.[1]

For a proud woman like Elizabeth Mafeking, revealing financial struggles and asking for help, as in her letter to Ray Alexander, had to have been incredibly difficult. Just a few years earlier, Mafeking had been a leading trade union activist with enough income to be considered the breadwinner in her large family. Now, however, she was

5 "One day we are going home"

nearly destitute and could not afford to cover her children's school fees. Mafeking also had a difficult time keeping a roof over their heads. The network of sources she'd been able to access upon her arrival in 1959 had, by 1968, all but disappeared, leaving Mafeking in the unenviable position of having to solicit funds from a former colleague.

When the friends next spoke, Mafeking's financial worries had increased. By early 1970, one of Mafeking's sons had been forced, by the death of his father, to relocate from Paarl to Lesotho to live with his mother. As the new man in the house, Mafeking's son endeavored to support the family and took one of the only jobs available to unskilled African men in the tiny country: working in the mines. Mafeking bemoaned the fact that when he suffered a broken leg on the job his only reward was "that little compensation" and indefinite unemployment.[2] Mafeking had recently received a long-awaited house from the government, but the responsibility of repairs on the property were hers alone, and her son's so-called compensation was only R30 – just half of the R60 the family needed to complete the repairs and move into the house.[3]

5 "One day we are going home"

This was the first of two missives Alexander received on the same day from the Mafeking household, and the second echoed concerns from the first, but from a very different source.

Mafeking's second eldest daughter in exile and sixth child, twenty-one year-old Nomahlubi Rhoda, had also begun to write Alexander at the encouragement of her mother. While Rhoda clearly intended to speak with Alexander about a possible educational opportunity away from home and subsequent travel details, Rhoda could not help but share her concern that "my mummy looks a little bit worried because of some financial matters."[4] Rhoda seemed unsure of the exact details, but was sure her mother had spoken to her good friend about the family's situation. Rhoda wasn't the only Mafeking child to turn to Alexander, and within a matter of weeks, Nomsa Catherine, Mafeking's eighth child, contacted Alexander in Zambia to introduce herself. Eighteen year-old Nomsa – a student at Lesotho High School – had failed to earn her matric certificate in recent testing, but achieved Class II status, which granted her the opportunity to attend secondary

5 "One day we are going home"

school in local Bereng.[5] Nomsa felt she was "really in trouble, especially when I recall my hard reading period." Nomsa had been seven years-old when her mother's allies smuggled her into Basutoland, but grew up speaking primarily isiXhosa in the Cape. Upon arrival in Basutoland, however, Nomsa had to learn to speak, read, and write SeSotho, skills that developed frustratingly slow. In spite of these challenges, Nomsa wanted to press forward with her education, but she needed sponsorship for that to happen.

Months passed as Mafeking attempted to navigate a violent, political coup that had erupted in Lesotho. When Mafeking next spoke to Alexander, she apologized for the delay in a response, but claimed she "was always handicapped by the police ever since after the elections."[6] Mafeking would not give Alexander exact details about what that entailed until she could "make sure whether you have received this letter and ... the date written and posted." Mafeking was concerned Basutoland officials were monitoring her mail, and the activist had every right to be suspicious. What Mafeking would share, however, was the fact that she'd recently exchanged correspondence with

5 "One day we are going home"

Sonia Bunting – another South African anti-apartheid activist in exile in London – who forwarded Mafeking £15 to help with moving expense for the girls. Mafeking was consumed with thoughts of how to pay for the needed supplies, uniforms, and bedding the girls would need – on top of feeling as if she was the "first target" of Basutoland National Party (BNP) officials who'd effectively assumed control of Lesotho. She had not yet been arrested, but Mafeking seemed sure it was imminent. The 1970s ushered in an era of political change and instability in Lesotho, and Mafeking's alliance with the defeated Basutoland Congress Party (BCP) made her position in the country that much more difficult. While Mafeking spent the remainder of 1970 attempting to avoid the attention of Basutoland officials, daughters Rhoda and Nomsa continued to correspond with Alexander, who continually encouraged their success.

When Alexander learned of the sisters' achievements, she pledged "As soon as I get your school report and I also would like Rhoda's school report, I will start working for scholarships for you."[7] In an earlier letter to Alexander, Nomsa had made a request for new clothes

5 "One day we are going home"

in anticipation of reporting to boarding school, and Alexander was happy to let the teen know she was "writing to friends in South Africa and [would] make an appeal to them to help." In the meanwhile though, Alexander needed Nomsa to speak with her mother about the whereabouts of South African political exiles in Lesotho.[8]

Nomsa was happy to glean information from her mother for Alexander, but the teenager insisted the activist get her name right first. Nomsa gently reminded Alexander in a subsequent letter that, "firstly, my name I am sure you know is NOMSA CATHERINE MAFEKING," most certainly in response to Alexander's previous correspondence wherein she'd misspelled Nomsa's middle name.[9] Eighteen year-old Nomsa went on to tell "Mrs. Ray" about her budding interest in medicine and law, and how she hoped that after receiving her school report Alexander would "decide accordingly to my ability what is good." More than anything, however, Nomsa wanted to leave the confines of Lesotho and travel to Zambia where she could live with Alexander. Nomsa was unable to obtain a passport from Lesotho authorities, but she was hopeful there was "still a

5 "One day we are going home"

chance of having it before 1972." Future desires aside, Nomsa was aware of her mother's immediate needs at home, and she pleaded with Alexander for assistance:

> Mrs. Ray, my mother really suffers a lot as to support us with clothes. If it can really be possible for you to help please do help. She has four kids of roughly 7 years, 10 years, 12 years, and 14 years at home . . . please send her blankets, it [is] very cold.[10]

Nomsa was away at school in bustling Maseru, but her mother and younger siblings were miles away on the outskirts of rural Mafeteng struggling, as previous chapters detail – to eke out an existence in the unforgiving countryside. Nomsa worried that the strain of having to provide for both her and Rhoda away at boarding school meant undue suffering for everyone else. Rhoda, too, had concerns about the expenses associated with being at boarding school, but for seemingly less altruistic reasons.

In July of 1970, Rhoda wrote Alexander updating her on the struggle to obtain her school records in the wake of political unrest that "caused some disturbance in school and for the teachers," who experienced high enough turnover in the ranks as to cause administrative issues – like delays in issuing grade reports.[11] Rhoda seemed less hopeful about her marks in comparison to previous conversations, suggesting any bad grades she did make would be the result of inconsistencies in schooling. Finally, near the end of the letter, Rhoda tells Alexander that Mafeking had recently been hospitalized due to high blood pressure. Rhoda seemed chagrined to admit this was actually the second time her mother had been admitted to the hospital in recent months, but more importantly, with Mafeking incapacitated there was no financial support coming in.

> Pity on us for we need some things for school, but we wouldn't be able to get them for our dear mother is not around to see that we get everything before we get to school. It's a pity for our father is no more, leaving no help for her when she's not well.

5 "One day we are going home"

On the surface, the wording of Rhoda's message and the timely mention of a father who'd died years ago, sounds both manipulative and selfish. Moreover, her primary concern over her mother's health crisis appears to be how it would affect Rhoda's need for material items away at school. Rhoda was not selfish, however, but she was likely very anxious. As the eldest Mafeking daughter living in exile, if anything happened to their mother, Rhoda would be expected to leave school and return to Mafeteng where she would assume responsibility of raising her younger siblings. For a twenty-one year-old who'd struggled early in life but now stood at the precipice of independence that had to have been worrying.

Alexander did not misunderstand Rhoda's words, thankfully, and continued to work with both her and Nomsa to arrange the much-needed funding for school. Mafeking was 52 years-old, had just spent two weeks in the hospital, and always seemed sick to Rhoda. The twenty-one year-old was simply overwhelmed with the responsibilities she took on in her mother's stead. Yes, leaving Lesotho would mean leaving her aging mother and young siblings behind, but it

5 "One day we are going home"

would also mean that Rhoda might be able to taste true freedom for the first time in her life.

For now, however, both Rhoda and Nomsa were needed at home. Mafeking was ill in the winter months leading up to the girls' departure for boarding school, and as Nomsa remembered it, "no month ends with her being healthy."[12] Mafeking was "always attended by a doctor," which further inspired Nomsa's desire to become a physician. She echoed Rhoda's fear that political instability in Lesotho "might interfere with the education of the country," as educators were assigned and reassigned to schools based on shifting political alliances. In January 1970, Lesotho had held its first general elections since achieving independence in 1966. Although the BCP – the very party Elizabeth Mafeking had aligned herself with upon arrival in in the territory in 1959 – won the elections, the ruling BNP declared a state of emergency, annulled the election, dissolved parliament, and suspended the constitution. The 1970 coup culminated in the exile of King Moshoeshoe II by BNP leaders, and coordinated harassment, torture, and murder of BCP members, their families, and sympathizers.

5 "One day we are going home"

As Rhoda plainly put it, "life is quite bad these days in Lesotho," and both she and sister Nomsa were "prepared to leave at any time."[13]

Leaving Lesotho for greener pastures began to look like more and more of a possibility in 1971. Mafeking was back on her feet, working, she and Alexander had rekindled their communications, and Alexander was redoubling her efforts to secure financial aid for Nomsa and Rhoda. She told Mafeking she'd appealed to the International University Exchange Fund on the girls' behalf and expected a reply before the end of the year, so it was crucial the sisters provide her with every piece of documentation she needed – in spite of any difficulty.[14] Alexander had been experiencing her own fair share of difficulty in exile in Lusaka in 1971, though the activist downplayed the real danger. In one communique to Mafeking, Alexander apologized for the delay in her response, but she "had trouble which disorganized my way of life."[15] Alexander immediately changed the subject, inquiring about Mafeking's health and asking her to send regards to fellow, exiled comrades like Gilbert Hani and John Motloheloa.

5 "One day we are going home"

What Alexander does *not* do is explain to Mafeking that the "trouble" she's downplaying is in regard to Alexander's own, endangered refugee status in Zambia.

When the South African government banned the ANC in 1960, the party did not dissolve, rather, it continued to operate underground both inside and outside of the country, and nearby Lusaka, Zambia, was a prime location for the transition.[16] Lusaka was a small but rapidly growing town, had a population of just over 100,000, and the government had just broken ground on two major construction projects nearby – a new university and the parliament buildings. By 1971 when Alexander and her husband arrived, they joined a small group of white radicals vital to the support structure of the ANC underground. This support structure, however, was rapidly falling out of favor with the Zambian government, and authorities were beginning to refuse the right of some South African refugees to remain in the country. The "trouble" Alexander references in her letter most likely refers to her witnessing a round of deportations that occurred in Lusaka in 1971, like that of Barney Gordon, a former trade union activist in

5 "One day we are going home"

South Africa, and his wife, Sonia. In spite of watching some of her closest allies be expelled from Zambia, Alexander remained an active part of the ANC underground network, utilizing connections with people in exile like Elizabeth Mafeking to connect friends and family separated by the dictates of Apartheid. Gilbert Hani, in particular, became a regular name mentioned in the missives exchanged between Alexander and Mafeking, with the latter passing messages along to the former for Hani's family back in South Africa.[17]

The Mafeking children in exile were doing relatively well in the opening months of 1972: everyone except Rhoda had passed their yearly exams, baby Uhuru was thirteen and completing Standard 7, and Catherine Nomsa was – like any teenager – pushing to spread her wings and get away from home. In April, however, when final grades were released, Nomsa learned she'd done poorly, achieving what she called "a lousy pass," only successfully completing her Biology and Health Science courses.[18] The teen was still desperate to get out of Lesotho, and terrified her recent grades would dash those hopes. Nomsa wrote:

5 "One day we are going home"

> I really want to be out of this country by December, really because there is no work in this country you won't believe me when I tell you that side [I have] been applying ever since I left school but up to this blessed day I've got no post I am still at home.

Nomsa wanted to leave Lesotho so badly, she even considered South Africa – colloquially referred to as "that side" by BaSotho – as a possible destination. There were few to no job opportunities for young women in Lesotho that did not involve poorly paid domestic work, and Nomsa had dreams of becoming a doctor, an attorney, or even a typist if it meant a way out of Lesotho. Life outside of the protected environment of boarding school was harsh, and Nomsa quickly learned what life in the so-called real world might entail for her. At school, she'd been "given everything" from clothes to shoes, but now winter approached in Lesotho and, not returning to school, Nomsa did not have a proper winter coat or shoes to combat the chilly weather. For Uhuru, the climate in Lesotho seemed

5 "One day we are going home"

analogous to the cold treatment she received from her Standard 7 classmates.

Despite Sesotho being her first and primary language, during her youth in Basutoland classmates teased Uhuru. Sometimes they rudely dismissed her as "that Xhosa girl," an insult she really didn't understand.[19] She'd left South Africa behind when only two months old, well before she began forming her first words. When she did begin to speak, it was SeSotho, the language of Basutoland rather than isiXhosa, the language spoken in the Mafeking household in the Cape in South Africa. A simple bowl of *ipap*, rather than the more elaborate *umngqusho*, most frequently graced the dinner table in Mafeteng.[20] It was in Lesotho, not the Union, where Uhuru first understood the meaning of community by watching her mother involve herself in everything from local politics to social outreach. When she prayed over meals, at church, or even at school, it was to *Ntate Molimo*, not to some unknown entity called *uThixo*.[21] She did everything just like everyone else around her, but she was still "that Xhosa girl," and it hurt. Even

5 "One day we are going home"

Uhuru's older sister, Nominki, was subject to the taunts and jeers of classmates:

> They used to call us names at school. "You Xhosa have to go back to South Africa, you don't belong here!" You have to ask exactly what is happening. Why are we here? What is Xhosa?

When Nominki and Uuhru were old enough to start asking questions about the things local children said to them, their mother took the time to sit all of the children down – just once – to explain what all of the teasing at school was about, and why the family was in Lesotho. Nominki recalls the explanation her mother used was short and to the point:

> I was fighting for people who were working and getting small wages, and some of our people couldn't even get jobs. It was tough, [but] I had to stand up and make people realize this [was not right], and the *Boers* wanted to kill me and I had to run away. This is the reason why we ended up being [in Lesotho].

5 "One day we are going home"

It was one of the few times Nominki remembered her mother taking the time to explain something to the children, and it was the only time. On subsequent occasions when Uhuru would come home crying about something a classmate said to her about her supposed roots, Mafeking told her to just ignore the girls because "One day, we are going home." It became her mother's most-repeated refrain for the rest of their years in Lesotho: "One day, we are going home." For a thirteen year-old struggling with group bullying to, from, and at school, however, it was an entirely unsatisfactory response to her concerns. It also offered neither strategies to combat nor protection from the slights, insults, and probing questions, that dogged Uhuru's most formative years in Lesotho. For her, however, Lesotho *was* home – albeit it a conflicted one, and when her mother said, sang, or even shouted, "One day we are going home," Uhuru didn't know what to think. For years she'd just been curious about the mythical "home" her mother spoke of frequently, but as an adolescent she was growing suspicious, and questioned her mother's past exploits.[22] But never to her face. Older sister Nominki had once received

5 "One day we are going home"

what even she admits to this day was a well-deserved "smack" when once, around the age of 13, she'd made the mistake of saying aloud, "I wonder if you'll see that South Africa again?" as her mother – singing the words "one day we're going home" over and over again – busily prepared dinner.[23] Uhuru was no fool, however, and just learned to keep her mouth shut when her mother started talking about "home."

While the Union was clearly the home of Elizabeth Mafeking's heart, her family lived in Basutoland, and in the 1970s, the political atmosphere of the territory-turned-country was both frustrating and dangerous for exiles. While her very public persona and generosity had initially been welcomed – celebrated, even – in Lesotho upon her arrival, Mafeking's community and political activism slowly became an issue for Lesotho officials, who necessarily had to tighten their control of the refugee population at large as the country drew closer and closer to independence in 1966. By the early 1970s, the landlocked country of Lesotho – which heavily depended upon South Africa – just could not afford to continue to appear to offer unconditional

5 "One day we are going home"

support to political exiles. Under great, indirect pressure from the South African government, Lesotho officials began to toughen their stance on political refugees, their movements, and actions inside the country. Mafeking's close affiliation with members of the Basotho Congress Party (BCP) made her an easy target. Mafeking lost her temporary residence status and was forced to undergo an additional application and appeal process to retain the right to remain in Lesotho with her children. The strain, stress, and worry of the application process – in addition to concerns about household finances – drove Mafeking even further from the public eye, and by January of 1970, she had all but disappeared from the media spotlight. Ironically, this was fortuitous timing for Mafeking, who managed to avoid the worst of the fallout from a post-election coup instigated by Prime Minister Jonathan, who placed the King, opposition leaders, and many of their supporters in detention when Ntsu Mokhehle's BCP defeated Jonathan's BNP in the first, post-independence elections.[24] Over the course of the next year, Mafeking poured all of her energies into her family – biological and extended. Mafeking's

5 "One day we are going home"

relationship with Gilbert Hani was publically known of and respected by both the members of the Mafeteng community and their respective families. Subsequently, when Hani's family traveled to Lesotho to visit him in exile, Mafeking received and cared for them as if she were the lady of the house, and they accepted her as such.

In fact, Nompumelelo "Npumi" Hani – the former classmate of Nyati Mafeking who'd first laid eyes on the green suit-clad activist back in 1959 and never forgotten how "smart" Mafeking looked – was also the niece of Gilbert Hani, and when she and her sister visited their uncle in exile in 1971, it was very clear who ran the two households that operated as one. For three weeks, Npumi watched *Mme Fix* organize children, chores, and meals. She saw the mutual respect her uncle and Mafeking had for one another, and it felt natural to accept the place of Mafeking and her children in his life. During her visit, Npumi watched interactions between Mafeking, her uncle, and other political refugees who constantly passed through the two households. It seemed to Npumi that even in her fifties, Mafeking "had the character of a man," when it came to

5 "One day we are going home"

discussing the anti-apartheid struggle, never feigning ignorance or retreating from difficult conversations. Npumi's visit occurred during a rare and brief period of calm in the Mafeking family in Lesotho, but the increase in political repression in the early 1970s brought that time to a close, and Mafeking's daughter Nominki vividly recalled an evening in 1973 when the Mafeking family felt anything *but* welcome in Lesotho.

Nomvula Martha "Nominki," the tenth of Elizabeth Mafeking eleven children, was only two-and-a-half years-old in 1960 when her mother's comrades spirited her and seven other siblings across South Africa and into Basutoland. Nominki – affectionately known now in the family as "The Cake-Eater" – was too young to remember specific details about the escape, but vividly recalls how difficult it was living in Lesotho in the 1970s. She'd grown up watching her mother provide food, clothing, and shelter – sometimes at the expense of her own children – to scores of desperate young men in the early days and weeks of their exile, and indigent street children in Mafeteng. Her mother's generosity had been praised, celebrated even,

5 "One day we are going home"

which was why Nominki could not understand what happened late one evening in 1973:

> I remember one time it was around 1 o'clock in the morning, and there were cars surrounding the house. There was a woman at the door who was talking, my mom's friend. Her husband was an officer [with the Lesotho police], but [he] decided to send his wife because they knew immediately that when [my mother] heard her friend's voice she'd open the door. My mom opened the door, and [just like that] when she opened the door the house was full! [Police] were searching *every* where, but nobody knew why. They never needed to tell you.

Police harassment did not, surprisingly, end with Lesotho officials. Although South African officials had technically rescinded Mafeking's banning orders after the death of her husband, Moffat, Nominki distinctly recalled "seeing Special Forces cars passing by" their home throughout the 1970s.[25] Once the very thin veneer of British protection had

5 "One day we are going home"

worn away to reveal a fully independent Lesotho in 1966, South African officials felt increasingly free to send agents across the borders into the landlocked country – with or without the consent of the Lesotho government.

> It was very easy [for Special Forces to enter Lesotho], it was *very* easy. They never had a problem by doing that, so it was easy for them to come in and out. I don't think the Lesotho government was aware of them, but I think some of the Lesotho officials were working with the *Boers*. It's not easy for some Special Branch [officers] to enter another country without people knowing something like that is going to happen. Certainly when there's more than one car!

While there was no way to prove the large, unmarked vehicles with South African plates belonged to members of the Special Forces, Nominki swore when "somebody would just pass the house, and look, and come back and pass again ... you could feel in your blood" that the family was under surveillance. As evidence from declassified government

5 "One day we are going home"

documents analyzed in Chapters Two and Three illustrate, the feeling of being watched was not just simple paranoia on the part of Elizabeth Mafeking or her children. Mafeking conveyed this very sentiment to Ray Alexander when the friend asked Mafeking to return to political organizing amongst mine workers in Lesotho.

Mafeking admitted that at 54 years of age and having been repeatedly hospitalized and diagnosed with high blood pressure, her health was likely too poor for her to "ever be able to do" that kind of work again. Moreover, Mafeking had learned her lesson about dabbling in politics in Lesotho and told Alexander she could not "try an inch to do something" with the current government restrictions against her. By 1973, Mafeking's family – once comprised of infants, toddlers, and young children – had matured into young adults, some with families of their own, and she seemed content to witness their progress. Rhoda was "quite happy with her family out at Maseru," Uhuru was in her second year of boarding school, and two of her other daughters were training to be a nurse and a teacher.[26] There was cause for celebration in February of 1975, and

5 "One day we are going home"

Mafeking wrote her dear friend to brag on her baby. Fifteen year-old Uhuru completed her final testing with a "first class" pass in her Form D schooling.[27] While all of her children worked hard in their courses, even she had to admit that "Uhuru [was] an exception." Mafeking seemed amazed that she had been the one to produce Uhuru since the activist had "never gone so far for [her own] education." Mafeking was not the only one who was incredibly proud of Uhuru, in fact, "even some of the South African refugees" expressed how happy they were with the news. To have the child of one of their own ascend to the top of her class in spite of the trials of exile was a victory for the entire South African refugee community.

Mafeking assured her friend she was doing well, and still enjoying the financial support Alexander had helped to arrange through the International Defense and Aid Fund for Southern Africa, a British-based, anti-apartheid organization that provided financial support for the legal defense of political activists and their dispossessed families. Mafeking was apparently feeling more like her old self, too, sounding invigorated rather than drained by talking politics:

5 "One day we are going home"

> The question is, who is there to go on with the work as people are so scared these days, and this is the time that our people should really stand together.

For more than a year, the ANC had been suffering devastating losses both at home and abroad as a spate of assassinations took the lives of high-ranking activists, their allies, and even family members unfortunate enough to be in the immediate vicinity. While the losses of many were mourned as tragic, the passing of some, like Chief Albert Lutuli, was an opportunity for celebration. A few months shy of the eight-year anniversary of the death of Chief Albert Lutuli, Mafeking attended a rally in his honor and sang the praises of his veneration.

> Ray that was a wonderful day for all of us of the ANC. We were all in uniforms at the National Maseru *pitso* [meeting] ground so we were able that evening to meet the old lady, Mrs. Luthuli (sic) and people like Gatsha Buthelezi happened to be very fortunate those two days and we met all

5 "One day we are going home"

> representatives from some of the African states and we discussed quite a good number of things with them and even with Mrs. Luthuli (sic).

Mafeking seemed to no longer care about the undertaking she'd signed years earlier to remain distanced from political dealings while in Lesotho. She also no longer seemed to fear writing about the details of her exploits. Mafeking attended a meeting celebrating a highly controversial political figure, wore the official uniform of her banned organization, met with international political dignitaries, and discussed strategy with Mangosuthu "Gatsha" Buthelezi, the founder of the South African-based Inkatha Freedom Party (IFP). Alexander replied with great interest to Mafeking's seemingly newfound energy for political work. She first updated Mafeking on the recent success of her home union back in Cape Town with the H. Jones Canning Factory in staging a work stoppage in spite of the murder of its leader.[28] Alexander even consulted with Mafeking regarding the most democratic method of selecting the

5 "One day we are going home"

next leader. Mafeking remained intimately tied to the movement, and it continued to cost her

The anti-apartheid struggle in South Africa entered a new, militant phase, and Mafeking's mere affiliation with supposed "radicals" within the exiled ANC population again made her the target of the South African government, which in 1974 attempted to pressure the government of Lesotho into arresting both Mafeking and Chris Hani for allegedly operating MK camps in Lesotho. While Mafeking and Hani did not operate underground training camps in Lesotho, Mafeking *did* provide material support – hot meals, a home, and safe passage out of South Africa – to many young comrades who'd fled the country bound for ANC underground training camps in Tanganyika and Angola. In a September 1975 letter, Mafeking had to admit she was "not quite well."[29] A few months earlier, local police arrested her, her partner Gilbert Hani, his son Chris, and another of their allies on unspecified charges, and sent 57 year-old Mafeking to jail "for a sixty day detention and a week on top."[30] Being detained "in the peak of winter" had an adverse effect on Mafeking's health, and now in addition

5 "One day we are going home"

to high blood pressure, Mafeking was experiencing complications with her kidneys. She was convinced the poor condition of the jails during her incarceration was the culprit.

What Mafeking does not reveal, however, is that after her release from prison, she continued drinking, which only served to exacerbate her age-related health problems. Still, she remained a vital link in the exile community, describing political conditions in Lesotho as "settled and normal."[31] According to Mafeking, "all comrades in Lesotho" were in good health and able to "meet freely" following the "tough time" many of them had with the extended incarceration in the previous year. Mafeking claimed to be "running a complicated piece of work" and had "some more important matters" to discuss with Alexander, but cagily sidestepped providing her friend with details at the moment, imploring patience as she coordinated whatever plan she hoped to present to Alexander. Where work was demanding, family was a relief, and Mafeking continued to take pride in the educational accomplishments of her youngest – and most willful child –

5 "One day we are going home"

Uhuru, whose success gave Mafeking "hope that one of these fine days the struggle will come to an end." She just hoped that day was "not too far" away. Mafeking was convinced exile was only temporary, and that one day, "each and every one of us will meet each other" again. Mafeking could "see things are changing very fast," and felt that something was "very near" to breaking in South Africa.

Something was close to breaking in South Africa, most particularly in the townships of Soweto one month later in 1976. On June 16, 1976, thousands of students from numerous high schools took to the streets to protest the introduction of Afrikaans – the language of Apartheid – as the language of instruction in schools. Heavily armed South African police forces opened fire on the crowd of unarmed, chanting schoolchildren wearing their uniforms, killing twenty-three and wounding over 1000. Mafeking was heartbroken by the events in Soweto, devastated that children sacrificed their lives when and where adults would not, and the June killings haunted Mafeking for months. In December two weeks before Christmas as the Mafeking children began looking forward to holiday preparations,

5 "One day we are going home"

their mother came home and summarily canceled Christmas. Catherine Nomsa remembered her saying, "If the children who died in Soweto can't enjoy Christmas, we won't either," and wasn't the least bit surprised when her mother stayed true to her word. December 25, 1976 was just another Saturday in the Mafeking household. Not one gift, not one special dish, not one song. In the aftermath of the student uprisings and an incredibly solemn Christmas Day, Mafeking felt compelled to again aid the struggle in any way she could, in spite of the potential personal costs.

Hundreds of African youths fled South Africa in the wake of the Soweto uprising, and security forces swept through townships arresting alleged agitators and those supposedly responsible for the carnage. This flight of South African youths from South Africa to places like Tanzania, Angola, Zambia, and Zimbabwe – critically supportive locales in the South African liberation struggle – was often facilitated by Elizabeth Mafeking when those young men passed through Lesotho. As Lauretta Ngcobo demonstrates in *Prodigal Daughters*, Lesotho had been "a vital outpost" for the ANC since the 1960 State of Emergency in South

5 "One day we are going home"

Africa that ushered in the banning of political organizations both in material and actual support for the anti-apartheid movement.[32] Ngcobo's text offers rich insight into the experiences of exiled women, and inadvertently demonstrates the ways in which Mafeking's experience of self-imposed exile remains unique. There were seventeen women under study in *Prodigal Daughters*, from varying racial backgrounds – African, white, Indian – all of whom were exiled *after* Mafeking in 1959. The majority of the women were affiliated with the ANC, while the rest were split equally between either the PAC or SACP. Nine of the group were married women with living husbands who could/did contribute to their welfare, and twelve of the women had some sort of familial or financial support. At least fifteen of the women could identify as middle-class (or better), primarily due to their degrees earned at university. None of the women under study spent any significant time in Lesotho during their exiles, rather, in the UK, Zambia, Kenya, Botswana, Zimbabwe, and the United States. Mafeking had neither institutional connections, husband,

5 "One day we are going home"

status, nor educational background to rely upon for support when she faced exile in Lesotho.

One of Ngcobo's respondents in *Prodigal Daughters*, Nomvo Booi, worked "as a courier for groups in Lesotho and Botswana" for the duration of her two-year banishment in Lesotho, actively participating in the underground at the time despite the dangers to herself or residency status. While Mafeking's residency in Lesotho ultimately forced her to abandon her public support and work for the ANC, over the decades following the Soweto Uprising, she continued to offer material support to the ANC by taking part in the intricate, underground transportation network that funneled young, political refugees from South Africa to either military camps on the Continent or abroad to Europe to attend colleges and universities.[33] It was because of those very specific underground networks that two of Mafeking's daughter's – Nomonde Mary and Nomsa Catherine – were able to make it out of Lesotho without legal passports.[34] Both young girls had ultimately decided the potential rewards far outweighed the risks associated with international travel without the proper

5 "One day we are going home"

documentation. They feared, however, this was causing problems for their mother back home, since everyone knew neither Elizabeth Mafeking nor her children had ever obtained passports from the Lesotho government. According to Nomsa, people likely could "not understand what could have happened to us."

Over the course of the next two years, Alexander was a crucial informational conduit between Elizabeth Mafeking and her daughters studying abroad in the Soviet Union.[35] Both global and local political alliances made it impossible for Mafeking to receive international post directly from a socialist country, but Alexander could and did receive, re-package, and re-post correspondence from Lusaka to Lesotho. Thanks to the community of activists and allies of which Alexander was a part in Zambia, when a trusted comrade passed through Lusaka bound for Lesotho, Alexander would secret letters and photographs from the girls to their mother. Alexander continued to provide her dear friend with material support and clothing, most especially when winter came to Lesotho. Alexander also reminded her friend that in spite of their hardships, they needed to celebrate their accomplishments.

Alexander once met with the Mafeking girls in Dar es Salaam during a school break in 1979, and the meeting made her reminisce about the feverish work of women in South Africa to organize in 1954 in her next letter to her friend in Lesotho:

> There we gathered in Johannesburg with women of all colours (sic) from all provinces and established the Federation on 19th April, 1954. In a short space of time we made history in the struggle against passes, against the apartheid regime's brutality to our men, women, young and old, and we were working for a society in which our children could know a life of peace, freedom and progress. In the Charter for women that we adopted, we as mothers had our children's needs as the main focal point.[36]

Alexander likely saw in both Nomonde and Nomsa a realization of the opportunities for which she and their

5 "One day we are going home"

mother fought and sacrificed. No amount of adversity could detract from the fact that the system of Apartheid had not trapped two of Mafeking's girls – unlike thousands of other African schoolgirls doomed to lives of substandard education, domestic servitude, and poverty in Southern Africa. Thus, when Alexander wished Mafeking "many, many Happy Returns" on the occasion of her 61st birthday, Mafeking had a lot to be thankful for: one of her children was a happily married mother, three of her daughters were studying abroad, and another child was poised to excel academically at the country's leading university.[37] It was hard for Mafeking to see this silver lining due to decades of drinking, however, and it literally showed in her letters to Alexander in the early 1980s. At first glance, it appeared as if the then 63 year-old activist was suffering the aftereffects of a mild stroke. Mafeking's handwriting was incredibly unsteady, and entire passages of the letter were largely illegible. Conversations with Mafeking's daughter's, however, shed a very different light on the true cause of their mother's poor penmanship in the early 1980s, and the

5 "One day we are going home"

unbelievable "solution" devised by her comrades in the ANC underground.

In 1981, from her school in Russia, 22 year-old Uhuru begged ANC administrators to allow her to travel to neighboring Romania when she learned that her mother was there. Ray Alexander had heard too many stories, from too many people, about Mafeking's drinking, and she'd begun to see with her own eyes the physical toll it was taking on her friend. Alexander determined to get Mafeking help – even if it meant risking capture and arrest – and smuggled the activist out of Lesotho, presumably under the guise of visiting her daughters, Nomsa and Uhuru, in Europe. According to Uhuru, however, in actuality Mafeking was admitted to a state-run facility to "cure her from the drinking." Elizabeth Mafeking was not mentally ill, but she *did* have a long-term drinking problem, and the Romanian institution was believed to be the best-designed program to address Mafeking's drinking problem. There are no records available that allow for a reconstruction of her time in the treatment facility, but one can only imagine the scene Elizabeth Mafeking made when she realized she was being

5 "One day we are going home"

admitted to a rehabilitation facility, rather than visiting her children.[38]

Drinking might have been taking a toll on her body, but it had little to no effect on her spirit of defiance. In short order, she was en route back to Lesotho, and along the way established friendships with other South African anti-apartheid activists living in exile, like Albert "Albie" Sachs, who was well known in the Union for having been arrested and placed in solitary confinement for over five months.[39] Mafeking's route back to Lesotho included a trip through Mozambique, and when she wrote to Alexander about her time in Europe, she mentioned what a "pleasure" it was to have finally met Sachs there. Back home in Lesotho, Mafeking's drinking resumed nevertheless, and portions of letters after her return from a failed attempt at institutionalization indicate that finally both age and alcohol were affecting her mental faculties. Lines from one of the last few letters written by Elizabeth Mafeking to her dear friend Ray Alexander were peppered with isiXhosa – something none of the Mafeking family had ever written in over the course of almost twenty years – and it is unclear

5 "One day we are going home"

whether Alexander could even understand those parts of her friend's message to her.

Almost three years passed before Mafeking and Alexander began writing one another again, and unfortunately, it was only due to tragedy: Mafeking was in mourning. In July of 1983, Alexander typed a brief letter of condolence:

> My dear Elizabeth,
> I was shocked to hear of your sudden
> severe loss, the untimely tragic murder of
> your daughter.
>
> Elizabeth dear, be strong – this murder is
> one other beastly action by our enemies.
> SACTU (South African Congress of Trade
> Unions) sent you a telegram and have asked
> our Women Secretariat to do likewise.
> Dear one, how can one help to console you
> at your great loss. Know that we feel with
> you and wish we could comfort you.
> Please convey to all your family Jack's and
> my sincere condolences. Yours with love.[40]

5 "One day we are going home"

Violence characterized life in Lesotho in the early 1980s, and Mafeking's notoriety from decades bygone did not guarantee protection from the realities of life. In 1982 the South African army raided Maseru in search of ANC-activists and killed 42 people – most of whom were ANC-activists living as political refugees, alongside a handful of innocent bystanders who were Lesotho nationals. The Maseru Massacre, which South African authorities defended as justified, sparked a wave of retributive justice that spread from the capital city into neighboring Mafeteng, and within a year had enveloped one of Mafeking's beloved children. Mafeking's seventh child, 28 year-old Sisinyana Suzan, was a grade school teacher who routinely used public transport, and one fateful afternoon as her *khumbi* traveled through the streets of Maseru during evening traffic their conveyance was attacked and Sisinyana and her fellow passengers were killed.

Mafeking was devastated, and suspected – as did Alexander – that her child was murdered. It took more than a year for Mafeking to begin to emerge from a depression that threatened to take her life. Her health had begun to

5 "One day we are going home"

recover and her letters returned to the clear, pointed style of writing that characterized her first letters to Alexander years ago, but it was clear Mafeking wasn't very happy that her children were "scattered all over," but they all continued to write her and that provided a measure of comfort.[41] Catherine Nomsa was a second year student studying Pedagogy at Sophia University, and she was doing so well in her studies she contemplated a graduate degree. She diligently wrote from Bulgaria to her mother in Lesotho, entrusting Aunt Ray's international, underground mail system to deliver letters, trinkets, and even small gifts for "Mama Elizabeth and Dad," which she hoped would bring her mother and Ntate Hani pleasure.[42] Catherine Nomsa's gifts were of great comfort to her parents, as was the mere presence of herself and two of her sisters at international colleges earning degrees. In the ability of her daughters to walk a pathway to a life better than what Lesotho begrudgingly had to offer the children of a refugee, in the educational successes of her daughters, Mafeking was able to retain her belief that one day Apartheid would fall, and when it did, she, Alexander, and everyone else displaced by the pernicious system would finally be able – and prepared – to return home to a free and democratic South Africa. Mafeking still believed Apartheid's defeat was imminent, telling Alexander, "Victory is ours although we are in the midst of the frost. But [if] we hold hands together we won't fall."[43]

"More than a blessing"

As Elizabeth Mafeking aged from a vibrant young woman to an elderly individual in need of constant care, daughter Nominki – who recognized that her mother "was a rock [and still] very strong" – decided to remain by her side when the time came for Nominki to go to boarding school abroad when she completed matric in Lesotho. All of the other Mafeking girls in exile – save Rhoda – had ventured out of Lesotho for greener educational pastures due to Mafeking's insistence that a woman should be educated, but Nominki "was scared that if we [left] her alone something bad would happen to her." Nominki stayed by Mafeking's side, and as the years passed and family members sent their children to

5 "One day we are going home"

the Mafeking home in Lesotho, Nominki helped her mother raise the assortment of nieces and nephews that came to the family home.[44] "No matter how long it was going to take" for Mafeking to return to South Africa, Nominki was prepared to wait for her mother. In truth, Nominki was preparing to help her mother die in peace, because by the late 1980s when NP leaders were forced to begin negotiating a transition to democracy and no one came to speak with, consult, or consider Elizabeth Mafeking's return to South Africa, Nominki believed "the whole thing was a lie," and that people wouldn't actually care if the Mafeking family ever returned to Paarl.

So when Mafeking did return to South Africa in 1993, Nominki – who remained in Lesotho to care for the family's property – was humbled to hear about the response of the local populace in Paarl upon her mother's arrival.[45] When community members, local politicians, and high-ranking ANC members came to visit Mafeking, welcoming her back to South Africa, Nominki finally began to understand just how central her mother had been to the anti-apartheid struggle in the Cape.

5 "One day we are going home"

> I was told that there were so many cars to go when she arrived in Cape Town [at the airport]. [The people] knew she was coming. She arrived at my sister's place and everybody knew she was coming! There were so many people, everybody was so happy, some people couldn't believe she was still alive. That was a blessing ... everything she was fighting for at last she's seen that. She got to see it.

One of the most remarkable manifestations of Elizabeth Mafeking's newfound freedom as a South African citizen was gaining the franchise, and Nominki recalled with great pride the first opportunity her mother had to vote. Nominki laughed as she reminisced on the evening before the 1994 South African General Elections, claiming Mafeking acted like a child the night before Christmas, too excited for a good night's rest. "She couldn't sleep, she just couldn't sleep." When Nominki awoke in the morning, Mafeking had been up for hours, was fully dressed, and waiting to walk to the polling station. Nominki felt the distance was too far for

5 "One day we are going home"

her 75 year-old mother to walk, so she arranged for a car to pick her up. "She was so happy. She couldn't believe it [was really happening]." Nominki accompanied her mother to the local polling place, and when they arrived someone in the crowd recognized Mafeking and insisted she bypass the long line and go directly to the front of the queue. No one in line – not even those who had been waiting for hours to cast a vote – objected. "She was so excited," and on her way to the front of the line people "joked with her 'Rokie, what are you going to vote for?' and she said, 'Everybody knows!'" On April 27, 1994, Elizabeth Mafeking cast the first vote of her life as a citizen in the land of her birth, and her daughter Nominki stood by her side proudly. A local newspaper published a photograph of Mafeking post-vote, smiling broadly, giving the mid-twentieth century "Africa" salute with one hand with her thumb raised to display the mark made by election officials signifying her vote, and holding her ID in the other.[46]

While Nominki felt "blessed" to witness these events in her mother's life, it still could not completely ameliorate the pain of growing up dispossessed from the

5 "One day we are going home"

life she was supposed to have. Nominki had grown to resent hearing "one day we're going home" over the course of thirty-two years. Mafeking had *said* it with conviction, she had *shouted* it in frustration, and she'd even *sung* it gleefully as the only lyric to the tune of whichever favorite "love songs, church songs, [or] *mzabalazo* songs" that popped into her mind.[47] After the first and only time decades ago when she'd verbally doubted her mother's return to "that South Africa" while Mafeking was cooking dinner and gotten the business end of the stick her mother was using to make *pap*, Nominki learned not to question her mother's idea of "home," regardless of how it made her feel.

> The reality [was] that Lesotho had been our home . . . it's so difficult to lose your identity. You are in Lesotho and you are called a refugee. When you come back to the Cape you are called a BaSotho! You're in between, you don't have a balance. You're not South African, you're not [Ba]Sotho. Who are you? What are you?

5 "One day we are going home"

Three of Mafeking's four surviving daughters all echo this sentiment: feeling trapped between two cultures, and never fully belonging to either. Uhuru articulated it best, stating, "We were always too amaXhosa for the BaSotho, and too BaSotho for the amaXhosa." Language, in particular played a significant factor in the difficult adjustment to life back "home" in South Africa. While SeSotho and amaXhosa are two of the eleven official languages of South Africa, they are *not* – as in the case of isiXhosa and isiZulu – mutually intelligible. For Nominki, the switch from SeSotho to isiXhosa, a language she hadn't spoken since she was a toddler, was hard. It was almost impossible to communicate with friends and extended family members who spoke isiXhosa, isiZulu, Afrikaans, and even English – the languages of the Cape. In truth, over the past 32 years, the only experience Nominki had with isiXhosa was when her mother became very angry. At those times, Mafeking spoke exclusively in isiXhosa, and Nominki was grateful to *not* understand. Outside of those instances, however, the only thing Nominki and her siblings knew about the amaXhosa world was that they did *not* want to be associated with the faceless entity that had been the reason for years of childhood trauma. Even today, Uhuru refuses to claim being either amaXhosa or BaSotho. "I am a South African. Full stop." Sadly, communication was not the most difficult obstacle to overcome when the Mafeking family returned to the Cape.

Following Mafeking's banning in 1959, the NP was able to finally designate Paarl as a "whites only" living zone and push the last African families out of the city further north, past the Coloured buffer-zone of Huguenot, to the black resettlement township of Mbekweni. When Nominki finally joined her mother in Mbekweni one year after Mafeking's return, while she was grateful to see so many individuals paying their respect to her mother, she was dismayed at Mafeking's living conditions. In the words of Nomphumelelo Hani, the niece of Gilbert Hani who'd visited the Mafeking family in the 1970s, the activist had gone from living in "a very nice house in Lesotho" to a "one-room shack" like you would see in the worst South African shantytown.[48] When Mafeking returned to the Cape, former political comrades publicly announced they would

5 "One day we are going home"

build a new house for the activist to show their gratitude for her sacrifices, but that didn't happen. For more than one year, Mafeking lived in "deplorable" conditions that fellow activists and community leaders felt was "embarrassing" for a woman of her stature. What many did not see, however, was the true extent of financial support the ANC provided for Mafeking and her children upon their return. Mafeking's children report their mother lived a rather dignified life because of generous pension funds provided by the government—funds far in excess of the average pension provided to returning activists. The ANC pension removed from Mafeking's children the financial burden of caring for their mother in her final years, allowing them, as Uhuru said, to truly "cater for all her needs." It seemed as if the respect and appreciation ANC-leaders felt for a former national Vice President of the ANC-Women's League who'd sacrificed everything for the struggle stopped at handshakes and well wishes. Nominki sighed, "My mother loved the ANC so much, she would do anything for them," but it seemed as if the ANC was not willing to *work* for the

5 "One day we are going home"

elderly Elizabeth Mafeking or include her in any in the new system of governance.

Comrade Nomathemba "Themsi" Nkewu was elected chairperson of the Paarl branch of the ANC shortly after Mafeking's return to the Cape, and recalled with dismay the ways in which she felt the organization "failed" Mafeking upon her return to South Africa.[49] In spite of her recognized centrality to the anti-apartheid movement decades earlier, Elizabeth Mafeking did not receive a hearty, coordinated welcome from the organizations she once represented – a welcome many other activists enjoyed. There were no parades in her honor, no awards in her name, and there were no invitations to participate in meetings discussing the national transition to democracy. There was, however, plenty of judgment regarding how Mafeking had spent her time in exile.

> She went through pain and bitterness ... after they came back, things were very, very difficult for her. I'm going to be honest and tell you the truth. After she came back, I don't think that the welcoming was what she

deserved as a heroine. There were many squabbles . . . and I remember when we had to name our branch . . . we raised her name as one of [the potential names]. And then there was a lot of discussion. They didn't want to take her name!

Figure 5.1 Nomathemba "Themsi" Nkewu and Koko Ndinisa at the Mafeking home in Mbekweni (Summer 2017).

Photograph taken by author

Cmde. Nkewu was "bitter" about the lack of support to name the Paarl branch of the ANC after Mafeking. She'd only been two years-old when Mafeking escaped to Lesotho, but she'd grown up hearing stories from her aunt

5 "One day we are going home"

about the activist, and as a grown woman who witnessed Mafeking's return, Nkewu could not understand why *everyone* wasn't excited to celebrate Mafeking. Unbeknownst to most, however, in 2001 – almost one decade after she returned from exile in Lesotho – the ANC-government provided Mafeking a financial remuneration in recognition of her contributions and sacrifices. Similar to other former political refugees and returned exiles, Mafeking received a single, lump sum, then a monthly allowance for her needs.[50]

In 2006, Nkewu had attempted to organize members of the branch – predominantly women – *as* women to recognize someone who had "sacrificed so much" for the movement. Nkewu felt naming the branch after Mafeking would ensure that her work was "not in vain," and more importantly, since Mafeking was still alive at the time of the naming of the branch, it would have been a tangible and enduring recognition of her life's work. The branch, however, was not the least bit interested in being named after Elizabeth Mafeking.

5 "One day we are going home"

> The problem was her drinking. They said they just could not support it. I asked them, "Did you go to her? Did you find out *why* she drank? Do you know what she's [gone] through? Do you know the reasons behind it? . . . She didn't have anything [in exile], and that was the only coping tool!"

Every argument Nkewu attempted to present to the ANC on Mafeking's behalf was met with unyielding African cultural stigmas against female drinking. Everyone knew about Mafeking's drinking problems and enough people felt naming the branch after her would besmirch the good name of the ANC that Mafeking's name was removed from contention and the branch was, instead, named after Dr. Alfred. B. Xuma. Nkewu could not understand it. Mafeking "was strong, she was courageous, [and] she was an organizer" who would "go from door to door organizing men and women, educating them about their rights." Moreover, she'd given everything to the struggle, and it felt wrong to simply ignore her work. Nkewu argued that plenty of male activists possessed a laundry list of shortcomings,

5 "One day we are going home"

but there were streets, bridges, buildings, and entire communities, named after them.[51] Why not Mafeking? Nkewu had grown up hearing about this woman named Elizabeth Mafeking who "never led from the back, always the front," but when the time came to honor her efforts, the ANC seemed to turn its back on "Auntie Rockie."

> [Many of us] felt no one is taking care of Auntie Rockie. We don't have money. We don't have power . . . [but] we have an icon in our community, a legend, and *nobody* is saying anything about this icon? Nobody is saying *anything* about this legend?

The best Nkewu could manage was to organize a small function at a local elementary school recognizing ten women from the local community who'd been active in the movement. She presented Mafeking with a simple certificate printed in the school office because:

> We had nothing [else] to give her, [but we wanted to at least say] "We recognize you."
> The African National Congress doesn't

5 "One day we are going home"

> recognize you, they can say whatever they are saying, but *we* are saying "You are our hero. You are our legend. You are our icon. We will always keep your name shining wherever we go."

In spite of the modesty of the event, Nkewu believed it was important to do something – anything – for Mafeking because it was "very rare" to find someone who had made such lasting contributions to the liberation struggle. Even rarer to find that someone was largely being ignored by the very organization she'd helped to build. When asked if the ANC would have cared about honoring a male comrade with a drinking problem, Nkewu responded "no," without hesitation. Mafeking still cared for her family, still cared for the children of others, and still provided material support for the ANC underground and other political refugees during her 32-year exile. The drinking "didn't make her bad" or invalidate Mafeking's experiences, but the way in which the ANC treated her upon her return made Nkewu feel as if the organization believed differently.

5 "One day we are going home"

> They wrote her off. They wrote her out [of
> the victory of our liberation]. It [was like it]
> all meant nothing.

Elizabeth Mafeking was an original "foot soldier" who "broke barriers and opened doors" during the liberation struggle, and helped to lead South Africa to its freedom. Her exile resulted in a marked loss of momentum for both the FCWU and the AFCWU, organizational momentum that did not recover for decades. How the ANC could bear to ignore Mafeking's "pain of longing" for her children, for her people, for her husband, for her mother, for her true home in exile was beyond comprehension.

> It hurts me that nobody ever speaks about
> her. [The ANC] never mentions her name.

It is truly unfortunate that Nkewu—and many others—could not see the true lengths to which the ANC went to provide for Mafeking and her children upon their repatriation to South Africa. While Mafeking had not been deployed to any structure of the ANC, it is important to note

5 "One day we are going home"

that both her age and her health would not have allowed for the needs of government work. The ANC, however, *did* ensure that Mafeking's children received an education in exile, and during the transition, were named to senior posts in government. Indeed, Uhuru recalled with great pride the first time she entered Parliament as a government official. "I felt that even though my mother did not work for government, I, her lastborn, have been given the authority and power by the ANC government to enter the Parliament building. This was a great moment for me. I felt at that moment that my mum's role in the struggle had been worth it." The ability of the multiple generations of Mafeking's to earn degrees, serve in government, and even (eventually) own a family game farm, simply would not have been possible without the (sometimes silent) support of the ANC. COSATU joined the cadre of organizations that paid respect to Mafeking upon her return by celebrating the activist with numerous awards—one of which was received by the family at a Johannesburg event where (then President) Thabo Mbeki was a guest of honor. Whereas the eyes of the world had been on Mafeking when the strictures of

5 "One day we are going home"

Apartheid expelled her from South Africa, the attention paid to the fall of Apartheid and the election of the nation's first African president far eclipsed the return of an elderly activist, quite frankly. The residents of Paarl and Mbekweni never forgot their prodigal daughter, however, and in the waning years of her hard-lived life, countless individuals continued to pay their modest respects to one they considered *iqhawe lamaqhawe*, a hero among heroes.

Figure 5.2 Elizabeth Mafeking makes her grand entrance into the banquet hall where friends and family prepare to celebrate her 90th birthday, which was hosted and fully sponsored by FAWU.

Courtesy of Mafeking Family

Figure 5.3 Elizabeth Mafeking dancing with her eighth child, daughter Catherine Nomsa.

Courtesy of Mafeking Family

Figure 5.4 Mafeking's enduring admiration for the ANC was reflective in many elements of her 90th birthday celebration, most especially the cake, ordered especially by FAWU to honor Mafeking's contributions.

Courtesy of Mafeking Family

5 "One day we are going home"

Notes

1 Letter from Elizabeth Mafeking to Ray Alexander. February 10, 1968. Ray Alexander Collection: General Correspondence (Box 21). Special Collections, University of Cape Town, South Africa. Subsequent references from this archival source will appear as "Alexander Papers: Special Collections, UCT."

2 Letter from Elizabeth Mafeking to Ray Alexander. January 1, 1970. Alexander Papers: Special Collections, University of Cape Town.

3 R60 in South African currency (ZAR) – used interchangeably in both South Africa and Lesotho – in 1970 is equivalent to R589 today, or approximately $40 (USD).

5 "One day we are going home"

4 Letter from Rhoda Mafeking to Ray Alexander. January 7, 1970. Alexander Papers: Special Collections, University of Cape Town.

5 Letter from Nomsa Catherine Mafeking to Ray Alexander. January 29, 1970. Alexander Papers: Special Collections, University of Cape Town.

6 Letter from Elizabeth Mafeking to Ray Alexander. March 1, 1970. Alexander Papers: Special Collections, University of Cape Town.

7 Letter from Ray Alexander to Nomsa Catherine Mafeking. March 14, 1970. Alexander Papers: Special Collections, University of Cape Town. In the original correspondence, Alexander mistakenly spells Nomsa's name "Katherine."

8 Robert Matji, Gilbert Hani, and Anderson Ganyile and his brother Daniel had all taken refuge in Lesotho when their welcome expired in the Union in the

5 "One day we are going home"

1960s, and Alexander had specific information to share with each man. Within weeks of Alexander inquiring about the location of Anderson Ganyile, he was kidnapped by South African police, who illegally crossed into Lesotho to capture Ganyile and transport him back across the border where he was promptly arrested and jailed. Alexander also wanted to inform Gilbert Hani that his sons – whom he had presumably been looking for – had been located in Johannesburg. One of Hani's sons, twenty-eight year-old Chris, went on to become a fierce opponent of the Apartheid government in the wake of his father's exile. Chris Hani was the leader of the South African Communist Party and chief of staff for Umkhonto we Sizwe, the armed wing of the ANC. At the height of his influence and

5 "One day we are going home"

in the last moments of Apartheid, Chris Hani was assassinated on April 10, 1993.

9 Letter from Nomsa Mafeking to Ray Alexander. April 1970. Alexander Papers: Special Collections, University of Cape Town. Words appear in all caps in original correspondence. Nomsa's correction of Alexander in 1970 can most likely be attributed to a misguided sense of teenage pride or umbrage, but in 2016, it's just ironic. It was not long after this correspondence that Nomsa – so fiercely proud of her middle name as to correct Ray Alexander – dropped it entirely. "As I grew up I realized that Catherine name was just irrelevant in my life as a black person and found that my parents for one reason or the other followed the trend of giving children Christian names as they were being baptized. When I started acquiring legal documents

and having the right to decide for myself what I wanted I dropped that Catherine name and all my legal and any other documents only reflect 'Nomsa' since 1972." Conversation, Nomsa Mafeking with author, summer 2016.

10 Ibid.

11 Letter from Rhoda Mafeking to Ray Alexander. July 1970. Alexander Papers: Special Collections, University of Cape Town.

12 Letter from Nomsa Mafeking to Ray Alexander. October 19, 1970. Alexander Papers: Special Collections, University of Cape Town.

13 Letter from Rhoda Mafeking to Ray Alexander. December 22, 1970. Alexander Papers: Special Collections, University of Cape Town.

14 The International University Exchange Fund (IUEF), headquartered in the Netherlands, aimed to assist

refugees – most particularly South African students via scholarships; Letter from Ray Alexander to Elizabeth Mafeking. August 5, 1971. Alexander Papers: Special Collections, University of Cape Town.

15 Letter from Ray Alexander to Elizabeth Mafeking. April 20, 1971. Alexander Papers: Special Collections, University of Cape Town.

16 Macmillan, Hugh, The Lusaka Years: The ANC in Exile in Zambia, 1963 to 1994 (Johannesburg, South Africa: Jacana Media, 2013), 23–25.

17 Letter from Elizabeth Mafeking to Ray Alexander. November 16, 1971. Alexander Papers: Special Collections, University of Cape Town.

18 Letter from Nomsa Mafeking to Ray Alexander. April 24, 1972. Alexander Papers: Special Collections, University of Cape Town.

5 "One day we are going home"

---

19 Conversation, Uhuru Mafeking with author, Summer 2013, Johannesburg, South Africa.

20 Umngqusho is widely accepted as the quintessential amaXhosa dish. It is comprised of "samp" (stamp mielies), sugar beans, butter, potatoes, and onions. The dried maize and bean mélange has several variants that include (but are not limited to) chilies and lemons.

21 Ntate Molimo is Father God in Sesotho, whereas uThixo is the same in isiXhosa.

22 Uhuru admits that as she and her mother aged in Lesotho, she learned to simply nod indulgently when Mafeking seemed to lapse into a place of nostalgia and say, "One day we are going home."

23 Interview, Nominki Mafeking with author, summer 2013, Paarl, Western Cape, South Africa.

24 Khaketla, B. Makalo, Lesotho 1970: An African Coup under the Microscope (Oakland: University of California Press, 1972).

25 When Mafeking's husband died in Paarl in 1965, South African officials coincidentally rescinded her banning orders. According to Nominki this was most likely a tactic to trick her mother into returning to the Republic, thereby setting the stage for a re-arrest. Neither Mafeking nor the children returned to South Africa to bury their husband and father, and they all later learned that members of the Special Forces had attended the funeral services, clearly in search of Mafeking.

26 Letter from Elizabeth Mafeking to Ray Alexander. 1973. Alexander Papers: Special Collections, University of Cape Town. While there is no exact date for this letter, information in the communique suggests it

5 "One day we are going home"

---

was written by Mafeking in either April or May of 1973.

27 Letter from Elizabeth Mafeking to from Ray Alexander. February 5, 1975. Alexander Papers: Special Collections, University of Cape Town.

28 Letter from Ray Alexander to Elizabeth Mafeking. March 12, 1975. Alexander Papers: Special Collections, University of Cape Town.

29 Letter from Elizabeth Mafeking to Ray Alexander. September 11, 1975. Alexander Papers: Special Collections, University of Cape Town.

30 Ibid.

31 Letter from Elizabeth Mafeking to Ray Alexander. January 7, 1976. Alexander Papers: Special Collections, University of Cape Town.

5 "One day we are going home"

---

32 Ngcobo, Lauretta (ed.), Prodigal Daughters: Stories of South African Women in Exile (Pietermaritzburg: UKZN Press, 2012), 34.

33 There was an extensive South African exile network throughout "southern, central, western and northern Africa" with tentacles into Europe, the Caribbean and North America," and the path of many young men and women transitioning through Lesotho began at the home of Elizabeth Mafeking. Ngcobo, Lauretta (ed.), Prodigal Daughters: Stories of South African Women in Exile (Pietermaritzburg: UKZN Press, 2012), 43.

34 Letter from Nomonde Mary Mafeking to Ray Alexander. August 21, 1977. Alexander Papers: Special Collections, University of Cape Town.

5 "One day we are going home"

35 Letter from Ray Alexander to Elizabeth Mafeking. July 12, 1978. Alexander Papers: Special Collections, University of Cape Town.

36 Letter from Ray Alexander to Elizabeth Mafeking. April 17, 1979. Alexander Papers: Special Collections, University of Cape Town.

37 Letter from Ray Alexander to Elizabeth Mafeking. September 8, 1979. Alexander Papers: Special Collections, University of Cape Town; According to Uhuru, Nomonde left Lesotho in late 1975, she followed in April of 1977, and finally, sister Nomsa followed shortly after.

38 Ultimately, Uhuru and Mafeking missed the opportunity to see one another, because as Uhuru recognizes, "the ANC had many children who were living in different countries without their parents, [and it would have set] a very wrong precedence to

5 "One day we are going home"

pay for my ticket to go to Romania to see my mum if the ANC would not be able to do the same for other kids." Uhuru was still grateful to the ANC, because at the time it felts as if they "never abandoned" her and "appreciated the challenges that she faced in Lesotho." There were dozens of comrades and families with serious challenges during the 1980s, when the anti-apartheid movement was at war with South Africa, yet the ANC still managed to send Mafeking to Romania for treatment.

39 Seven years after their first meeting in Maputo, Albie Sachs received a parcel bomb in the mail that exploded upon opening, costing Sachs one arm and sight in one eye.

5 "One day we are going home"

---

40 Letter from Ray Alexander to Elizabeth Mafeking. July 8, 1983. Alexander Papers: Special Collections, University of Cape Town.

41 Mafeking was, again, truly fortunate in this regard. While she considered her children "scattered all over," she was still able to take part in their lives and actually knew where they were. Badat's, The Forgotten People recounts the banishment of Frances Baard, who was banned then incarcerated for a total of eleven years, who traveled home to Port Elizabeth following the expiration of her banning orders to find her children. "She discovered that they were dispersed, having found shelter with other families . . . [because] following her conviction, her children were evicted from their home and all the furniture and goods had been taken away in a truck by the location

5 "One day we are going home"

superintendent." Badat, The Forgotten People, 202–203.

42 Letter from Elizabeth Mafeking to Ray Alexander. March 8, 1984. Alexander Papers: Special Collections, University of Cape Town.

43 Ibid.

44 Nominki's unwavering commitment to her mother earned her the nickname "Cake-Eater" in the family, because all of the siblings were convinced she would be rewarded in heaven with limitless, confectionary delights.

45 Mafeking repatriated to South Africa under a United Nations program, and left behind three of her children, whom she buried in Lesotho.

46 The second time Elizabeth Mafeking voted was a much more bittersweet moment. When the second General Elections were held in 1999, Elizabeth

5 "One day we are going home"

Mafeking was 78 years-old and could not go to the poll to cast her vote. Polling officials came to the Mafeking home the day of the election, however, and allowed Nominki to help Mafeking cast her vote.

47 Elizabeth Mafeking was known for starting each trade union meeting with a protest song, encouraging everyone present to lend their voices to the collective chorus. Her daughter, Nominki, could not stop laughing when I shared this detail about her mother's life that I'd come across in my research. Nominki shook her head and laughed, saying, "My mother absolutely could not sing. She liked to sing, but she just could not."

48 More than one year later when the promise had yet to be fulfilled, with the help of Liz Abrahams and members of the Food and Allied Workers Union

5 "One day we are going home"

(FAWU), Mafeking's adult children put enough pressure on enough organizations and individuals to see the home constructed. According to the family, "FAWU built [Mafeking] a house." The Mafeking family recognizes FAWU as one of the few organizations that stepped into the void for their mother immediately following her return.

49 Interview with author in Mbekweni, Western Cape, South Africa, Summer 2017.

50 Upon her death, the direct dependents of Elizabeth Mafeking received the second, lump sum designated for survivors of former political refugees.

51 The reception area at COSATU headquarters in Johannesburg is named after Elizabeth Mafeking, and the FAWU office in Kelrksdorp in the North West Province is called named the Elizabeth

5 "One day we are going home"

Mafeking House. It is important to note that there was a tri-partite relationship between the ANC, COSATU, and the Communist Party during and following the fall of Apartheid, and the organizations worked closely with one another rather than in competition with one another. Any recognition by COSATU was a tacit recognition by the ANC, and any recognition by COSATU was possible because of the recognition of the affiliate member—FAWU.

Conclusion

The story of Elizabeth Rokie Mafeking *is* a victorious one, but it is *not* romantic. It is the amazing, true story of a woman who lost costly battles, but ultimately won the war against Apartheid. Unlike hundreds of banned individuals, political refugees, and exiles who died – most often largely forgotten – beyond the borders of South Africa during and after the decades of Apartheid, Mafeking lived to return home to the Western Cape, effectively redeeming her cause, her family, and herself. Mafeking's long-awaited repatriation was both a celebration of her defeat over institutionalized, racial discrimination, and a commemoration of the memories of those unable to return to a free South Africa in their lifetimes. In her lifetime, Mafeking played a direct role in challenging long-standing perceptions of African women from unnecessary members of the South African citizenry, to a radicalized demographic determined to have a place in the economic, social, and industrial development of the nation. Mafeking leveled sharp critiques of the social conditions that restricted the citizenship of Africans at home to international audiences, drawing the ire of Apartheid architects who had in recent years been rather successful at whitewashing the true ills of the system to the global community. Mafeking consistently defied government regulations and policies in her efforts to educate her fellow workers on their rights, and to establish crucial alliances with international organizations capable of aiding in the destruction of Apartheid.

But the story of Elizabeth Mafeking is also one of a woman whose life was irrevocably damaged by institutionalized race discrimination. Mafeking was no different from the scores of exiles, political refugees, and banished individuals who suffered from the loneliness, depression, and anger their condition inspired. Her progressive descent into a severe drinking problem greatly affected her relationships with her children who, though they loved their mother deeply, learned to dread being sent to the bottle store to retrieve her brandy in their youths.[1] Mafeking's thirty year relationship with Gilbert Hani, whom she first respected as a comrade then came to care for and

Conclusion

depend upon as a man, ended abruptly in the early 1990s when Mafeking returned to Mbekweni outside Paarl while Hani went to Cofimvaba in the Transkei, almost 1,000km away.[2] Societal expectations and cultural judgment separated the two widows, who had worked hard to and succeeded in constructing their own sort of family in exile. Sadly, for the second time in her life, a family that she had built was torn asunder, and there was nothing Mafeking could do about it. While the Mafeking and Hani families remain close to this day, the separation of their "parents" in the early 1990s meant that for the second time in their lives, the Mafeking children lost a beloved father. The loss of Ntate Hani's everyday presence in the lives of Mafeking's children only compounded the pains of adjusting to life in the supposedly "new" South Africa. In their childhood they'd struggled with their cultural identity in exile, and the highly sectarian South Africa they encountered as adults made it almost impossible to reconcile their BaSotho upbringing with new, cultural, and societal expectations.

Most amazingly, perhaps, about the story of Elizabeth Mafeking is the incredible personal cost she willingly paid in devotion to the struggle. Mafeking was the married mother of eleven children at the time of her banning in 1959, and rather than be parted from her entire family indefinitely, Mafeking made the difficult decision to *split* her family in half in order to raise the eight youngest children in exile, alone in Lesotho. Moreover, during her decades of exile Mafeking lost both a husband and a mother, and the activist regretted not being able to return to South Africa to mourn for them properly. She was neither cowed by these pressures, nor was she passively acceptant of her new lot in life as a political refugee. The memories of Mafeking's children – both natural and adopted – provide intimate details regarding the struggles and (sometimes surprising) joys associated with rearing a family in exile. They also reveal Mafeking as tireless in her efforts as a community leader, activist, and mother. From the outside looking in, Mafeking weathered the storm of exile admirably – providing a home to the homeless, food to the hungry, and surviving the political backlash of three countries – but from the inside looking out, the view was much less rosy. As Jan Theron articulates in *Solidarity Road*,

Conclusion

Mafeking "had by all accounts been broken by her years in exile," and the testimony of her children, extended family members, and comrades, are sad confirmations of this assessment.[3]

In reconstructing the years of Elizabeth Mafeking's life spent battling Apartheid, *"One day we are going home"* perceives the intersections of race, gender, class, and international politics as fertile ground for new historical conversations that challenge conventional topical, socio-economic, or geographical boundaries. Elizabeth Mafeking's story is about much more than black women's early work in international arenas in South Africa in the twentieth century, their conversations about imperialism, and the attractions of radicalism to working-class African women in the nation. It is the story of a system of racial discrimination, its epic rise, its remarkable endurance, and its eventual downfall. It is the story of women in protest willing to sacrifice everything – even those things most precious to them – in the hopes of ushering in new eras of opportunity, dignity, and respect in their beloved homelands. Ultimately, it is the story of one woman's

Conclusion

struggle, resistance, and long-awaited triumph over Apartheid.

Notes

1 Perhaps most tragically in connection to Mafeking's drinking was that "by the time she passed away she had Alzheimer's," and the family is unsure whether their mother's health problems at the time of her death were due to her drinking or the onset of Alzheimer's. In truth, it was likely a combination of both, further exacerbated by Mafeking's advanced age. The family is unsure when the disease – a type of dementia that causes problems with memory, thinking, and behavior – began to affect Mafeking, who could have gone undiagnosed for years, possibly up to the last decade of her life. Uhuru Zikalala Mafeking, correspondence to author, Summer 2017.

Conclusion

2 Badat, Saleem, The Forgotten People: Political Banishment under Apartheid (Leiden: Brill, 2013), 170.

3 Theron, Jan, Solidarity Road: The Story of a Trade Union in the Ending of Apartheid (Johannesburg, South Africa: Jacana Media, 2016), 8.

Epilogue

Lala kahle, qhawe la maqhawe (rest well, hero of heroes)

Five months before her 91st birthday in 2009, Elizabeth Rokie Mafeking passed away at her home in Mbekweni, Western Cape Province, South Africa – the home of her heart, and the land of her birth.[1] She was surrounded by four of her adult children, more than one dozen grandchildren and great-grandchildren, extended family members, and beloved community supporters.[2] Mafeking dedicated her entire adult life to the anti-apartheid struggle in South Africa, and in the last moments of her life, she knew her decades of sacrifice had not been in vain. Mafeking lived to see the system of Apartheid crumble, her long-held dreams of an equitable, non-racialized South Africa come to life, and her children inherit the opportunity to live their lives with dignity and respect in the land of *their* birth.[3] The memorial and funeral services for Elizabeth

Mafeking were a truly moving testament to her well-lived life.[4]

More than two hundred mourners – some from as far away as Lesotho – journeyed to Paarl in the Drakenstein Municipality for a two-day celebration of Mafeking's life. A stream of representatives from local and national organizations spoke before the crowd of two hundred, each in their turn offering their condolences to the Mafeking family, many saying "we are with you in your pain."[5] Two, full-color, 15 ft banners were hung from the ceiling at the front of a vast reception hall on either side of two 12 ft tables on a dais with a speaker's podium in the center. The banners featured an image of the elderly Mafeking, with "Elizabeth, Hero of the Workers" written across the top, and *Hamba Kahle Qabane* (Farewell, Comrade) across the bottom. Logos of the ANC, FAWU, SACP, and COSATU appeared prominently just above the words wishing Mafeking rest in peace. Both the tables and the podium were draped in ANC green, black, and yellow, and elaborate flower displays banked both tables, where almost one dozen speakers sat facing a crowd of two hundred. The atmosphere at the memorial service was more festive than solemn, as one after another speakers rose to lead the audience in songs and chants celebrating the memory of "Ma Rokie," "Mme. Fiki," or "Mme. Mafeking" as many of the speakers affectionately referred to Mafeking.[6] One after another, speakers shared personal accounts of their relationship with Ma Rokie or her influence in their lives, and when each in their turn reflected upon her generosity of self or spirit, dozens in the audience responded with calls of "Amen." The painful emotions evoked by speakers were far outweighed, however, by the joy expressed by mourners in the songs that interspersed these emotional accounts and drew dozens out of their chairs (and sometimes from the dais) to participate in elaborate circle dances at the front of the reception hall and even alongside the isles. Rather than tears and sorrow, Elizabeth Mafeking's memorial service was filled with song, dance, smiles, joy, and the cherished memories of people who had the opportunity to know her on a personal level.

Mafeking's funeral service the following day was a four-hour tribute filled with traditional customs and

Epilogue

heartfelt words of gratitude from family, friends, and a very long list of political organizations and offices both local and national. The services were held on a chilly, overcast June morning, typical of those in the Western Cape in the late spring as winter approaches. An early morning drizzle of rain had left the streets wet with a thin sheen of water and the air chilly enough to warrant heavy coats, scarves, and traditionally worn blankets. A small group of eleven mourners – some in full combat fatigues and all save an ANC flag-bearer raising their right fist in the "Africa" show of solidarity – led a lengthy procession from the funeral home to the reception hall where the services would be held. Eight stretched, white limousines followed Mafeking's hearse, which proceeded slowly through the streets of Mbekweni and accumulated mourners who joined the procession along its route. Along either side of Mafeking's hearse were her escorts, more than two dozen of her sisters in service from the Women's Missionary Society of the Maranantha AME Church in Mbekweni, where Mafeking had been an active member prior to her banning in 1959 and ever since her return in 1991. The numbers of people lining the streets with raised fists increased as the procession neared the reception hall and everyone in attendance sang the national anthem, *Nkosi Sikelele' iAfrica*. Three male, family elders led a sheep to the back of the hearse, and the crowd silenced as pallbearers drew Mafeking's casket from the hearse just enough to lift the cover.[7] The eldest of the men offered a moving prayer in isiXhosa welcoming Mafeking back home after her years away, and thanking everyone present for being a part of the service.

Unlike the previous day's more informal memorial service, the group of speakers sitting at the dais for the funeral service were both larger in number and clearly more senior representatives of their respective organizations. The dais was filled with local municipal leaders in their regalia, high-ranking members of FAWU, COSATU, the SACP, and the ANC wearing their group's t-shirt or official colors, and clergy in their official robes. In particular, the purple and gold ceremonial vestments of the keynote speaker, Rev. Andrew Lewin, Presiding Elder of the South African AME Church, stood out prominently amidst the sea of black, green, yellow, and red. So too had the numbers of mourners increased, making Mafeking's funeral service standing-room only. When the crowd could no longer fit inside the two hundred-seat capacity hall or along the walls and throughout the back of the hall, mourners simply amassed outside in the chilly, overcast morning. The service itself was a reflection of both the cooperative, multi-racial society Mafeking hoped to create in South Africa, and the multi-racial community she surrounded herself with in life. Prayers, singing, and remarks about Mafeking were made in a fluid mix of isiXhosa, SeSotho, Afrikaans, and English depending upon the racial or ethnic identity of the speaker. Race, gender, and ethnicity had no bearing, however, on the jubilant dancing that intermittently erupted in the reception hall, drawing a diverse crowd of all generations into praise dances honoring Mafeking.

Approximately two dozen speakers – representatives from FAWU, the ANC, the ANC-Women's League, the Umkhonto WeSizwe Military Veterans Association (MKVA), and the local Drakenstein Municipality – were seated on the dais. Those who knew Mafeking spoke of her impact on their lives, and those who were only children when Mafeking escaped to Lesotho and learned of her through their elders expressed their gratitude for her sacrifices each maintained contributed to the demise of Apartheid. Each speaker relied upon the call-and-response tradition, rousing the crowd with shouts of *"Amandla!"* or *"Mayibuye!"* prompting respective responses of *"Ngawethu!"* and *"Afrika!"* The Regional Chairman of the ANC-Worlon District welcomed everyone, proclaiming:

> We praise this very special service! All of us came to show our respects to someone we looked up to for many years. We do not always realize that we are walking in the shadows and footsteps of giants. People led this revolution for years without asking anything for themselves ... [people] who understood the concept of selfless service. Those are the values we should treasure and return to ... Ma Rokie was one of those rare breed of people. They're leaving us one by one, and we grant them their rest.

Epilogue

The ANC representative maintained that Mafeking was a model of service to both her community and her nation, and assured the family that the efforts Mafeking put forth to improve the lives of people across South Africa would never be forgotten. "Long live the spirit of Ma Rokie Mafeking," she implored before yielding the podium. Over the course of the next few hours, a succession of speakers from the ANC and it alliance partners addressed the crowd of more than two hundred, many of whom were FAWU comrades representing all nine provinces of South Africa.

One of the most moving features of Mafeking's funeral services were the struggle songs sung in her honor. During the reading of her obituary, the entire audience began singing:

Ehla moya oyingcwele . . .

Come, Holy Spirit . . .

Two dozen women from the AME church, wearing black and white uniforms and leopard-skin hats – the traditional uniform of the South African branches of the Women's

Epilogue

Missionary Society – organized themselves as a choir at the front of the reception hall, just to the right of Mafeking's casket, which was draped by the ANC flag and surrounded by ornate sprays of white lilies. Her sisters from the Missionary Society led many songs, but they gladly yielded the floor to speakers like the ANC Deputy Secretary of the Western Cape Province, who led a stirring rendition of *Ngibambe ngesandla* (Hold My Hand).

> Ngibambe ngesandla ngingashi emlilweni.
> Inhliziyo Ma Rokie inene sengizocasha kuyona.

> Hold my hand that I may not burn in the fire.
> This pure heart of Ma Rokie is where I will hide.[8]

Almost half of those present rose to their feet to dance in whatever spaces were available in the packed reception hall. Dozens wore commemorative t-shirts identifying Mafeking as a "trade unionist, gender activist, liberation fighter, and a communist comrade," and the noise level increased to a fever pitch during the song when ANCWL members alternated between ululating and blowing whistles. The ANCWL, in particular, honored Mafeking as being "a rock in the province of the Western Cape. She made sure that a woman's role was not only in the kitchen, it was in the forefront of the struggle to liberate people, particularly workers." Representatives emphasized the importance of Mafeking's struggles in light of the politics of the mid-twentieth century.

> Mama Rokie was fighting against the triple exploitation of women, which was . . . the discrimination of women according to their race, discrimination of women because of their sex, [and] discrimination as a part of the working class. She worked to show us that we have to play a role in fighting that. It was through women like Mama Rokie that women were taught to fight discrimination.

Mafeking helped an entire generation of women reconceptualize their role in life as having a part in the social and political betterment of the nation. She also greatly influenced the next generation of male, anti-apartheid activists like Charles Setsubi, a member of the Central Committee of the SACP and MK veteran, who lived in the Mafeking household from 1977–1986. Setsubi considered himself a "son" of "'Me Mafeking" after having spent almost one decade under Mafeking's care when he fled South Africa following the Soweto uprisings. At the time, Mafeking was the first South African native living in the Mafeteng District of Lesotho, but she would not be last. According to Setsubi, "almost all members of the MK" fleeing South Africa in those days "passed through the hands and guidance of Mama Mafeking."

Artwell Nazo, National President of FAWU began his tribute to Mafeking with a song that drew mourners from the back rows of the reception hall to the front for a massive dance of concentric circles revolving in opposite directions, carefully timed body dips, and expressive arm movements.

Ayaduma'makhosikazi!

Ayaduma'makhosikazi,
ayaduma'makhosikazi, ayangena Jerusalem!

Epilogue

The women are roaring!

The women are roaring, the women are roaring, they are entering Jerusalem![9]

Nazo reminded the audience that they were not present to mourn Mafeking's passing, but to celebrate her life. Mafeking was a "stalwart" whose history was that of the nation, and whose energy and determination to crush the Apartheid society contributed to building a vibrant and militant FAWU. Finally, Nazo recognized that "FAWU was led by women, comrades, for a number of years," and that he felt privileged to have inherited an organization that was built upon the shoulders of leaders like Elizabeth Mafeking. A subsequent representative from the ANC National Executive Committee thanked the Mafeking family for "borrowing us Mama Rokie and for allowing her to serve the nation," and two members of the Women's Missionary Society recounted Mafeking's centrality to the establishing of the AME Church in Paarl prior to her banning and her dedicated service to the church throughout her exile, as evidenced by the fact that "she raised one of the most dedicated missionaries in Sister Puleng (Malawa), one of her daughters."[10] After more than one half dozen representatives from various political organizations and offices offered brief tributes to Mafeking, Rev. Lewin the Presiding Elder of the Fifteenth District of the AME Church of South Africa, delivered the sermon.

Rev. Lewin recalled his first meeting with Mafeking in 1992 upon her return to South Africa when he was first appointed Presiding Elder. The initial meeting was arranged by Mafeking's first pastor, and when Lewin initially met her, he was struck by the aging activist's liveliness. Mafeking had a "wonderful sense of humor and, [was a] wonderful woman of faith." Rev. Lewin considered it a "privilege" to have met what he considered a remarkable woman of faith who met her just rewards after a lifetime of struggle and, "like Madiba and many others, became a legend in their own lifetime."

> We are touched by the passing of a mother, of a friend, of a comrade, [and] in our united grief ... we must admit this day that our

lives are a little bit richer because of her life, because for a brief spell God permitted us to bask in the warmth and in the sunshine of her life. We are not done, we will never be done, but today we are united in grief but we are also united in our determination to continue to build on the legacy left behind by Ma Rokie. The struggle against racial injustices and inequality, the struggle against poverty, against violence and crime, gender and child abuse, is a righteous struggle, so the struggle continues, and we must never rest until these issues are eradicated from our society. I want you to thank God that Elizabeth "Ma Rokie" was yours, and you were hers. Now let her memory live on.

The scripture for Mafeking's funeral service came from Mark 14:3–9, and Rev. Lewin delivered a moving sermon that drew both tears and shouts of praise from the mourners.

Epilogue

Mark 14:3–9

3: And being in Bethany in the house of Simon the leper, as he sat at meat, there came a woman having an alabaster box of ointment of spikenard (perfume) very precious; and she brake the box, and poured it on his head.

4: And there were some that had indignation within themselves, and said, Why was this waste of the ointment made?

5: For it might have been sold for more than three hundred pence, and have been given to the poor. And they murmured against her.

6: And Jesus said, Let her alone; why trouble ye her? She hath wrought a good work on me.

7: For ye have the poor with you always, and whensoever ye will ye may do them good: but me ye have not always.

8: She had done what she could: she is come aforehand to anoint my body to the burying.

9: Verily I say unto you, Wheresoever this gospel shall be preached throughout the whole world, *this* also that she hath done shall be spoken of for a memorial of her.

Rev. Lewin likened Mafeking to the poor woman with the alabaster box who poured out her life, her everything, to pay homage to Jesus. In the scripture, the poor woman of note has nothing to offer Jesus other than a prized container of expensive perfume worth "three hundred pence," or one year's wages. The container and its contents are the only source of material wealth for the woman, who observers criticize for wasting the potential proceeds from its sale. Jesus silences everyone by stating the woman "hath wrought good work" in his honor, and pointedly reminds his disciples that they have not always served him as selflessly. "She hath done what she could," Jesus proclaims, praising the woman for sacrificing her riches. So too did Mafeking sacrifice her riches in devotion to the struggle, even though it meant loneliness, deprivation, and untold hardship for her and her family in exile.

> What a woman and what a testimony. Never did she allow herself to be resentful or bitter. She gave her heart, she gave her whole, [and] she opened her purse and her pocket for others. *She did what she could.* In spite of the viciousness of the Apartheid state and its brutal response to those that resisted it, Ma Rokie never ceased to hope that tomorrow would be better than today. She never permitted the years to kill her hopes. How wonderful that God permitted her to live to

Epilogue

> witness that dawning of a free and democratic South Africa!

Rev. Lewin imagined that "even in her darkest moments Ma Rokie never ceased" to have faith, and that her lifetime of service and devotion was well and truly rewarded in her ability to see the birth of a new South Africa. Rev. Lewin closed his remarks on the life of Elizabeth Mafeking by imagining her final moments, when "her soul and spirit [were] in perfect harmony." Mafeking was no doubt able to lift up her face without shame in the presence of the Lord, forgive her oppressors, and say, "Tell them that even if history does not record anything I've ever said or done, that is all right with me because I have found a higher place." She hath done what she could.

Epilogue

Notes

1 In death, Elizabeth Mafeking suffered one last slight at the hands of the South African government. The official death certificate for "Rokie Elizabeth Mafeking" issued by the Department of Home Affairs lists the activist as "NEVER MARRIED." These two words officially nullified her legal union with husband Moffat Henry Mditjana and branded all eleven of their children as illegitimate; Death certificate furnished to author by Mafeking family.

2 At the time of her death, Elizabeth Mafeking had buried seven of her eleven children.

3 Indeed, Mafeking's children are now mothers and grandmothers themselves, and are building families in the new South Africa, taking advantages

of opportunities created by the freedom Mafeking and many others fought for.

4 Mafeking's funeral services were coordinated by a funeral coordinating committee comprised of several national and community organizations – including the ANC, South African Communist Party (SACP), and the South African National Civic Organization – working in conjunction with a family representative, and a third-party chair.

5 Memorial & Funeral Service of the late Elizabeth "Rokie" Mafikeng (sic), 11 September 1918–28 May 2009 (Bereshith Productions) DVD. Source provided by Mafeking family.

6 "Mama" (isiXhosa) and "Me" (SeSotho) can both be used to communicate mother, Mrs., or ma'am, and are the culturally appropriate ways to refer or speak to a female elder. Moreover, the practice serves as an

indication to the speaker that s/he is connected to the person being addressed – if not by blood most certainly by culture.

7 Tradition dictates that when someone dies – usually away from their homeland/family – a sheep is slaughtered and eaten by all mourners as a way of calling the spirit of the departed back home to rest.

8 In the original version of Ngibambe ngesandla, the lyrics translate "the pure heart of Jesus is where I will hide." Mourners at Mafeking's funeral substituted "Ma Rokie" for Jesus, singing, "the pure heart of Ma Rokie is where I will hide."

9 Like most amaXhosa, amaZulu, and BaSotho songs, this one is open to alteration. Singers can substitute preferred proper nouns as the destination being entered. For example, in 2014 when the Democratic Alliance (DA) won a surprising victory

Epilogue

over the ANC in the Western Cape, at a celebration rally, Mam'Veliswa Mvenya opened the proceedings with this same song, singing instead "Sizongena Parliament!" (We are entering Parliament).

10 Artwell Nazo, Memorial & Funeral Service of the late Elizabeth "Rokie" Mafikeng (sic), 11 September 1918–28 May 2009 (Bereshith Productions) DVD. Source provided by Mafeking family.

Appendix

The children of Elizabeth Mafeking

Figure A.1 This treasured family photo hangs in the Mafeking home in Mbekweni. In the center is Elizabeth Mafeking, surrounded by images of nine of her eleven children.

Courtesy of Mafeking Family

Appendix

1. ***Nozipho Sophie Nqigashe "Khekhemani"*** (June 13, 1939 – Present; Born Paarl, Western Cape, South Africa)

    - Nozipho Sophie completed Grade 8, and was employed as a factory worker. She and her husband, Mbuthi Nqigashe, had seven children – Mongameli, Nobomvu, Mavayi, Nori, Vukile, Khaya, and Luzuko.

2. ***Nozkhumbuzo Gertrude Mafeking*** (December 16, 1940 – July 2001; Born Paarl, Western Cape, South Africa; Died Pretoria, Gauteng, South Africa)

    - Nozkhumbuzo completed Grade 8, was employed as a factory worker, and the single mother of three children – Mimi, Papali, and Vova. One of her grandchildren, Gugu Karabo Hlatshwayo graduated as a civil engineer from the University of Johannesburg.

Appendix

3   ***Atti Stanley Mafeking*** (April 4, 1942 – August 2000; Born Paarl, Western Cape, South Africa; Died Paarl, Western Cape South Africa)

- Atti Stanley completed Grade 8, never married, but had two children – Elizabeth and Stanley Jr.

4   ***Ngubenyathi Melford Mafeking*** (June 11, 1945 – January 1995; Born Paarl, Western Cape, South Africa; Died Paarl, Western Cape South Africa)

- Ngubenyathi Melford completed Grade 10 and earned his Junior Certificate. He never married and never had children.

5   ***Mehlo Andrew Mafeking*** (September 23, 1947 – Unknown; Born Paarl, Western Cape, South Africa; Died Mafeteng, Lesotho)

- Mehlo Andrew completed Grade 7, never married, and never had children.

Appendix

6   ***Nomahlubi Rhoda Maranyane*** (October 21, 1949 – December 1, 2005; Born Paarl, Western Cape, South Africa; Died Stellenbosh, Western Cape, South Africa)

- Nomahlubi Rhoda earned a diploma in Fashion Design and was employed in her field prior to her death. She was survived by her husband, Oupa Maranyane, their children – Liqabang, Babane, Mamile, and Mapolo—and three grandchildren, Malia, Ramoshana, and Khola Realeboha.

7   ***Sisinyana Suzan Mafeking*** (February 6, 1950 – September 1984; Born Paarl, Western Cape, South Africa; Died Mafeteng, Lesotho)

- Sisinyana Suzan earned a diploma in nursing and worked in her field prior to her untimely death. She was survived by her

Appendix

husband, Khotso Mokuena, and their children, Mandela and Sechaba.

8   *Nomsa Mohlathe Mafeking* (November 7, 1952 – Present; Born Paarl, Western Cape, South Africa)

- Nomsa Catherine Mohlathe earned a Bachelors in Education, and is a retired director of the Department of Social Development in Mpumalanga. She is divorced with one child, Noddy, and a granddaughter Motshegi.

- Nomsa was amongst the first ANC candidates for Senate in the first democratic elections in 1994, earning her place in a formal leadership role through years of dedication to the party. She was subsequently appointed as one of the first Commissioners of in the Reconstruction and Development Programme in

Appendix

Mpumalanga/RDP. In 1995, when President Nelson Mandela launched the Masakhane Campaign, Nomsa became the Mpumalanga Provincial Masakhane Coordinator. In 2002, she became the District/Regional Director of the Department of Social Development in Mpumalanga until retirement in 2014 at the age of 62.

9   *Nomonde Mary Mafeking* (September 19, 1955 – June 1988; Born Paarl, Western Cape, South Africa; Died Maseru, Lesotho)

- Nomonde Mary complete a degree in dentistry, and was employed as a dentist prior to her death. She never married, nor did she have children.

10 *Nominki Martha Mafeking* (May 11, 1958 – Present; Born Paarl, Western Cape, South Africa)

Appendix

- Nominki Martha completed matric and is a retired public servant. She never married, but has one child, Mthetheleli.

11   *Uhuru Zikalala Mafeking* (August 24, 1959 – Present; Born Paarl, Western Cape, South Africa)

- Uhuru Zikalala earned an MSc in Civil Engineering from Patrice Lumumba University in Moscow, and is currently employed as the Managing Director of Bio Moringa, the company she owns with her husband Siphiwe Zikalala. Uhuru worked for four years as Deputy Director General in the National Department of Human Settlement, making her the second highest official in the country in authority for housing development. Uhuru served as the head of housing for the City of Johannesburg for almost one decade, the most senior official in the City responsible for policy formulation and implementation of human settlements in the city.

- Uhuru's first born, Boitumelo (who is deaf) completed a course in jewelry design and manufacturing at the National Institute for the Deaf in Worcester in the Western Cape. Uhuru has three step-daughters; Nomathemba, Thembi and Thato and a grandson, Chad – Lee.

- In her own words: "I was only three months old when my mother left Paarl for Lesotho. I grew up in Lesotho and completed my primary education in Lesotho. I was 18 years-old when I joined the ANC and went to Tanzania and eventually to Russia to study. I grew up not knowing my country of birth. For 18 years my mother had said 'One day we are going home' and for 16 years the ANC had said to us that one day we will return home. I have to make special mention of Getrude Shope who was in the leadership of the then ANC Women Section. Mothers in South Africa must thank this comrade who took it upon herself to mother girl children in exile. Ma Shope as she was affectionately called, used to say to us young girls then 'what will we tell your parents when we return home and in that excitement parents are hugging their returning children and your parents can't find you amongst us? How do we tell them that your daughter got married and left for another country with the husband and she is not here with us?'" In 1992 I was a trainee at the London Borough of Lambeth. As I made arrangements to return to South Africa through the United Nations Office of Refugees, a colleague asked why I wanted to return to South Africa especially because there was so much political violence in South Africa at the time. This lady,

Appendix

Margaret, was from Ghana and had made London her new home. I told her that for 33 years I never had a country; I never had a place I called home. I lived all my life knowing that one day I will return home and not even the political violence could stop me. When I left Lesotho in 1977, I had a forged passport with a false name and later got a travel document in Tanzania which clearly stated that I was not a Tanzanian national. This was an A4 size paper and every time I traveled I used this paper instead of a normal passport. I am forever grateful to the people of Tanzania for providing us a home in our greatest time of need; but every time I had to produce this document, I was reminded that I had no country, that I did not belong. I was 34 years-old when I finally returned to South Africa and had to learn to be a South African.

Index

A

Abrahams, Elizabeth "Liz", v, 2, 20, 27, 60, 69, 75, 100, 135, 142, 154, 187, 198, 240, 273, 406
African National Congress (ANC), 115, 147
Angola, 323, 359, 362
anti-apartheid activism, 19, 149
Apartheid, vii, x, 2, 4, 6, 8, 18, 21, 22, 25, 26, 27, 29, 31, 32, 34, 37, 40, 48, 51, 54, 71, 77, 78, 79, 81, 89, 91, 92, 94, 100, 105, 109, 112, 114, 122, 133, 135, 144, 150, 151, 152, 155, 182, 190, 199, 208, 219, 221, 222, 231, 238, 240, 243, 247, 262, 264, 272, 279, 281, 283, 285, 298, 319, 324, 325, 329, 330, 344, 361, 367, 372, 389, 394, 408, 409, 413, 416, 417, 423, 428, 432
Atti Stanley, Mafeking, 46, 68, 297, 440
Auschwitz, 131

B

banishment, vi, 1, 3, 4, 18, 22, 40, 43, 45, 49, 51, 52, 54, 147, 148, 154, 155, 157, 159, 187, 199, 200, 204, 205, 208, 211, 225, 233, 235, 241, 242, 244, 248, 265, 283, 307, 308, 364, 404
Basotho, xiii, 231, 296, 299, 350
Basutoland, vii, 1, 3, 11, 21, 22, 23, 48, 55, 56, 98, 183, 210, 211, 213, 214, 215, 217, 218, 221, 222, 223, 226, 227, 228, 230, 232, 233, 234, 236, 238, 242, 251, 252, 253, 254, 255, 256, 257, 258, 259, 260, 261, 262, 264, 267, 269, 270, 272, 273, 275, 276, 277, 279, 282, 283, 284, 286, 289, 290, 291, 293, 294, 295, 298, 299, 305, 310, 311, 312, 313, 314, 315, 316, 317, 318, 319, 320, 321, 322, 323, 324, 335, 346, 349, 352, *See* Basotho
Basutoland Congress Party (BCP), 228, 269, 282, 336
Basutoland National Party (BNP), 336
Bechuanaland, 215, 242, 251, 252, 310, 319, 324
Botswana, 215, 363, 364
Bulgaria, 127, 129, 131, 132, 279, 372
Buthelezi, Mangosuthu "Gatsha", 358

C

canning industry, 2, 42, 64, 71, 125, 138, 149
Cape Town, x, xii, 12, 28, 30, 33, 34, 37, 57, 58, 67, 70, 82, 84, 100, 101, 103, 108, 110, 111, 112, 125, 134, 155, 159, 168, 169, 170, 171, 174, 186, 218, 233, 242, 246, 268, 284, 315, 316, 317, 330, 331, 358, 375, 392, 393, 395, 396, 397, 399, 400, 401, 402, 404, 405

Index

Capello, Cecil, 64
China, 131, 132, 320
church, 157, 213, 346, 377, 424, 428
Church, 16, 156, 420, 421, 428
Coloureds, so-called, 19, 67, 152, 184, 197
communism, 90, 117
Communist Party of South Africa (CPSA), 82
Copenhagen, viii, 278, 280
Czechoslovakia, 122, 132

D

decolonization, 265
Drum, 14, 263, 314

E

education, 51, 57, 91, 119, 120, 215, 287, 328, 335, 341, 356, 367, 388, 445
education policy, 91
escape, vii, 20, 47, 124, 183, 193, 196, 199, 210, 221, 222, 225, 226, 235, 239, 240, 241, 282, 283, 287, 323, 352
escape, Mafeking's flight, 21, 241, 262, 263
exile/exiles/exiled, vi, vii, 1, 2, 4, 5, 8, 9, 14, 15, 18, 21, 22, 23, 24, 25, 36, 39, 40, 48, 50, 53, 54, 150, 160, 187, 191, 200, 202, 212, 213, 215, 216, 217, 220, 223, 224, 225, 228, 232, 271, 272, 277, 283, 284, 285, 286, 289, 290, 291, 292, 293, 294, 295, 296, 297, 298, 299, 300, 301, 305, 306, 309, 310, 311, 312, 319, 323, 325, 329, 334, 336, 337, 340, 341, 342, 344, 349, 350, 351, 352, 356, 359, 360, 361, 363, 364, 369, 373, 381, 383, 384, 386, 387, 388, 394, 401, 409, 410, 411, 412, 413, 428, 432, 446

F

factories, 57, 61, 62, 124, 137, 143, 145, 146
Federation of South African Women (FEDSAW), 2, 70, 97, 104, 105, 116, 128, 162, 170, 171, 181
Food and Allied Workers Union (FAWU), 407

G

Garment Workers Union (GWU), 104
Ghana, 265, 447
Guardian, the, 60, 85, 112, 113

H

H. Jones Canning Factory, 58, 60, 63, 65, 117, 122, 358
Hani, Chris, 359, 394, 395
Hani, Gilbert, 291, 298, 325, 326, 342, 344, 351, 359, 379, 393, 394, 410
Hani, Nompumelelo "Npumi", 351
Hashe, Viola, 89, 115, 116
Hertzog, J.B.M., 52

I

immigrant, 236, 268
influx control, 79, 150
Inkatha Freedom Party (IFP), 358

J

jail, incarceration, 147, 359, 360
Jerusalem, 232, 283, 427, 428
Johannesburg, 13, 14, 27, 29, 30, 33, 67, 87, 95, 99, 105, 114,

Index

117, 162, 168, 183, 321, 328, 366, 388, 394, 397, 398, 407, 416, 439, 444
Joseph, Helen, 1, 13, 34, 51, 95, 96, 295

K

Kenya, 363
Kimberly, 57

L

Lan, Rebecca "Becky", 2
Leselinyana, 220, 224, 252, 278, 280, 320
Lesotho, vii, viii, ix, xii, xiii, 1, 10, 14, 31, 55, 56, 184, 197, 211, 212, 214, 215, 220, 222, 225, 226, 228, 229, 231, 252, 253, 260, 272, 273, 280, 281, 287, 289, 296, 309, 317, 320, 323, 324, 325, 327, 328, 333, 334, 335, 337, 340, 341, 342, 344, 345, 346, 347, 348, 349, 352, 353, 354, 355, 358, 359, 360, 362, 364, 365, 366, 368, 369, 371, 372, 373, 374, 377, 379, 382, 392, 393, 398, 399, 401, 402, 403, 405, 412, 418, 423, 427, 440, 441, 443, 445
Lusaka, 329, 342, 343, 365, 397
Luthuli, Chief Albert John, 147
Luthuli, Mrs., 357, 358

M

Mafeking Affair, The, 14, 16, 26, 39, 48, 49, 239, 258
Mafeking children, 24, 45, 197, 199, 211, 272, 286, 323, 344, 361, 411
Mafeking, Mehlo Andrew, 46, 297, 440
Mafeking, Ngubenyathi Melford, 46, 297, 440
Mafeking, Nomahlubi Rhoda Maranyane, 91, 441
Mafeking, Nomonde Mary, 46, 133, 297, 364, 401, 443
Mafeking, Nomsa Catherine, 46, 92, 97, 103, 121, 150, 151, 183, 297, 299, 318, 334, 364, 393, 442
Mafeking, Nomvula Nominki "Minki" Martha, 46, 142, 150, 297, 352
Mafeking, Nozipho "Sophia" Khekhemani, 43, 63
Mafeking, Nozkhumbuzo Gertrude, 46, 63, 297, 439
Mafeking, Sisinyana Suzan, 46, 92, 121, 297, 371, 441
Mafeking, Uhuru Teresa Zikalala, vii, 11, 36, 46, 145, 147, 195, 196, 211, 212, 214, 220, 225, 227, 228, 229, 230, 231, 264, 282, 290, 291, 295, 297, 299, 307, 308, 344, 345, 346, 347, 348, 349, 355, 356, 361, 368, 378, 379, 380, 388, 398, 402, 403, 415, 444, 445
Mafeteng, 236, 258, 278, 279, 281, 282, 290, 299, 312, 318, 338, 340, 346, 351, 352, 371, 427, 440, 441
Mandela, Nelson Rolihlahla "Madiba", 294, 442, 443
Maphathe, N.S., viii, 278, 279, 280, 320
Maseru, 21, 213, 214, 228, 232, 234, 235, 237, 239, 254, 255, 256, 258, 267, 269, 276, 292, 314, 315, 316, 317, 318, 338, 355, 357, 371, 443
Maxeke, Charlotte, 77
Mbekweni, viii, 183, 184, 197, 379, 382, 389, 407, 411, 417, 420, 438

Index

Mditjane, Moffat Henry, 17, 46, 63, 102, 318, 434
Media coverage, 48
Mokhehle, Ntsu, vii, 228, 231, 232, 269, 292, 293, 294, 304, 350
Molaoa, Puleng, 323, 327
Moshoeshoe II, Paramount Chief of Lesotho (Constantine Bereng Seeiso), 276, 277, 318, 341
Motloheloa, John, 289, 342
Mozambique, 369
Mpetha, Oscar, 2, 44, 124, 126

N

National Council of Women in South Africa (NCWSA), 159
National Party (NP), 73, 80
newspapers, vii, x, 12, 14, 48, 54, 135, 160, 229, 278
Ngoyi, Lilian, vii, 89, 228, 230, 282, 283
Nkewu, Nomathemba "Themsi", viii, 381, 382
Nthunya, Mpho 'M'atsepo, 222
Nyasaland, 147

O

oral histories, 8, 9, 34, 54
organizing workers, 64

P

Paarl, vi, ix, xii, 3, 4, 11, 14, 21, 28, 37, 42, 44, 46, 47, 53, 57, 64, 66, 69, 70, 71, 95, 103, 105, 125, 133, 147, 152, 158, 161, 179, 183, 185, 188, 192, 197, 199, 204, 207, 209, 211, 223, 226, 235, 256, 262, 271, 273, 274, 285, 297, 306, 317, 333, 374, 379, 381, 382, 389, 398, 399, 411, 418, 428, 439, 440, 441, 442, 443, 444, 445
pass law and protests, women's, 6
Poland, 128, 131
police, Basutoland, 233, 234, 235, 237, 238, 239, 240, 243, 263, 267, 291
police, South African Police (SAP), 3
political alliances, 152, 227, 234, 341, 365
political refugees, 228, 232, 310
Prime Minister Jonathan, 309, 350

R

radicalism, 75, 112, 413
refugees, 22, 40, 215, 216, 219, 221, 227, 228, 231, 232, 243, 270, 276, 277, 283, 291, 292, 294, 298, 309, 312, 323, 325, 343, 350, 351, 356, 364, 371, 383, 386, 397, 407, 409, 410
Rhodesia, 99, 147
Roma, Lesotho, 14, 185, 220, 231, 252, 260, 280
Romania, 368, 403

S

Sachs, Albert "Albie", 369
Sachs, Emil Solomon "Solly", 87
Simons, Ray Alexander, 2, 13, 19, 23, 26, 33, 63, 64, 69, 99, 128, 168, 310, 311, 329, 330, 331, 332, 355, 368, 369, 392, 393, 395, 396, 397, 399, 400, 401, 402, 404, 405
Southey, vi, 44, 53, 147, 160, 187, 200, 201, 202, 203
Soviet Union, 35, 122, 127, 132, 365
Soweto, 319, 323, 361, 362, 364, 427
Swaziland, 215, 242, 251, 252, 324

Index

Swaziland Chronicle, 216

T

Tanganyika, 310, 359
Tanzania, 320, 323, 362, 445
trade unions, 4, 17, 20, 25, 66, 70, 75, 78, 81, 88, 89, 92, 101, 119, 122, 130, 140, 143, 149, 160, 169
Trotsky, Leon, 127

V

Verwoerd, Hendrik Frensch, vii, 206, 240, 241
Vorster, Balthazar Johannes, 307, 328
Vryburg, vi, 3, 44, 45, 202, 203

W

Western Cape, vi, ix, xii, 2, 17, 27, 28, 43, 46, 70, 73, 74, 75, 92, 97, 101, 120, 134, 138, 149, 160, 168, 183, 193, 207, 240, 246, 285, 398, 407, 409, 417, 420, 425, 426, 437, 439, 440, 441, 442, 443, 444, 445
Women's March, 1956, 2, 89

X

Xuma, Alfred Bathini, 384

Z

Zambia, 329, 334, 337, 343, 362, 365, 397
Zimbabwe, 362

www.ingramcontent.com/pod-product-compliance
Lightning Source LLC
Chambersburg PA
CBHW032013230426
43671CB00005B/68